1,000,000 Books

are available to read at

Forgotten Books

www.ForgottenBooks.com

Read online
Download PDF
Purchase in print

ISBN 978-1-330-13019-3
PIBN 10033157

This book is a reproduction of an important historical work. Forgotten Books uses state-of-the-art technology to digitally reconstruct the work, preserving the original format whilst repairing imperfections present in the aged copy. In rare cases, an imperfection in the original, such as a blemish or missing page, may be replicated in our edition. We do, however, repair the vast majority of imperfections successfully; any imperfections that remain are intentionally left to preserve the state of such historical works.

Forgotten Books is a registered trademark of FB &c Ltd.
Copyright © 2018 FB &c Ltd.
FB &c Ltd, Dalton House, 60 Windsor Avenue, London, SW19 2RR.
Company number 08720141. Registered in England and Wales.

For support please visit www.forgottenbooks.com

1 MONTH OF FREE READING

at

www.ForgottenBooks.com

By purchasing this book you are eligible for one month membership to ForgottenBooks.com, giving you unlimited access to our entire collection of over 1,000,000 titles via our web site and mobile apps.

To claim your free month visit:

www.forgottenbooks.com/free33157

* Offer is valid for 45 days from date of purchase. Terms and conditions apply.

English
Français
Deutsche
Italiano
Español
Português

www.forgottenbooks.com

Mythology Photography **Fiction**
Fishing Christianity **Art** Cooking
Essays Buddhism Freemasonry
Medicine **Biology** Music **Ancient Egypt** Evolution Carpentry Physics
Dance Geology **Mathematics** Fitness
Shakespeare **Folklore** Yoga Marketing
Confidence Immortality Biographies
Poetry **Psychology** Witchcraft
Electronics Chemistry History **Law**
Accounting **Philosophy** Anthropology
Alchemy Drama Quantum Mechanics
Atheism Sexual Health **Ancient History**
Entrepreneurship Languages Sport
Paleontology Needlework Islam
Metaphysics Investment Archaeology
Parenting Statistics Criminology
Motivational

DISCOURSES

ON

HUMAN NATURE.

HUMAN LIFE,

AND THE

NATURE OF RELIGION.

BY
ORVILLE DEWEY, D.D.
PASTOR OF THE CHURCH OF THE MESSIAH, IN NEW YORK.

NEW YORK:
C. S. FRANCIS & CO., 252 BROADWAY.
BOSTON:
J. H. FRANCIS, 128 WASHINGTON-STREET
1847.

Entered according to Act of Congress, in the year 1846,
BY C. S. FRANCIS & CO.
In the Clerk's Office of the District Court for the Southern District of New York.

NEW YORK.

PRINTED BY
MUNROE AND FRANCIS,
BOSTON.

PREFACE.

I HAVE collected into these Volumes, most of the Sermons and Essays that have been published with my name; and have added some Sermons not before printed, together with Articles from Reviews, and Occasional Discourses. A new arrangement is made, in order to bring the Discourses under certain heads. The title of the Volume first published, "Discourses on Various Subjects," is dropped. The first Series in this Edition, "On Human Nature," embraces several of those Discourses; others are omitted; and others, placed under another Head. Discourses on "Human Life," follow; and then, a number of Discourses, for which I could find no more definite title than "The Nature of Religion." In the first Sermon of the succeeding series, on "Commerce and Business," I have attempted by a revision of the Argument, to reply to an objection sometimes urged against its main doctrine, with regard to the use of superior knowledge, power or opportunity. I have met with those who argued thus: "We have a right to take every advantage of each other; it is perfectly honest to do so, because we have agreed to do so. It is a matter of compact, whose chances and risks we mutually agree to take." Now I maintain that the general *moral policy* of trade formas such *compact*. The remainder of the Second Volume is occupied by a Miscellaneous Collection of Discourses on Politics and Society, and by reprints of Reviews and Occasional Sermons and Addresses. The Third Volume, or the one which is to occupy that place in the Edition, is already published—as it has been some time out of print, and was called for—under the title of " Discourses and Reviews upon Questions in Controversial Theology and Practical Religion." My apology for these details is, that they seemed to be necessary to explain to those who have purchased my publications, the character of the present Edition.

Let me add, that no attempt is made at a full discussion of any of the subjects embraced in these Volumes. I suppose that a Treatise is not usually expected in a Volume of Sermons. Pulpit Discourses are, from the nature of the case, more like separate Essays, than successive portions of a regular Treatise.

I have now said all that is necessary, perhaps, in a Preface; and yet, in sending forth a revised Edition of my Publications, I am disposed to add one or two remarks.

I have sometimes regretted that it has been my fortune to communicate with the Public through Sermons. I doubt whether there is any one vehicle of communication—Art, Literature, Poetry, Fiction, the Journal, or the Newspaper —in the way of which public opinion has thrown so many obstructions and difficulties. In the first place, it has laid a jealous restriction upon the *topics* of the Sermon, the style, the modes of illustration—the whole manly freedom of utterance. In the next place, having thus helped to make it tame and common-place, it has branded what is partly its own work, with that fatal epithet, *dull*. In fact, the Sermon, the printed Sermon, has scarcely any recognised place among the great and noble arts of expression or communication. It is not appreciated as such. It has not the stimulus either of praise or blame from any high court of Literary Criticism.

I do not say, I am far from saying, that all this is the fault of the public, or of public opinion. It is the fault of the preacher rather; it is the error essentially of our religious ideas and feelings. In this view I know of no more significant fact connected with the history of Christianity than this, that the Sermon should in all ages have been proverbially *dull*. I confess that I am stung to indignation and shame at the bitter taunt implied in it, and would willingly take upon my hands all the disabilities and difficulties of this kind of communication, if I could give the feeblest demonstration, that it is not altogether deserved. The Essayist, Foster, says: " Might not all the Sermon-books in the English language, after the exception of three or four dozen volumes, be committed to the fire without any cause of regret?" I am not bold enough to expect that these volumes of mine could escape the doom; it would be a solace to me if I could believe, that they might stimulate others to do better, and that, from their ashes, something should arise, that would be worthy to live.

CONTENTS.

Discourses on Human Nature.

		PAGE.
I.	ON HUMAN NATURE,	9
II.	THE SAME SUBJECT,	28
III.	ON THE WRONG WHICH SIN DOES TO HUMAN NATURE,	41
IV.	ON THE ADAPTATION WHICH RELIGION, TO BE TRUE AND USEFUL, SHOULD HAVE TO HUMAN NATURE,	56
V.	THE APPEAL OF RELIGION TO HUMAN NATURE,	71
VI.	THE CALL OF HUMANITY AND THE ANSWER TO IT,	88
VII.	HUMAN NATURE CONSIDERED AS A GROUND FOR THANKSGIVING,	103

Discourses on Human Life.

VIII.	THE MORAL SIGNIFICANCE OF LIFE,	123
IX.	THAT EVERY THING IN LIFE IS MORAL,	137
X.	LIFE CONSIDERED AS AN ARGUMENT FOR FAITH AND VIRTUE,	154
XI.	LIFE IS WHAT WE MAKE IT,	169
XII.	ON INEQUALITY IN THE LOT OF LIFE,	184
XIII.	ON THE MISERIES OF LIFE,	198
XIV.	ON THE SCHOOL OF LIFE,	212
XV.	ON THE VALUE OF LIFE,	227
XVI.	LIFE'S CONSOLATION IN VIEW OF DEATH,	241
XVII.	THE PROBLEM OF LIFE, RESOLVED IN THE LIFE OF CHRIST,	255
XVIII.	ON RELIGION, AS THE GREAT SENTIMENT OF LIFE,	276
XIX	ON THE RELIGION OF LIFE,	285
XX.	THE VOICES OF THE DEAD,	306

Discourses on the Nature of Religion.

XXI.	THE IDENTITY OF RELIGION WITH GOODNESS, AND WITH A GOOD LIFE,	322
XXII.	THE SAME SUBJECT,	343
XXIII.	THE SAME SUBJECT,	365
XXIV.	SPIRITUAL INTERESTS, REAL AND SUPREME,	379

DISCOURSES.

ON HUMAN NATURE.

I.

WHAT IS MAN, THAT THOU ART MINDFUL OF HIM? AND THE SON OF MAN THAT THOU VISITEST HIM? FOR THOU HAST MADE HIM A LITTLE LOWER THAN THE ANGELS, AND HAST CROWNED HIM WITH GLORY AND HONOUR.—Psalm viii. 4, 5.

You will observe, my brethren, that in these words two distinct, and in a degree opposite views are given, of human nature. It is represented on the one hand as weak and low, and yet on the other, as lofty and strong. At one moment it presents itself to the inspired writer as poor, humble, depressed, and almost unworthy of the notice of its Maker. But in the transition of a single sentence, we find him contemplating this same being, man, as exalted, glorious and almost angelic. "When I consider thy heavens, the work of thy fingers, the moon and the stars, which thou hast ordained," he says, "what is man that thou art mindful of him?" And yet, he adds, "thou hast made him a little lower than the angels, and hast crowned him with glory and honour."

But do not these contrasted statements make up, in fact, the only true view of human nature? Are they not conformable to the universal sense of mankind, and to the whole tenor and spirit of our religion? Whenever the human character is portrayed in colours altogether dark, or altogether bright; whenever the misanthrope pours out his scorn upon the wickedness and baseness of mankind, or the enthusiast lavishes his admiration upon their virtues, do we not always feel that there needs to be some qualification; that there is something to be said on the other side?

Nay more; do not all the varying representations of human nature imply their opposites? Does not virtue itself imply, that sins and sinful passions are struggled with, and overcome? And on the contrary, does not sin in its very nature imply that there are high and sacred powers, capacities and affections, which it violates?

In this view it appears to me, that all unqualified disparagement as well as praise of human nature, carries with it its own refutation; and it is to this point that I wish to invite your particular attention in the following discourse. Admitting all that can be asked on this subject by the strongest assertors of human depravity; admitting every thing, certainly, that can be stated as a matter of fact; admitting that men are as bad as they are said to be, and substantially believing it too, I shall argue that the conclusion to be drawn is entirely the reverse of that which usually is drawn. I shall argue, that the most strenuous, the most earnest and indignant objections against human nature imply the strongest concessions to its constitutional worth. I say then, and repeat, that objection here carries with it its own refutation; that the objector concedes much, very much to human nature, by the very terms with which he inveighs against it.

It is not my sole purpose, however, to present any abstract or polemic argument. Rather let me attempt to offer some general and just views of human nature;

and for this purpose rather than for the sake of controversy, let me pass in brief review before you, some of the specific and disparaging opinions, that have prevailed in the world concerning it; those for instance, of the philosopher and the theologian.

In doing this, my purpose is to admit that much of what they say, is true; but to draw from it an inference quite different from theirs. I would admit on one hand, that there is much evil in the human heart, but at the same time, I would balance this view, and blend it with others that claim to be brought into the account. On the one hand, I would admit the objection that there is much and mournful evil in the world; but, on the other, I would prevent it from pressing on the heart, as a discouraging and dead weight of reprobation and obloquy.

It may appear to you that the opinions which I have selected for our present consideration are, each of them, brought into strange company; and yet they have an affinity which may not at once be suspected. It is singular indeed, that we find in the same ranks and waging the same war against all human self-respect, the most opposite descriptions of persons; the most religious with the most irreligious, the most credulous with the most sceptical. If any man supposes that it is his superior goodness or purer faith, which leads him to think so badly of his fellow-men and of their very nature, he needs to be reminded that vicious and dissolute habits almost invariably and unerringly lead to the same result. The man who is taking the downward way, with almost every step, you will find thinks worse of his nature and his species; till he concludes, if he can, that he was made only for sensual indulgence, and that all idea of a future, intellectual, and immortal existence, is a dream.

And so if any man thinks that it is owing to his spirituality and heavenly mindedness, that he pronounces the world so utterly corrupt, a mere mass of selfishness and deceit; he may be admonished that nobody so thoroughly agrees with him as the man of the world, the shrewd, over-reaching and knavish practicer on the weakness or the wickedness of his fellows. And in the same way, the strict and high-toned theologian, as he calls himself, may unexpectedly find himself in company with the sceptical and scornful philosopher. No men have ever more bitterly decried and vilified human nature, than the Infidel philosophers of the last century. They contended that man was too mean and contemptible a creature, to be the subject of such an interposition as that recorded in the Gospel.

I. But I am to take up in the first place, and more in detail, the objection of the sceptical philosopher.

The philosopher says, that man is a mean creature; not so much a degraded being, as he is originally, a poor, insignificant creature; an animal, some grades above others perhaps, but still an animal; for whom, to suppose the provision of infinite mercy and of immortality to be made, is absurd.

It is worth noticing, as we pass, and I therefore remark, the striking connection which is almost always found, between different parts of every man's belief or scepticism. I never knew one to think wrongly about God, but he very soon began to think wrongly about man: or else the reverse is the process, and it is not material which. The things always go together. He who conceives of the Almighty as a severe, unjust and vindictive being, will regard man as a slave, will *make* him the slave of *superstition*, will take a sort of superstitious pleasure or merit in magnifying his wickedness or unworthiness. And he who thinks meanly of human nature, will think coldly and distrustfully of the Supreme Being, will think of him as withdrawing himself to a sublime distance from such a nature. In other words, he who does not take the Christian view, and has no apprehension of the infinite love of God, will not believe that he has made man with such noble faculties, or for such noble ends, as we assert. The discussion proposed is obviously, even in this view, one of no trifling importance.

Let us, then, proceed to the objection of our philosopher. He says, I repeat, that man is a mean creature, fit only for the earth on which he is placed, fit for no higher destination than to be buried in its bosom, and there to find his end. The philosopher rejects what he calls the theologian's dream about the fall. He says that man needed no fall in order to be a degraded creature; that he is, and was, always and originally, a degraded creature; a being, not fallen from virtue, but incapable of virtue; a being, not corrupted from his innocence, but one who never possessed innocence; a being never of heaven, but a being only of earth aud sense and appetite, and never fit for any thing better.

Now let us go at once to the main point in argument, which is proposed to be illustrated in this discourse. What need, I ask, of speaking of human debasement, in such indignant or sneering tones, if it is the real and only nature of man? There is nothing to blame or scorn in man, if he is naturally such a poor and insignificant creature. If he was made only for the senses and appetites, what occasion, I pray, for any wonder or abuse, that he is sensual and debased? Why waste invectives on such a being? The truth is, that this zealous depreciation of human nature betrays a consciousness, that it is not so utterly worthless, after all. It is no sufficient reply to say, that this philosophic scorn has been aroused by the extravagance of human pretensions. For if these pretensions were utterly groundless, if the being who aspired to virtue were fit only for sensation, or if the being whose thoughts swelled to the great hope of immortality, were only a higher species of the animal creation, and must share its fate; if this were true, his pretensions could justly create only a feeling of wonder, or of sadness.

We might say much to rebut the charge of the philosopher; so injurious to the soul, so fatal to all just self-respect, so fatal to all elevated virtue and devotion. We might say that the most ordinary tastes and the most trifling pursuits of man carry, to the observant eye, marks of the nobler mind. We might say that vain trifling, and that fleeting, dying pleasure, does not satisfy the immortal want; and that toil does not crush the soul, that the body cannot weigh down the spirit to its own drudgery. We might ask our proud reasoner, moreover, whence the moral and metaphysical philosopher obtains the facts with which he speculates, and argues, and builds up his admirable theory? And our sceptic must answer, that the metaphysical and moral philosopher goes to human nature; that he goes to it in its very attitudes of toil and its free actings of passion, and thence takes his materials and his form, and his living charm of representation, which delight the world. We might say still more. We might say that all there is of vastness and grandeur and beauty in the world, lies in the conception of man; that the immensity of the universe, as we term it, is but the reach of his imagination; that immensity in other words is but the image of his own idea; that there is no eternity to him, but that which exists in his own unbounded thought; that there is no God to man, but what has been conceived of in his own capacions and unmeasured understanding.

These things we might say; but I will rather meet the objector on his own ground, confident that I may triumph even there. I take up the indignant argument, then. I allow that there is much weight and truth in it, though it brings me to a different conclusion. I feel that man is, in many respects and in many situations, and above all, compared with what he should be, that man is a mean creature. I feel it, as I should if I saw some youth of splendid talents and promise plunging in at the door of vice and infamy. Yes, it *is* meanness, for a MAN—who stands in the presence of his God and among the sons of heaven; it is meanness in him to play the humble part of sycophant before his fellows; to fawn and flatter, to make his very soul a slave, barely to gain from that fellow-man his smile, his nod, his hand; his favour, his vote, his patronage. It is meanness for a *man* to prevaricate and falsify, to sell his conscience for advantage, to barter his soul for gain, to give his noble brow to the smiting blush of shame, or his cheek to the deadly paleness of convicted dishonesty. Yes, it is a degradation unutterable, for a man to steep his soul in gross, sensual, besotting indulgence; to live for this, and in this one, poor, low sensation to shut up the mind with all its boundless range; to sink to a debasement more than beastly; below where an animal can go. Yes, all this, and much beside this is meanness; but why, now I ask—why do we speak of it thus, unless it is because we speak of a being who might have put on such a nobility of soul, and such a loftiness and independence, and spiritual beauty and glory, as would fling rebuke upon all the hosts of sin and temptation, and cast dimness upon all the splendour of the world?

It may be proper under the head of philosophical objections to take notice of the celebrated maxim of Rochefoucauld; since it is among the written, and has as good a title as others, to be among the philosophic objections. This maxim is, that we take a sort of pleasure in the disappointments and miseries of others, and are pained at their good fortune and success. If this maxim were intended to fix upon mankind the charge of pure, absolute, disinterested malignity, and if it could be sustained, it would be fatal to my argument. If I believed this, I should believe not only in total, but in diabolical depravity. And I am aware, that the apologists for human nature, receiving the maxim in this light, have usually contented themselves with indignantly denying its truth. I shall, however, for myself take different ground. I suppose, and I admit, that the maxim is true, to a certain extent. Yet I deny that the feelings on which it is founded, are malignant. They may be selfish, they may be bad; but they are not malicious and diabolical. But let us explain. It should be premised, that there is nothing wrong in our desiring the goods and advantages of life, provided the desire be kept within proper bounds. Suppose then that you are pursuing the same object with your neighbour, a situation, an office, for instance; and suppose that he succeeds. His success, at the first disclosure of it to you, will of course, give you a degree of pain; and for this reason: it immediately brings the sense of your own disappointment. Now it is not wrong perhaps, that you do regret your own failure; it is probably unavoidable that you should. You feel perhaps that you need, or deserve the appointment, more than your rival. You cannot help, therefore, on every account, regretting that he has obtained it. It does not follow that you wish him any less happy. You may make the distinction in your own mind. You may *say*—"I am glad he is happy; but I am sorry he has the place; I wish he could be as happy in some other situation." Now all this, so far from being malignant, is scarcely selfish; and even when the feeling in a very bad mind is altogether selfish, yet it is very different from a malignant pain, at another's good fortune. But now, let us extend the case a little, from immediate rivalship to that general competition of interests which exists in society; a competition which the selfishness of men makes to be far more than is necessary, and conceives to be far greater than it is. There is an erroneous idea, or imagination shall I call it—and certainly it is one of the moral delusions of the world —that something gained by another, is something lost to one's self: and hence the feeling, before described, may arise at almost any indifferent instance of good fortune. But it always rises in this proportion: it is stronger, the nearer the case comes to direct competition. You do not envy a rich man in China, nor a great man in Tartary. But if envy, as it has been sometimes called, were pure malignity, a man should be sorry that any body is happy, that any body is fortunate or honoured in the world. But this is not true; it does not apply to human nature. If you ever feel pain at the successes or acquisitions of another, it is when they come into comparison or contrast with your own failures or deficiencies. You feel that those successes or acquisitions might have been your own; you regret, and perhaps rightly, that they are not; and then, you insensibly slide into the very wrong feeling of regret, that they belong to another. This is envy; and it is sufficiently base; but it is not purely malicious, and it is, in fact, the perversion of a feeling originally capable of good and valuable uses.

But I must pursue the sceptical philosopher a step farther; into actual life. The term, philosopher, may seem to be but ill applied here; but we have probably all of us known or heard those, who, pretending to have a considerable *knowledge of the world*, if not much other knowledge, take upon them with quite an air of philosophic superiority, to pronounce human nature nothing but a mass of selfishness; and to say that this mass, whenever it is refined, is only refined into luxury and licentiousness, duplicity and knavery. Some simple souls they suppose there may be, in the retired corners of the earth, that are walking in the chains of mechanical habit or superstitious piety, who have not the knowledge to understand nor the courage to seek, what they want. But the moment they do act freely, they act, says our objector, upon the selfish principle. And this he maintains is the principle which, in fact, governs the world. Nay more, he avers, that it is the only reasonable and sufficient principle of action; and freely confesses that it is his own.

Let me ask you here to keep distinctly in view the ground, which the objector now assumes. There are talkers against human virtue, who never think however of going to this length; men in fact, who are a great deal better than their theory; whose example, indeed, refutes their theory. But there are worse objectors and worse men; vicious and corrupt men; sensualists; sensualists in philosophy, and in practice alike; who would gladly believe all the rest of the world as bad as themselves. And these are objectors,

I say, who like the objections before stated, refute themselves.

For who is this small philosopher, that smiles, either at the simplicity of all honest men, or at the simplicity of all honest defenders of them? He is, in the first place, a man who stands up before us, and has the face to boast, that he is himself without principle. No doubt, he thinks other men as bad as himself. A man necessarily, perhaps, judges the actions of other men by his own feelings. He has no other interpreter. The honest man, therefore, will often presume honesty in another; and the generous man, generosity. And so the selfish man can see nothing around him but selfishness; and the knave, nothing but dishonesty; and he who never felt any thing of a generous and self-devoting piety, who never bowed down in that holy and blessed worship, can see in prayer nothing but the offering of selfish fear; in piety, nothing but a slavish superstition.

In the next place, this sneerer at all virtue and piety, not only imagines others to be as destitute of principle as himself; but to some extent, he makes them such, or makes them seem such. His eye of pride chills every goodly thing it looks upon. His breath of scorn blights every generous virtue where it comes. His supple and crafty hand puts all men upon their guard. They become like himself, for the time; they become more crafty while they deal with him. How shall any noble aspiration, any high and pure thoughts, any benevolent purposes, any sacred and holy communing, venture into the presence of the proud and selfish scorner of all goodness! It has been said, that the letters your friends write to you, will show their opinion of your temper and tastes. And so it is, to a certain extent, with conversation.

But in the third place, where, let us ask, has this man studied human nature? Lord Chesterfield observes—and the observation is worthy of a man who never seems to have looked beneath the surface of any thing—that the Court and the Camp are the places, in which a knowledge of mankind is to be gained. And we may remark, that it is from two fields not altogether dissimilar, that our sceptic about virtue always gains his knowledge of mankind: I mean, from fashion and business; the two most artificial spheres of active life. Our objector has witnessed heartless civilities, and imagines that he is acquainted with the deep fountains of human nature. Or he has been out into the paths of business, and seen men girt up for competition, and acting in that artificial state of things which trade produces; and he imagines that he has witnessed the free and unsophisticated workings of the human heart; he supposes that the laws of trade, are also the laws of human affection. He thinks himself deeply read in the book of the human heart, that unfathomable mystery, because he is acquainted with notes and bonds, with cards and compliments.

How completely, then, is this man disqualified from judging of human nature! There *is* a power, which few possess, which none have attained in perfection; a power to unlock the retired, the deeper and nobler sensibilities of men's minds, to draw out the hoarded and hidden virtues of the soul, to open the fountains which custom and ceremony and reserve have sealed up: it is a power, I repeat, which few possess—how evidently does our objector possess it not—and yet without some portion of which, no man should think himself qualified to study human nature. Men know but little of each other, after all; but little know how many good and tender affections are suppressed and kept out of sight, by diffidence, by delicacy, by the fear of appearing awkward or ostentatious, by habits of life, by education, by sensitiveness, and even by strong sensibility, that sometimes puts on a hard and rough exterior for its own check or protection. And the power that penetrates all these barriers, must be an extraordinary one. There must belong to it charity, and kindness, and forbearance, and sagacity, and fidelity to the trust which the opening heart reposes in it. But how peculiarly, I repeat, how totally devoid of this power of opening and unfolding the real character of his fellows, must be the scoffer at human nature!

I have said that this man gathers his conclusions from the most formal and artificial aspects of the world. He never could have drawn them from the holy retreats of domestic life—to say nothing of those deeper privacies of the heart of which I have just been speaking; he never could have drawn his conclusions from those family scenes, where unnumbered, nameless, minute, and indescribable sacrifices are daily made, by thousands and ten thousands all around us; he never could have drawn them from the self-devoting mother's cares, or from the grateful return, the lovely assiduity and tenderness of filial affection; he never could have derived his contemptuous inference from the sick-room, where friendship, in silent prayer, watches and tends its charge. No: he dare not go out from our dwellings, from our temples, from our hospitals—he dare not tread upon the holy places of the land, the high places where the devout have prayed, and the brave have died, and proclaim that patriotism is a visionary sentiment; and piety a selfish delusion; and charity a pretence; and virtue, a name!

II. But it is time that we come now to the objection of the Theologian. And I go at once to the single and strong point of his objection. The Theologian says that human nature is bad and corrupt. Now, taking this language in the practical and popular sense, I find no difficulty in agreeing with the Theologian. And, indeed, if he would confine himself—leaving vague and general declamation and technical phraseology—if he would confine himself to facts; if he would confine himself to a description of actual bad qualities and dispositions in men, I think he could not well go too far. Nay more, I am not certain that any Theologian's description so far as it is of this nature, has gone deep enough into the frightful mass of human depravity. For it requires an acute perception, that is rarely possessed, and a higher and holier conscience, perhaps, than belongs to any, to discover and to declare, *how* bad, and degraded and unworthy a being, a *bad man* is. I confess that nothing would beget in me a higher respect for a man, than a real—not a theological and factitious—but a real and deep sense of human sinfulness and unworthiness; of the grievous wrong which man does to himself, to his religion and to his God, when he yields to the evil and accursed inclinations that find place in him. This moral indignation is not half strong enough, even in those who profess to talk the most about human depravity. And the objection to them is, not that they feel too much or speak too strongly, about the actual wickedness, the actual and distinct sins of the wicked; but they speak too generally and vaguely of human wickedness, that they speak with too little discrimination to every man as if he were a murderer or a monster, that they speak in fine too argumentatively, and too much, if I may say so, with a sort of argumentative satisfaction, as if they were glad that they could make this point so strong.

I know then, and admit, that men and all men more or less, are, alas! sinful and bad. I know that the catalogue of human transgressions is long and dark and mournful. The words, pride and envy and anger and selfishness and base indulgence, are words of lamentation. They are words that should make a man weep when he pronounces them; and most of all when he applies them to himself, or to his fellow-men.

But what now is the inference from all this? Is it that man is an utterly debased, degraded, and contemptible creature; that there is nothing in him to be revered, or respected; that the human heart presents nothing to us but a mark for cold and blighting reproach? Without wishing to assert any thing paradoxical, it seems to me that the very reverse is the inference.

I should reason thus upon this point. I should say, it must be a noble creature that can so offend. I should say, there must be a contrast of light and shade, to make the shade so deep. It *is* no ordinary being, surely; it is a being of conscience, of moral powers and glorious capacities, that calls from us such intense reproach and indignation. We never so arraign the animal creation. The very power of sinning is a lofty and awful power! It is, in the language of our holiest poet, "the excess of glory obscured." Neither is it a power standing alone. It is not a solitary, unqualified, diabolical power of evil; a dark and cold abstraction of wickedness. No, it is clothed with other qualities. No, it has dread attendants; attendants, I had almost said, that dignify even the wrong. A waiting conscience, visitings—Oh! visitings of better thoughts, calls of honour and self respect come to the sinner; terrific admonition whispering in his secret ear, prophetic warning pointing him to the dim and veiled shadows of future retribution, and the all-penetrating, all-surrounding idea of an avenging God are present with him: and the right arm of the felon and the transgressor is lifted up, amidst lightnings of conviction and thunderings of reproach. I can tremble at such a being as this; I can pity him; I can weep for him; but I cannot scorn him.

The very words of condemnation which we apply to sin, are words of comparison. When we describe the act of the transgressor as mean for instance, we recognise I repeat, the nobility of his nature; and when we say that his offence is a degradation, we imply a certain distinction. And so *to do wrong* implies a noble power, the very power which constitutes the glory of heaven; the *power to do right*. And thus it is, as I apprehend, that the inspired Teachers speak of the wickedness and unworthiness of man. They seem to do it under a sense of his better capacities and higher distinction. They speak as if he had wronged himself. And when they use the words ruin and perdition, they announce, in affecting terms, the *worth* of that which is reprobate and lost. Paul when speaking of his transgressions says,—"not I, but the sin that dwelleth in me." There was a better nature in him that resisted evil, though it did not always successfully resist. And we read of the Prodigal Son —in terms which have always seemed to me of the most affecting import—that when he came to the sense of his duty, he "came—*to himself*." Yes, the sinner is beside himself; and there is no peace, **no reconciliation of his conduct to his nature, till he re-**

turns from his evil ways. Shall we not say then, that his nature demands virtue and rectitude to satisfy it?

True it is, and I would not be one to weaken nor obscure the truth, that man is sinful; but he is not satisfied with sinning. Not his conscience only, but his wants, his natural affections, are not satisfied. He pays deep penalties for his transgressions. And these sufferings proclaim a higher nature. The pain, the disappointment, the dissatisfaction that wait on an evil course, show that the human soul was not made to be the instrument of sin, but its lofty avenger. The desolated affections, the haggard countenance, the pallid and sunken cheek, the sighings of grief, proclaim that there are ruins indeed, but they proclaim that something noble has fallen into ruin—proclaim it by signs mournful, yet venerable, like the desolations of an ancient temple, like its broken walls and falling columns and the hollow sounds of decay, that sink down heavily among its deserted recesses.

The sinner, I repeat it, is a sufferer. He seeks happiness in low and unworthy objects; that is his sin: but he does not find it there; and that is his glory. No, he does not find it there: he returns disappointed and melancholy; and there is nothing on earth so eloquent as his grief. Read it in the pages of a Byron and a Burns. There is nothing in literature so touching as these lamentations of noble but erring natures, in the vain quest of a happiness which the world and the world's pleasure can never give. The sinner is often dazzled by earthly fortune and pomp, but it is in the very midst of these things, that he sometimes most feels their emptiness; that his higher nature most feels that it is solitary and unsatisfied. It is in the giddy whirl of frivolous pursuits and amusements, that his soul oftentimes is sick and weary with trifles and vanities: that "he says of laughter, it is mad; and of mirth, what doeth it?"

And yet it is not bare disappointment, nor the mere destitution of happiness caused by sin—it is not these alone that give testimony to a better nature. There is a higher power that bears sway in the human heart. It is remorse, sacred, uncompromising remorse; that will hear of no selfish calculations of pain and pleasure; that *demands* to suffer; that, of all sacrifices on earth, save those of benevolence, brings the only willing victim. What lofty revenge does the abused soul thus take, for its offences; never, no, never, in all its anger, punishing another, as in its justice, it punishes itself!

Such, then, are the attributes that still dwell in the dark grandeur of the soul; the beams of original light, of which amidst its thickest darkness it is never shorn. That in which all the nobleness of earth resides, should not be *condemned* even, but with awe and trembling. It is our treasure; and if this is lost, all is lost. Let us take care, then, that we be not unjust. Man is not an angel; but neither is he a demon; nor a brute. The evil he does is not committed with brutish insensibility, nor with diabolical satisfaction. And the evil, too, is often disguised under forms that do not, at once, permit him to see its real character. His affections become wrong, by excess; passions bewilder; semblances delude; interests ensnare; example corrupts. And yet no tyrant over men's thoughts, no unworthy seeker of their adulation, no pander for guilty pleasure, could ever make the human heart what he would. And in making it what he has, he has often found that he had to work with stubborn materials. No perseverance of endeavour, nor devices of ingenuity, nor depths of artifice, have ever equalled those which are sometimes employed to corrupt the heart from its youthful simplicity and uprightness.

In endeavouring to state the views which are to be entertained of human nature, I have, at present, and before I reverse the picture, but one further observation to make. And that is on the spirit and tone with which it is to be viewed and spoken of. I have wished, even in speaking of its faults, to awaken a feeling of reverence and regret for it, such as would arise within us, on beholding a noble but mutilated statue or the work of some divine architect, in ruins, or some majestic object in nature, which had been marred by the rending of this world's elements and changes. Above all other objects, surely, human nature deserves to be regarded with these sentiments. The ordinary tone of conversation in allusion to this subject, the sneering remark on mankind, as a set of poor and miserable creatures, the cold and bitter severity whether of philosophic scorn or theological rancour, become no being; least of all, him who has part in this common nature. He, at least, should speak with consideration and tenderness. And if he must speak of faults and sins, he would do well to imitate an Apostle, and to tell these things, even weeping. His tone should be that of forbearance and pity. His words should be recorded in a Book of Lamentations. "How is the gold become dim," he might exclaim in the words of an ancient lamentation—"how is the gold become dim, and the most fine gold changed! The precious sons of Zion, comparable to fine gold, how are they esteemed but as earthen vessels, the work of the hands of the potter!"

II.

ON HUMAN NATURE.

FOR THOU HAST MADE HIM A LITTLE LOWER THAN THE ANGELS, AND HAST CROWNED HIM WITH GLORY AND HONOUR.—Psalm viii. 5.

I HAVE endeavoured, in my last discourse, to show that the very objections which are usually brought against human nature, imply in the very fact, in the very spirit and tone of them, the strongest concessions to its worth. I shall now proceed to the direct argument in its favour. It is the constitutional worth of human nature that we have thus far considered rather than its moral worth, or absolute virtue. We have considered the indignant reproaches against its sin and debasement, whether of the philosopher or the theologian, as evidence of their own conviction, that it was made for something better. We have considered that moral constitution of human nature, by which it was evidently made not to be the slave of sin, but its conqueror.

Let us now proceed to take some account of its moral traits and acquisitions. I say its moral *traits* and acquisitions. For there are feelings of the human mind which scarcely rise to the character of acquisitions, which are involuntary impulses; and yet which possess a nature as truly moral, though not in as high a degree, as any voluntary acts of virtue. Such is the simple, natural love of excellence. It bears the same relation to moral effort, as spontaneous reason does to reflection or logical effort: and what is spontaneous, in both cases, is the very foundation of the acquisitions that follow. Thus, the involuntary perception of a few axioms lies at the foundation of Mathematical science; and so from certain spontaneous impressions of truth, springs all knowledge; and in the same manner, our spontaneous moral impressions are the germs of the highest moral efforts.

Of these spontaneous impressions, I am to speak in the first place; and then to produce in favour of human nature the testimony of its higher and more confirmed virtues.

But I am not willing to enter upon this theme, without first offering a remark or two, to prevent any misconception of the purpose for which I again bring forward this discussion. It is not to bring to the altar at which I minister, an oblation of flattery to my fellow worshippers. It is not to make any man feel his moral dangers to be less, or to make him easier in reference to that solemn, spiritual trust that is committed to his nature; but the very contrary. It is not to make him think less of his faults, but more. It is not in fine to build up any one theological dogma, or to beat down another.

My view of the subject, if I may state it without presumption, is this; that there is a treasure in human nature of which most men are not conscious, and with which none are yet fully acquainted! If you had met in a retired part of the country with some rustic youth who bore in his character, the indications of a most sublime genius, and if you saw that he was ignorant of it, and that those around him were ignorant of it, you would look upon him with extreme, with enthusiastic interest, and you would be anxious to bring him into the light, and to rear him up to his proper sphere of honour. This, may I be permitted to say, illustrates the view which I take of human nature. I believe that there is something in every man's heart upon which he ought to look as a found treasure; something upon which he ought to look with awe and wonder; something which should make him tremble when he thinks of sacrificing it to evil; something also, to encourage and cheer him in every endeavour after virtue and purity. Far be it from me to say, that that something is confirmed goodness, or is the degree of goodness which is necessary to make him happy, here or hereafter; or, that it is something to rest upon, or to rely upon, in the anticipation of God's judgment. Still I believe that he who says there is *nothing* good in him, *no* foundation, no feeling of goodness, says what is not true, what is not just to himself, what is not just to his Maker's beneficence.

I will refer now, to those moral traits, to those involuntary moral impressions, of which I have already spoken.

Instances of this nature might undoubtedly be drawn from every department of social life; from social kindness, from friendship, from parental and filial love, from the feelings of spontaneous generosity, pity and admiration, which every day kindles into life and warmth around us. But since these feelings are often alleged to be of a doubtful character, and are so, indeed, to a certain extent; since they are often mixed up with interested considerations which lessen their weight in this argument, I am about to appeal to cases, which, though they are not often brought into the pulpit, will appear to you I trust to be excused, if not justified, by the circumstance that they are altogether apposite cases; cases that is to say, of disinterested feeling.

The world is inundated in this age, with a perfect deluge of fictitious productions. I look, indeed, upon the exclusive reading of such works, in which too many employ their leisure time, as having a very bad and dangerous tendency: but this is not to my purpose at present. I only refer now to the well known extent and fascination of this kind of reading, for the purpose of putting a single question. I ask, what is the moral character of these productions? Not high enough, certainly; but then I ask still more specifically, whether the preference is given to virtue or to vice, in these books; and to which of them, the feelings of the reader generally lean? Can there be one moment's doubt? Is not virtue usually held up to admiration, and are not the feelings universally enlisted in its favour? Must not the character of the leading personage in the story, to satisfy the public taste, be good, and is not his career pursued with intense interest to the end? Now reverse the case. Suppose his character to be bad. Suppose him ungenerous, avaricious, sensual, debased. Would he then be admired? Would he then enlist the sympathies even of the most frivolous reader? It is unnecessary to answer the question. Here, then, is a right and virtuous feeling at work in the world; and it is a perfectly disinterested feeling. Here, I say, is a right and virtuous feeling, beating through the whole heart of society. Why should any one say, it is not a feeling; that it is conscience; that it is mere approbation! It *is* a feeling, if any thing is. There is intense interest; there are tears, to testify that it is a feeling.

If, then, I put such a book into the hands of any reader, and if he feels thus, let him not tell me that there is nothing good in him. There may not be goodness, fixed, habitual goodness in him; but there is something good, out of which goodness may grow.

Of the same character are the most favourite popular songs and ballads. The chosen themes of these compositions are patriotism, generosity, pity, love. Now it is known that nothing sinks more deeply into the heart of nations; and yet these are their themes. Let me make the ballads of a people, some one has said, and let who will, make their laws; and yet he must construct them on these principles; he must compose them in praise of patriotism, honour, fidelity, generous sympathy and pure love. I say, pure love. Let the passion be made a base one; let it be capricions, mercenary, or sensual, and it instantly loses the public sympathy: the song would be instantly hissed from the stage of the vilest theatre that ever was opened. No, it must be true-hearted affection, holding its faith and fealty bright and unsoiled, amidst change of fortunes, amidst poverty, and disaster, and separation, and reproach. The popular taste will hardly allow the affection to be as prudent as it ought to be. And when I listen to one of these popular ballads or songs that tells—it may be not in the best taste—but which tells the thrilling tale of high, disinterested, magnanimous fidelity to the sentiments of the heart; that tells of pure and faithful affection, which no cold looks can chill, which no storms of misfortune can quench, which prefers simple merit to all worldly splendour; when I observe this, I say, I see a noble feeling at work; and that which many will pronounce to be silly, through a certain shamefacedness about their own sensibility, I regard as respectable, and honourable to human nature.

Now I say again, as I said before, let these popular compositions set forth the beauties of vice; let them celebrate meanness, parsimony, fraud or cowardice; and would they dwell, as they now do, in the habitations, and in the hearts, and upon the lips, of whole nations? What a disinterested testimony is this to the charms of virtue! What evidence that men feel those charms, though they may not be won by them to virtuous lives! The national songs of a people do not embrace cold sentiments; they are not sung or heard with cold approbation. They fire the breasts of millions. They draw tears from the eyes of ten thousand listening throngs, that are gathered in the homes of human affection.

And the power of music, too, as a separate thing, lies, very much, as it seems to me, in the sentiments and affections it awakens. There is a pleasure to the ear, doubtless; but there is a pleasure also, to the heart; and this is the greater pleasure. But what kind of pleasure is it? Does that melody which addresses the universal mind, appeal to vile and base passions? Is not the state into which it naturally throws almost every mind favourable to gentle and kind emotions, to lofty efforts and heroic sacrifices? But if the human heart possessed no high nor holy feelings; if it were entirely alien to them, then the music which excites them, should excite them to voluptuousness, cruelty, strife, fraud, avarice, and to all the mean aims and indulgences of a selfish disposition.

Let not these illustrations—which are adopted, to be sure, partly because they are fitted to unfold a moral character where no credit has usually been given for it, and because, too, they present at once universal and disinterested manifestations of human feeling—let not these illustrations, I say, be thought to furnish an unsatisfactory inference, because they are drawn from the lighter actions of the human mind. The feeling in all these cases is not superficial nor feeble; and the slighter the occasion that awakens it, the stronger is our argument. If the leisure and recreations of men, yield such evidence of deep moral feeling, what are they not capable of, when armed with lofty purposes and engaged in high duties? If the instrument yields such noble strains, though incoherent and intermitted, to the slightest touch; what might not be done, if the hand of skill were laid upon it, to bring out all its sublime harmonies? Oh! that some powerful voice might speak to this inward nature—powerful as the story of heroic deeds, moving as the voice of song, arousing as the trumpet-call to honour and victory! My friends, if we are among those who are pursuing the sinful way, let us be assured that we know not ourselves yet; we have not searched the depths of our nature; we have not communed with its deepest wants; we have not listened to its strongest and highest affections; if we had done all this, we could not abuse it as we do; nor could we neglect it as we do.

But it is time to pass from these instances of spontaneous and universal feeling, to those cases in which such feeling, instead of being occasional and evanescent, is formed into a prevailing habit and a consistent and fixed character; to pass from good affections, transient, uncertain, and unworthily neglected, to good men, who are permanently such, and worthy to be called such. Our argument from this source is more confined, but it gains strength by its compression within a narrower compass.

I shall not be expected here to occupy the time, with asserting or proving, that there are good men in the world. It will be more important to reply to a single objection under this head, which would be fatal if it were just, and to point to some characteristics of human virtue which prove its great and real worth. Let me however for a moment indulge myself in the simple assertion, of what every mind, not entirely misanthropic, must feel to be true. I say then that there are good men in the world: there are good men every where. There are men who are good for goodness' sake. In obscurity, in retirement, beneath the shadow of ten thousand dwellings, scarcely known to the world and never asking to be known, there are good men. In adversity, in poverty, amidst temptations, amidst all the severity of earthly trials, there are good men, whose lives shed brightness upon the dark clouds that surround them. Be it true, if we must admit the sad truth, that many are wrong, and persist in being wrong; that many are false to every holy trust, and faithless towards every holy affection; that many are estranged from infinite goodness; that many are coldly selfish and meanly sensual; yes, cold and dead to every thing that is not wrapped up in their own little earthly interest, or more darkly wrapped up in the veil of fleshly appetites. Be it so; but I thank God, that is not all that we are obliged to believe. No, there are true hearts, amidst the throng of the false and the faithless. There are warm and generous hearts, which the cold atmosphere of surrounding selfishness never chills; and eyes, unused to weep for personal sorrow, which often overflow with sympathy for the sorrows of others. Yes, there are good men, and true men; I thank them; I bless them for what they are: I thank them for what they are to me. What do I say—why do I utter my weak benediction? God from on high, doth bless them, and he giveth his angels charge to keep them; and no where in the holy Record are there words more precious or strong, than those in which it is written that God loveth these righteous ones. Such men are there. Let not their precious virtues be distrusted. As surely and as evidently as some men have obeyed the calls of ambition and pleasure, so surely, and so evidently, have other men obeyed the voice of conscience, and " chosen rather to suffer with the people of God than to enjoy the pleasures of sin for a season." Why, every meek man suffers in a conflict keener far, than the contest for honour and applause. And there are such men, who amidst injury, and insult, and misconstruction, and the pointed finger, and the scornful lip of pride, stand firm in their integrity and allegiance to a loftier principle, and still their throbbing hearts in prayer, and hush them to the gentle motions of kindness and pity. Such witnesses there are, even in this bad world; signs that a redeeming work is going forward amidst its mournful derelictions; proofs that it is not a world forsaken of heaven; pledges that it will not be forsaken; tokens that cheer and touch every good and thoughtful mind, beyond all other power of earth to penetrate and enkindle it.

I believe that what I have now said, is a most legitimate argument for the worth of human nature. As a matter of fact, it will not be denied that such beings as I have represented, there are. And I now further maintain, and this is the most material point in the argument, that such men—that good men, in other words—are to be regarded as the rightful and legitimate representatives of human nature. Surely, not man's vices but his virtues, not his failure but his success, should teach us what to think of his nature. Just as we should look, for their real character, to the productions nourished by a favourable soil and climate, and not to the same plants or trees, as they stand withered and stunted in a barren desert.

But here we are met with the objection before referred to. It is said that man's virtues come from God; and his *sins* only from his own nature. And thus—for this is the result of the objection—from the estimate of what is human, all human excellence is at once cut off, by this fine discrimination of theological subtilty. Unreasonable as this seems to me, if the objector will forget his theology for one moment, I will answer it. I say, then, that the influence of the good spirit of God, does not destroy our natural powers, but guides them into a right direction; that it does not create any thing unnatural surely, nor supernatural in man, but what is suitable to his nature: that, in fine, his virtues are as truly the voluntary putting forth of his native powers, as his vices are. Else would his virtues have no worth. Human nature, in short, is the noble stock on which these virtues grow. With heaven's rain, and sunshine, and genial influence, do you say? Be it so; still they are no less human, and *show the stock* from which they spring. When you look over a grain-field, and see some parts more luxuriant than others, do you say, that they are of a different nature from the rest? And when you look abroad upon the world, do you think it right to take Tartars and Hottentots as specimens of the race? And why then shall you regard the worst of men, rather than the best, as samples of human nature and capability?

The way, then, is open for us to claim for human nature, however that nature is breathed upon by heavenly influences, all the excellent fruits that have sprung from it. And they are not few; they are not small; they are not contemptible.

They have cost too much—if there were no other consideration to give them value; they have cost too much, to be thus estimated.

The true idea of human nature, is not, that it passively and spontaneously produces its destined results;

but, that placed in a fearful contest between good and evil, it is *capable* of glorious exertions and attainments. Human virtue is the result of effort and patience, in circumstances that most severely try it. Human excellence is much of it gained at the expense of self-denial. All the wisdom and worth in the world, are a struggle with ignorance and infirmity and temptation; often with sickness and pain. There is not an admirable character presented before you, but it has cost years and years, of toil and watching and self-government to form it. You see the victor, but you forget the battle. And you forget it, for a reason that exalts and ennobles the fortitude and courage of the combatant. You forget it, because the conflict has been carried on, all silently, in his own bosom. You forget it, because no sound has gone forth, and no wreath of fame has awaited the conqueror.

And *what* has he gained?—to refer to but one more of the views that might be urged; what has he gained? I answer, what is worth too much to be slightly estimated. The catalogue of human virtues is not brief nor dull. What glowing words do we involuntarily put into that record! with what feelings do we hallow it! The charm of youthful excellence, the strong integrity of manhood, the venerable piety of age; unsullied honour, unswerving truth; fidelity, magnanimity, self-sacrifice, martyrdom; ay, and the spirit of martyrdom in many a form of virtue; sacred friendship, with its disinterested toil, ready to die for those it loves; noble patriotism, slain in its high places, beautiful in death; holy philanthropy, that pours out its treasure and its life! dear and blessed virtues of humanity! (we are ready to exclaim,) what human heart does not cherish you? Bright cloud that hath passed on with " the sacramental host of God's elect," through ages!—how dark and desolate but for you, would be this world's history!

My friends, I have spoken of the reality and worth of virtue, and I have spoken of it as a part of human nature, not surely to awaken a feeling of pride, but to lead you and myself, to an earnest aspiration after that excellence, which embraces the chief welfare and glory of our nature. A cold disdain of our species, an indulgence of sarcasm, a feeling that is always ready to distrust and disparage every indication of virtuous principle, or an utter despair of the moral fortunes of our race, will not help the purpose in view, but must have a powerful tendency to hinder its accomplishment.

Unhappy is it, that any are left, by any possibility, to doubt the virtues of their kind! Let us do something to wipe away from the history of human life, that fatal reproach. Let us make that best of contributions to the stock of human happiness, an example of goodness that shall disarm such gloomy and chilling scepticism, and win men's hearts to virtue. I have received many benefits, from my fellow-beings. But no gift, in their power to bestow, can ever impart such a pure and thrilling delight, as one bright action, one lovely virtue, one character that shines with all the enrapturing beauty of goodness.

Who would not desire to confer such benefits on the world as these? Who would not desire to leave such memorials behind him? Such memorials have been left on earth. The virtues of the departed, but forever dear, hallow and bless many of our dwellings, and call forth tears that lose half of their bitterness in gratitude and admiration. Yes, there are such legacies, and there are those on earth who have inherited them. Yes, there are men, poor men, whose parents have left them a legacy in their bare memory, that they would not exchange—no, they would not exchange it for boundless wealth. Let it be our care to bequeath to society and to the world, blessings like these. "The memorial of virtue," saith the wisdom of Solomon, "is immortal. When it is present, men take example from it; and when it is gone, they desire it; it weareth a crown, and triumpheth forever."

III.

ON THE WRONG WHICH SIN DOES TO HUMAN NATURE.

HE THAT SINNETH AGAINST ME WRONGETH HIS OWN SOUL.—Prov. viii. 36.

This is represented as the language of wisdom. The attribute of wisdom is personified throughout the chapter; and it closes its instructions with the declaration of our text: "He that sinneth against me, wrongeth his own soul." The theme, then, which, in these words, is obviously presented for our meditation, is the wrong which the sinner does to himself, to his nature, to his own soul.

He does a wrong, indeed, to others. He does them, it may be, deep and heinous injury. The moral offender injures society, and injures it in the most vital part. Sin is, to all the dearest interests of society, a desolating power. It spreads misery through the world. It brings that misery into the daily lot of millions. The violence of anger, the exactions of selfishness, the corrodings of envy, the coldness of distrust, the contests of pride, the excesses of passion, the indulgences of sense, carry desolation into the very bosom of domestic life; and the crushed and bleeding hearts of friends and kindred, or of a larger circle of the suffering and oppressed, are every where witnesses at once, and victims to the mournful presence of this great evil.

But all the injury, great and terrible as it is, which the sinner does or can inflict upon others, is not equal to the injury that he inflicts upon himself. The evil that he does, is, in almost all cases, the greater, the nearer it comes to himself; greater to his friends than to society at large; greater to his family, than to his friends; and so it is greater to himself than it is to any other. Yes, it is in his own nature, whose glorious traits are dimmed and almost blotted out, whose pleading remonstrances are sternly disregarded, whose immortal hopes are rudely stricken down; it is in his own nature that he does a work so dark and mournful, and so fearful, that he ought to shudder and weep to think of it.

Does any one say, "he is glad that it is so; glad that it is himself he injures most?" What a feeling, my brethren, of disinterested justice is that! How truly, may it be said, that there is something good in bad men. Doubtless, there are those, who in their remorse at an evil deed, would be glad if all the injury and suffering could be their own. I rejoice in that testimony. But does that feeling make it any less true,—does not that feeling make it more true, that such a nature is wronged by base and selfish passions? Or, because it is a man's self, because it is his own soul that he has most injured; because he has not only wronged others, but ruined himself; is his course any the less guilty, or unhappy, or unnatural?

I say, unnatural; and this is a point on which I wish to insist, in the consideration of that wrong which the moral offender does to himself. The sinner, I say, is to be pronounced an unnatural being. He has cast off the government of those powers of his nature, which as being the loftiest, have the best right to reign over him, the government, that is to say, of his intellectual and moral faculties; and has yielded himself to meaner appetites. Those meaner appetites, though they belong to his nature, have no right, and he knows they have no right, to govern him. The rightful authority, the lawful sovereignty belongs, and he knows that it belongs, not to sense, but to conscience. To rebel against this, is to sin against nature. It is to rebel against nature's order. It is to rebel against the government that God has set up within him. It is to obey, not venerable authority, but the faction which his passions have made within him.

Thus violence and misrule are always the part of transgression. Nay, every sin—I do not mean now the natural and unavoidable imperfection of a weak and ignorant being—but every wilful moral offence is a monstrous excess and excrescence in the mind, a hideous deformity, a loathsome disease, a destruction, so far as it goes, of the purposes for which our nature was made. As well might you say of the diseased plant or tree, which is wasting all its vigour on the growth of one huge and unsightly deformity, that it is in a natural condition. Grant that the natural powers of the plant or tree are converted, or rather perverted to this misuse, and help to produce this deformity; yet the deformity is not natural. Grant that evil is the possible, or supposable, or that it is the actual, nay, and in this world, the common, result of moral freedom. But it is evidently not the just and legitimate result; it is not the fair and natural result; it violates all moral powers and responsibilities. If the mechanism of a vast manufactory, were thrown into sudden disorder, the power which propels it might, indeed, spread destruction throughout the whole work; but would that be the natural course of things; the result for which the fabric was made? So passion, not in its natural state, but still natural passion, in its unnatural state of excess and fury, may spread disorder and destruction through the moral system; but wreck and ruin are not the proper order of any nature, whether material or moral.

The idea against which I am now contending, that evil is natural to us, and, in fact, that nothing else is natural; this popular and prevailing idea is one, it seems to me, so fearful and fatal in its bearings—is one of such comprehensive and radical mischief, as to infect the religious state of all mankind, and to overshadow, almost with despair, the moral prospects of the world. There is no error, theological or moral, that appears to me, so destructive as this. There is nothing that lies so near the very basis of all moral reform and spiritual improvement as this.

If it were a matter of mere doctrine it would be of less consequence. But it is a matter of habitual feeling, I fear, and of deep-settled opinion. The world, alas! is not only in the sad and awful condition of being filled with evil, and filled with misery in consequence, but of thinking that this is the natural order of things. Sin is a thing of course; it is taken for granted that it must exist very much in the way that it does; and men are every where easy about it: they are every where sinking into worldliness and vice as if they were acting out the principles of their moral constitution, and almost as if they were fulfilling the will of God. And thus it comes to pass, that that which should fill the world with grief and astonishment and horror, beyond all things else most horrible and lamentable, is regarded with perfect apathy as a thing natural and necessary. Why, my brethren, if but the animal creation were found, on a sudden, disobedient to the principles of *their* nature; if they were ceasing to regard the guiding instincts with which they are endowed, and were rushing into universal mad-ness, the whole world would stand aghast at the spectacle. But multitudes in the rational creation, disobey a higher law and forsake a more sacred guidance; they degrade themselves below the beasts, or make themselves as entirely creatures of this world; they plunge into excess and profligacy; they bow down divine and immortal faculties to the basest uses; and there is no wonder, there is no horror, there is no consciousness of the wrong done to themselves. They say, "it is the natural course of things," as if they had solved the whole problem of moral evil. They say, "it is the way of the world," almost as if they thought it was the order of Providence. They say, "it is what men are," almost as if they thought it was what men were designed to be. And thus ends their comment, and with it, all reasonable endeavour to make themselves better and happier.

If this state of prevailing opinion be as certainly erroneous, as it is evidently dangerous, it is of the last importance that every resistance, however feeble, should be offered to its fatal tendencies. Let us therefore consider, a little more in detail, the wrong which sin does to human nature. I say then, that it does a wrong to every natural faculty and power of the mind.

Sin does a wrong to reason. There are instances, and not a few, in which it absolutely destroys reason. There are other and more numerous cases, in which it employs that faculty, but employs it in a toil most degrading to its nature. There is reasoning, indeed, in the mind of a miser; the solemn arithmetic of profit and loss. There is reasoning in the schemes of unscrupulous ambition; the absorbing and agitating intrigue for office or honour. There is reasoning upon the modes of sensual pleasure; and the whole power of a very acute mind is sometimes employed and absorbed, in plans and projects and imaginations of evil indulgence. But what an unnatural desecration is it, for reason, sovereign, majestic, all comprehending reason, to contract its boundless range to the measure of what the hand can grasp; to be sunk so low, as to idolize outward or sensitive good; to make its god, not indeed of wood or stone, but of a sense, or a nerve! What a prostration of immortal reason is it, to bend its whole power to the poor and pitiful uses, which sinful indulgence demands of it!

Sin is a kind of insanity. So far as it goes, it makes man an irrational creature: it makes him a fool. The consummation of evil is, ever, and in every form, the extreme of folly. And it is that most pitiable folly which is puffed up with arrogance and self-sufficiency. Sin degrades, it impoverishes, it beggars the soul; and yet the soul in this very condition, blesses itself in its superior endowments and happy fortune. Yes, every sinner is a beggar: as truly as the most needy and desperate mendicant. He begs for a precarious happiness; he begs it of his possessions or his coffers, that cannot give it; he begs it of every passing trifle and pleasure; he begs it of things most empty and uncertain,—of every vanity, of every shout of praise in the vacant air; of every wandering eye he begs its homage: he wants these things, he wants them for happiness; he wants them to satisfy the craving soul; and yet he imagines that he is very fortunate; he accounts himself wise, or great, or honourable, or rich, increased in goods, and in need of nothing. The infatuation of the inebriate man, who is elated and gay, just when he ought to be most depressed and sad, we very well understand. But it is just as true of every man that is intoxicated by any of his senses or passions, by wealth, or honour, or pleasure, that he is infatuated; that he has abjured reason.

What clearer dictate of reason is there than to prefer the greater good, to the lesser good. But every offender, every sensualist, every avaricious man, sacrifices the greater good, the happiness of virtue and piety, for the lesser good, which he finds in his senses or in the perishing world. Nor, is this the strongest view of the case. He sacrifices the greater for the less, without any necessity for it. He might have both. He gives up heaven for earth, when in the best sense, he might, I repeat, have both. A pure mind can derive more enjoyment from this world, and from the senses, than an impure mind. This is true even of the lowest senses. But there are other senses, besides these; and the pleasures of the epicure are far from equalling even in intensity, those which piety draws from the glories of vision, and the melodies of sound; ministers as they are of thoughts and feelings, that swell far beyond the measure of all worldly joy.

The love of happiness might properly be treated as a separate part of our nature, and I had intended, indeed, to speak of it distinctly; to speak of the meagre and miserable provision which unholy gratification makes for it; and yet more of the cruel wrong which is done to this eager and craving love of happiness. But as I have fallen on this topic, and find the space that belongs to me diminishing, I must content myself with a single suggestion.

What bad man ever desired that his *child* should be like himself? Vice is said to wear an alluring aspect; and many a heedless youth, alas! rushes into its embraces for happiness; but what vicious man, what corrupt and dissolute man, ever desired that his child should walk in his steps? And what a testimony is this, what a clear and disinterested testimony, to the unhappiness of a sinful course! Yes, it is the bad man that often feels an interest about the virtue of others, beyond all, perhaps, that good men feel—feels an intensity, an agony of desire for his children, that *they* may be brought up virtuously; that they may never, never be, such as he is!

How truly, and with what striking emphasis, did the venerable Cranmer reply, when told that a certain man had cheated him, "No, he has cheated himself." Every bad man, every dishonest man, every corrupt man, cheats himself of a good, far dearer than any advantage that he obtains over his neighbour. Others he may injure, abuse and delude; but, another thing is true, though commonly forgotten, and that is, that he deludes himself, abuses himself, injures himself, more than he does all other men.

In the next place, sin does a wrong to conscience. There is a conscience in every man, which is as truly a part of his nature, as reason or memory. The offender against this, therefore, violates no unknown law, nor impracticable rule. From the very teaching of his nature, he knows what is right, and he knows that he can do it; and his very nature, therefore, instead of furnishing him with apologies for wilful wrong, holds him inexcusable. Inexcusable, I am aware, is a strong word; and when I have looked at mankind, and seen the ways in which they are instructed, educated and influenced, I have been disposed to feel as if there were palliations. But on the other hand, when I consider how strong is the voice of nature in a man, how sharp and piercing is the work of a restraining and condemning conscience, how loud and terrible is its remonstrance, what a peculiar, what a heaven-commissioned anguish it sometimes inflicts upon the guilty man; I am compelled to say, despite of all bad teaching, and bad influence, "this being is utterly inexcusable." For, I repeat it, there is a conscience in men. I cannot admit that human nature ever chooses evil as such. It seeks for good, for gratification, indeed. But take the vilest man that lives; and if it were so, that he could obtain the gratification he seeks—be it property or sensual pleasure—that he could obtain it, honestly and innocently, he would greatly prefer it, on such terms. This shows that there is conscience in him. But he *will* have the desired gratification. And to obtain it, he sets his foot upon that conscience, and crushes it down to dishonour and agony, worse than death. Ah! my brethren, we who sit in our closets, talk about vice, and dishonesty, and bloody crime, and draw dark pictures of them; cold and lifeless, though dark pictures. But we little know, perhaps, of what we speak. The heart, all conscious and alive to the truth, would smile in bitterness and derision, at the feebleness of our description. And could that heart speak; could "the bosom black as death" send forth its voice of living agony in our holy places, it would rend the vaulted arches of every sanctuary, with the cry of a pierced, and wounded, and wronged, and ruined nature!

Finally, sin does a wrong to the affections. How does it mar even that image of the affections, that mysterious shrine from which their revealings flash forth, "the human face divine;" bereaving the world of more than half its beauty! Can you ever behold sullenness clouding the clear, fair brow of childhood, or the flushed cheek of anger, or the averted and writhen features of envy, or the dim and sunken eye and haggard aspect of vice, or the red signals of bloated excess hung out on every feature, proclaiming the fire that is consuming within—without feeling that sin is the despoiler of all that the affections make most hallowed and beautiful?

But these are only indications of the wrong that is done, and the ruin that is wrought in the heart. Nature has made our affections to be full of tenderness, to be sensitive and alive to every touch, to cling to their cherished objects with a grasp, from which nothing but cruel violence can sever them. We hear much, I know, of the coldness of the world; but I cannot believe much that I hear; nor is it perhaps meant, in any sense, that denies to man naturally, the most powerful affections; affections that demand the most gentle and considerate treatment. Human love —I am ready to exclaim—how strong is it! What yearnings are there of parental fondness, of filial gratitude, of social kindness, every where! What impatient asking of ten thousand hearts for the love of others; not for their gold, not for their praise, but for their love!

But sin enters into this world of the affections, and spreads around the death-like coldness of distrust; the word of anger falls like a blow upon the heart; or avarice hardens the heart against every finer feeling; or the insane merriment, or the sullen stupor of the inebriate man, falls like a thunder-bolt amidst the circle of kindred and children. Oh! the hearts, where sin is to do its work, should be harder than the nether mill-stone; yet it enters in among affections, all warm, all sensitive, all gushing forth in tenderness; and deaf to all their pleadings, it does its work, as if it were some demon of wrath that knew no pity, and heard no groans, and felt no relenting.

But I must not leave this subject to be regarded as

if it were only a matter for abstract or curious speculation. It goes beyond reasoning; it goes to the conscience, and demands penitence and humiliation.

For of what, in this view, is the sensualist guilty? He is guilty not merely of indulging the appetites of his body; but of sacrificing to that body, a soul!—I speak literally—of sacrificing to that body a soul; yes, of sacrificing all the transcendent and boundless creation of God in his nature, to one single nerve of his perishing frame. The brightest emanation of God, a flame from the everlasting altar, burns within him; and he voluntarily spreads over it, a fleshy veil, a veil of appetites, a veil of thick darkness; and if from its awful folds, one beam of the unholy and insufferable light within breaks forth, he closes his eyes, and quickly spreads another covering of wilful delusion over it, and utterly refuses to see that light, though it flashes upon him from the shrine of the Divinity. There is, indeed, a peculiarity in the sensuality of a man, distinguishing it from the sensual gratification of which an animal is capable, and which, many men are exalted above the brutes, only to turn to the basest uses. The sensual pleasures of a human being derive a quality from the mind. They are probably more intense, through the co-operating action of the mind. The appetite of hunger or thirst, for instance, is doubtless the same in both animal and man, and its gratification the same in *kind;* but the mind communicates to it a greater intensity. To a certain extent, this is unquestionably natural and lawful. But the mind, finding that it has this power, and that by absorption in sense, by gloating over its objects, it can for a time, add something to their enjoyment; the mind, I say, surrenders itself to the base and ignoble ministry. The angel in man does homage to the brute in man. Reason toils for sense;

the imagination panders for appetite; and even the conscience—that no faculty may be left undebased—the divine conscience strives to spread around the loathsome forms of voluptuousness, a haze of moral beauty—calling intoxication, enthusiasm; and revelling, good fellowship; and dignifying every species of indulgence with some name that is holy.

Of what, again, is the miser, and of what is every inordinately covetous man, guilty? Conversant as he may be with every species of trade and traffic, there is one kind of barter, coming yet nearer to his interest, but of which, perchance, he has never thought. He barters virtue for gain! That is the stupendous moral traffic in which he is engaged. The very attributes of the mind are made a part of the stock, in the awful trade of avarice. And if its account-book were to state truly the *whole* of every transaction, it would often stand thus: " Gained, my hundreds or my thousands; lost, the rectitude and peace of my conscience:" "Gained, a great bargain, driven hard; lost, in the same proportion, the generosity and kindness of my affections." " Credit "—and what strife is there for that ultimate item, for that final record?—" Credit, by an immense fortune;" but on the opposing page, the last page of that moral, as truly as mercantile account, I read those words, written not in golden capitals, but in letters of fire—" a lost soul!"

Oh! my brethren, it is a pitiable desecration of such a nature as ours to give it up to the world. Some baser thing might have been given, without regret; but to bow down reason and conscience, to bind them to the clods of earth; to contract those faculties that spread themselves out beyond the world, even to infinity—to contract them to worldly trifles; it is pitiable; it is something to mourn and to weep over. He who sits down in a dungeon which another has made, has not such cause to bewail himself, as he who sits down in the dungeon which he has thus made for himself. Poverty and destitution are sad things; but there is no such poverty, there is no such destitution, as that of a covetous and worldly heart. Poverty is a sad thing, but there is no man so poor, as he who is poor in his affections and virtues. Many a house is full, where the mind is unfurnished and the heart is empty; and no hovel of mere penury ever ought to be so sad as that house. Behold, it is left desolate; to the immortal it is left desolate, as the chambers of death. Death *is* there indeed; and it is the death of the soul!

But not to dwell longer upon particular forms of evil; of what, let us ask, is the *man* guilty? *Who* is it that is thus guilty? To say that he is noble in his nature, has been sometimes thought a dangerous laxity of doctrine, a proud assumption of merit, "a flattering unction" laid to the soul. But what kind of flattery is it, to say to a man, "you were made but little lower than the angels; you might have been rising to the state of angels; and you have made—*what* have you made yourself? What you *are;* a slave to the world; a slave to sense; a slave to masters baser than nature made them, to vitiated sense, and a corrupt and vain world!" Alas! the irony implied in such flattery as this, is not needed to add poignancy to conviction. Boundless capacities shrunk to worse than infantile imbecility! immortal faculties made toilers for the vanities of a moment! a glorious nature sunk to a willing fellowship with evil!—it needs no exaggeration, but only simple statement, to make this a sad and afflicting case. Ill enough had it been for us if we had been *made* a depraved and degraded race. Well might the world even then, have sat down in sackcloth and sorrow; though repentance could properly have made no part of its sorrow. But ill is it indeed, if we have made *ourselves* the sinful and unhappy beings that we are; if we have given ourselves the wounds, which have brought languishment and debility and distress upon us! What keen regret and remorse would any one of us feel, if in a fit of passion, he had destroyed his own right arm, or had planted in it a lingering wound! And yet this, and this last especially, is what every offender does to some faculty of his nature.

But this is not all. Ill enough had it been for us, if we had wrought out evil from nothing; if from a nature negative and indifferent to the result, we had brought forth the fruits of guilt and misery. But if we have wronged, if we have wrested from its true bias, a nature made for heavenly ends; if it was all beautiful in God's design and in our capacity, and we have made it all base, so that human nature, alas! is but the by-word of the satirist, and a mark for the scorner; if affections that might have been sweet and pure almost as the thoughts of angels, have been soured and embittered and turned to wrath, even in the homes of human kindness; if the very senses have been brutalized and degraded, and changed from ministers of pleasure to inflictors of pain; and yet more, if all the dread authority of reason has been denied, and all the sublime sanctity of conscience has been set at naught in this downward course; and yet once more, if all these things, not chimerical, not visionary, are actually witnessed, are matters of history, in ten thousand dwellings, around us; ah! if they are actually existing, my brethren, in you and in me!—and finally, if uniting together, these causes of depravation have spread a flood of misery over the world, and there are sorrows and sighings and tears in all the habitations of men, all proceeding from this one cause; then, I say, shall penitence be thought a strange and uncalled-for emotion? Shall it be thought strange that the first great demand of the Gospel, should be for repentance? Shall it be thought strange that a man should sit down and weep bitterly for his sins; so strange that his acquaintances shall ask, "what hath he done?" or shall conclude that he is going mad with fanaticism, or is on the point of losing his reason? No, truly; the dread infatuation is on the part of those who weep not? It is the negligent world, that is fanatical and frantic in the pursuit of unholy indulgences and unsatisfying pleasures. It is such a world refusing to weep over its sins and miseries, that is fatally deranged. Repentance, my brethren, shall it be thought a virtue difficult of exercise? What can the world sorrow for, if not for the cause of all sorrow? What is to awaken grief, if not guilt and shame? Where shall the human heart pour out its tears, if not on those desolations which have been of its own creating?

How fitly is it written, and in language none too strong, that "the sacrifices of God are a broken and contrite heart." And how encouragingly is it written also, "a broken and contrite heart, thou wilt not despise." "Oh! Israel," saith again the sacred word, "Oh, Israel! thou hast destroyed thyself; but in me is thine help found."

IV.

ON THE ADAPTATION WHICH RELIGION, TO BE TRUE AND USEFUL, SHOULD HAVE TO HUMAN NATURE.

A BRUISED REED SHALL HE NOT BREAK, AND THE SMOKING FLAX SHALL HE NOT QUENCH.—Isaiah xlii. 3.

This was spoken by prophecy of our Saviour, and is commonly considered as one of the many passages, which either prefigure or describe, the considerate and gracious adaptation of his religion, to the wants and weaknesses of human nature. This adaptation of Christianity to the wants of the mind, is, indeed a topic that has been much, and very justly insisted on, as an evidence of its truth.

I wish however, in the present discourse, to place this subject before you in a light somewhat different, perhaps, from that in which it has usually been viewed. If Christianity is suited to the wants of our nature, it is proper to consider what our nature needs. I shall therefore in the following discourse, give considerable prominence to this inquiry. The wants of our nature are various. I shall undertake to show in several respects, what a religion that is adapted to these wants, *should be.* In the same connection, I shall undertake to show that Christianity is such a religion.

This course of inquiry, I believe, will elicit some just views of religious truth, and will enable us to judge whether our own views of it are just. My object in it, is to present some temperate and comprehensive views of religion, which shall be seen at once to meet the necessities of our nature, and to accord with the spirit of the Christian religion.

Nothing, it would seem, could be more obvious, than that a religion for human beings, should be suited to human beings; not to angels, nor to demons; not to a fictitious order of creatures; not to the inhabitants of some other world; but to *men*—to men of this world, of this state and situation in which we are placed, of this nature which is given us; to *men*, with all their passions and affections warm and alive, and all their weaknesses and wants and fears, about them. And yet evident and reasonable as all this is, nothing has been more common, than for religion to fail of this very adaptation. Sometimes, it has been made a quality all softness, all mercy and gentleness; something joyous and cheering, light and easy, as if it were designed for angels. At others, it has been clothed with features as dark and malignant, as if it belonged to fiends rather than to men. In no remote period, it has laid penances on men; as if their sinews and nerves were like the mails of steel, which they wore in those days. While the same religion, with strange inconsistency, lifted up the reins to their passions, as if it had been the age of Stoicism, instead of being the age of Chivalry. Alas! how little has there been in the religions of past ages; how little in the prevalent forms even of the Christian religion, to draw out, to expand and brighten, the noble faculties of our nature! How many of the beautiful fruits of human affection, have withered away under the cold and blighting touch of a scholastic and stern theology! How many fountains of joy in the human heart have been sealed and closed up for ever, by the iron hand of a gloomy superstition! How many bright spirits, how many comely and noble natures, have been marred and crushed, by the artificial, the crude and rough dealing of religious phrenzy and fanaticism!

It is suitable, then, it is expedient, to consider the adaptation which religion to be true and useful ought to have to human nature. It may serve to correct errors. It may serve to guide those who are asking what ideas of religion they are to entertain, what sentiments they are to embrace; what conduct to pursue.

In entering upon this subject, let me offer one leading observation, and afterwards proceed to some particulars.

I. I say, then, in the first place, that religion should be adapted to our *whole* nature. It should remember that we have understandings; and it should be a rational religion. It should remember that we have feelings; and it should be an earnest and fervent religion. It should remember that our feelings revolt at violence, and are all alive to tenderness; and it should be gentle, ready to entreat, and full of mercy. It should remember too that our feelings naturally lean to self-indulgence, and it should be, in its gentleness, strict and solemn. It should in a due proportion address all our faculties.

Most of the erroneous forms of religious sentiment that prevail in the Christian world, have arisen from the predominance that has been given to some one part of our nature, in the matters of spiritual concernment. Some religions have been all speculation, all doctrine, all theology; and, as you might expect, they have been cold, barren and dead. Others have been all feeling; and have become visionary, wild, and extravagant. Some have been all sentiment; and have wanted practical virtue. Others have been all practice; their advocates have been exclaiming " works works ! these are the evidence and test of all goodness." And so, with certain exceptions and qualifications, they are. But this substantial character of religion, this hold which it really has, upon all the active principles of our nature, has been so much, so exclusively contended for, that religion has too often degenerated into a mere, superficial, decent morality.

Religion, then, let it be repeated, if it be true and just, addresses our whole nature. It addresses the active and the contemplative in us ; reason and imagination ; thought and feeling. It is experience ; but it is conduct too: it is high meditation ; but then it is also humble virtue. It is excitement, it is earnestness ; but no less truly, is it calmness. Let me dwell upon this last point a moment. It is not uncommon to hear it said that excitement is a very bad thing, and that true religion is calm. And yet it would seem as if, by others, repose was regarded as deadly to the soul, and as if the only safety lay in a tremendous agitation. Now what saith our nature—for the being that is the very subject of this varying discipline may surely be allowed to speak—what saith our nature to these different advisers ? It says, I think, that both are to a certain extent wrong, and both, to a certain extent right. That is to say, human nature requires, in their due proportion, both excitement and tranquillity. Our minds need a complex and blended influence ; need to be at once aroused and chastened, to be at the same time quickened and subdued ; need to be impelled, and yet guided ; need to be humbled no doubt, and that deeply, but not that *only*, as it seems to be commonly thought—humbled, I say, and yet supported ; need to be bowed down in humility, and yet strengthened in trust : need to be nerved to endurance at one time, and at another to be transported with joy. Let religion, let the reasonable and gracious doctrine of Jesus Christ, come to us with these adaptations; generous to expand our affections, strict to restrain our passions; plastic to mould our temper, strong, ay, strong to control our will. Let religion be thus welcomed to every true principle and passion of our nature. Let it touch all the springs of intellectual and of moral life. Let it penetrate to every hidden recess of the soul, and bring forth all its powers, and enlighten, inspire, perfect them.

I hardly need say, that the Christian religion *is* thus adapted to our whole nature. Its evidences address themselves to our sober judgment. Its precepts commend themselves to our consciences. It imparts light to our understandings, and fervour to our affections. It speaks gently to our repentance; but terribly to our disobedience. It really does that for us, which religion should do. It does arouse, and chasten, quicken and subdue, impel and guide, humble and yet support: it arms us with fortitude, and it transports us with joy. It is profitable for the life that now is, and for that which is to come.

II. But I must pass now, to observe, that there are more particular adaptations which religion should have, and which the Gospel actually has, to the condition of human nature, and to the various degrees of its improvement.

One of the circumstances of our moral condition is danger. Religion then should be a guardian, and a vigilant guardian; and let us be assured that the Gospel is such. Such emphatically do we read. If we cannot bear a religion that admonishes us, watches over us, warns us, restrains us; let us be assured that we cannot bear a religion that will save us. Religion should be the keeper of the soul; and without such a keeper, in the slow and undermining process of temptation, or amidst the sudden and strong assaults of passion, it will be overcome and lost.

Again, the human condition is one of weakness. There are weak points, where religion should be stationed to support and strengthen us. Points, did I say? Are we not encompassed with weakness? Where, in the whole circle of our spiritual interests and affections, are we not exposed, and vulnerable? Where have we not need to set up the barriers of habit, and to build the strongest defences, with which resolutions and vows and prayers can surround us? Where, and wherein, I ask again, is any man safe? What virtue of any man is secure from frailty? What strong purpose of his is not liable to failure? What affection of his heart can say, "I have strength, I am established, and nothing can move me." How weak is man in trouble, in perplexity, in doubt; how weak in affliction, or when sickness bows the spirit, or when approaching death is unloosing all the bands of his pride and self-reliance! And whose spirit does not sometimes faint under its *intrinsic* weakness, under its *native* frailty, and the burthen and pressure of its necessities? Religion then should bring supply, and support, and strength to the soul; and the Gospel does bring supply, and support, and strength. And it thus meets a universal want. Every mind *wants* the stability which principle gives, wants the comfort which piety gives; wants it continually, in all the varying experience of life.

I have said, also, that religion should be adapted to the various degrees of mental improvement, and I may add, to the diversities of temperament. Now there are sluggish natures that need to be aroused.

All the machinery of spiritual terror can scarce be too much to arouse some persons; though it may indeed be very improperly applied. But on the contrary, there *are* minds so excitable and sensitive, that religion should come to *them* with all its sobering and tranquillizing influence. In how many cases do we witness this! How many are there whose minds are chilled, or stupified by denunciation! How many are repelled by severity, or crushed by a weight of fear and anxiety! How many such are there, that need a helping hand to be stretched out to them; that need to be raised, and soothed, and comforted; that need to be won with gentleness, and cheered with promises. The Gospel has terrors, indeed, but it is not all terror: and its most awful rebukes soften into pity, over the fearful, the dejected, the anxious and humble.

But the most striking circumstance in the adaptation of religion to the different degrees of mental improvement, is its character as supplying not merely the general necessities, but the conscious wants of the mind. There may be some who have never been conscious of these intrinsic wants, though they spring from human nature and must be sooner or later felt. To the very young, or to the unreflecting, religion can be scarcely any thing more, perhaps, than direction. It says, "do this, and do that; and refrain from this gratification, and beware of that danger." It is chiefly a set of rules and precepts to them. Speak to them of religion as the grand resort of the mind, as that which meets its inward necessities, supplies its deep-felt wants, fills its capacious desires; and they do not well understand you; or they do not understand, why this view of the subject should be so interesting to you. But another mind shall be bound to the Gospel by nothing so much as by its wants. It craves something, thus vast, glorious, infinite, and eternal. It sought, sought long perhaps, and anxiously, for something thus satisfying; and it has found what it long and painfully sought, in the teachings of Jesus, in the love of God, in that world of spiritual thoughts and objects which the great teacher has opened, in that solemn and majestic vision of immortality which he has brought to light. To such a religion the soul clings with a peace and satisfaction never to be expressed, never to be uttered. It says, " to whom shall I go—to whom shall I go? thou, O blessed religion, minister and messenger from heaven!—thou hast the words of eternal life, of eternal joy!" The language which proclaims the sufficiency of religion, which sets forth the attraction and the greatness of it, as supplying the great intellectual want, is no chimerical language; it is not merely a familiar language; but is *intimate* with the deepest and the dearest feelings of the heart.

In descending to the more specific applications of the principle of religion to human nature, I must content myself for the present, with one further observation ; and that is, that it meets and mingles with all the varieties of natural temperament and disposition.

Religion should not propose to break up all the diversities of individual character; and Christianity does not propose this. It did not propose this, even when it first broke upon the world with manifestation and miracle. It allowed the rash and forward Peter, the timid and doubting Thomas, the mild and affectionate John, the resolute and fervent Paul, still to retain all their peculiarities of character. The way of *becoming* religious, or interested in religion, was not the same to all. There was Cornelius, the Pagan, whose " alms and prayers were accepted;" and there were others, who became Christians, "without so much as hearing that there was any Holy Ghost." There were the immediate disciples of our Lord, who, through a course of gradual teaching, came to apprehend his spiritual kingdom; and there was Paul, to whom this knowledge came by miracle, and with a light brighter than the sun. There was the terrified jailer who fell down trembling and said, "what must I do to be saved?" and there was the cautious and inquiring Nicodemus, who, as if he had been reflecting on the matter, said, " we know that thou art a teacher come from God, for no man can do these miracles that thou doest, except God be with him."

Now it is painful to observe at this day, how little of this individuality there is, in the prevailing and popular experience of religion. A certain process is pointed out, a certain result is described; particular views and feelings are insisted on, as the only right and true state of mind; and every man strives to bring himself through the required process to the given result. It is common, indeed, to observe, that if you read one account of a conversion, one account of a religious excitement, you have all. I charge not this to any particular set of opinions, though it may be found to have been connected with some creeds more than with others; but it results too, from the very weakness of human nature. One man leans on the experience of another, and it contributes to his satisfaction, of course to have the same experience. How refreshing is it amidst this dull and artificial uniformity, to meet with a man whose religion is his own; who has thought and felt for himself; who has not propped up his hopes on other men's opinions: who has been willing to commune with the spirit of religion and of God, alone, and who brings forth to you the fruits of his experience, fresh and original, and is not much concerned for *your* judgment of them, provided they have nourished and comforted *himself*. I would not desire that every man should view all the matters of piety, as I do; but would rather that every man should bring the results of his own individual conviction, to aid the common cause of right knowledge and judgment.

In the diversities of character and situation that exists, there will naturally be diversities of religious experience. Some, as I have said before, are constitutionally lively, and others serious; some are ardent and others moderate: some, also, are inclined to be social, and others to be retired. Knowledge and ignorance, too, and refinement and rudeness of character, are cases to be provided for. And a true and thorough religion—this is the special observation I wish to make on the diversities of character—a true and thorough religion, when it enters the mind, will show itself by its naturally blending and mingling with the mind *as it is;* it will sit easily upon the character; it will take forms in accordance, not with the bad, but with the constitutional tempers and dispositions it finds in its subjects.

Nay, I will say yet further, that religion ought not to repress the natural buoyancy of our affections, the innocent gaiety of the heart. True religion was not designed to do this. Undoubtedly, it will discriminate. It will check what is extravagant in us, all tumultuous and excessive joy about acquisitions of little consequence, or of doubtful utility to us: it will correct what is deformed; it will uproot what is hurtful. But there is a native buoyancy of the heart, the meed of youth, or of health, which is a sensation of our animal nature, a tendency of our being. This, true religion does not propose to withstand. It does not war against our nature. As well should the cultivator of a beautiful and variegated garden, cut up all the flowers in it, or lay weights and encumbrances on them, lest they should be too flourishing and fair. Religion is designed for the *culture* of our natural faculties, not for their eradication!

It would be easy now, did the time permit, to illustrate the views which have been presented, by a reference to the teachings of our Saviour. He did not address one passion or part of our nature alone, or chiefly. There was no one manner of address; and we feel sure as we read, that there was no one tone. He did not confine himself to any one class of subjects. He was not always speaking of death, nor of judgment, nor of eternity; frequently and solemnly as he spoke of them. He was not always speaking of the state of the sinner, nor of repentance and the new heart; though on these subjects too he delivered his solemn message. There was a varied adaptation, in his discourses, to every condition of mind, and every duty of life, and every situation in which his hearers were placed. Neither did the preaching of our Saviour possess, exclusively, any one moral complexion. It was not terror only, nor promise only; it was not exclusively severity nor gentleness; but it was each one of them in its place, and all of them always subdued to the tone of perfect sobriety. At one time we hear him saying, with lofty self-respect, "neither tell I you by what authority I do these things:" at another with all the majesty of the Son of God, we hear him, in reply to the fatal question of the judgment-hall, "Art thou the Christ?"—we hear him say, "I am; and hereafter ye shall see the Son of man seated on the throne of power and coming in the clouds of heaven."

But it is the same voice that says, "come unto me, all ye that labour and are heavy laden, and I will give you rest; take my yoke which is easy, and my burden which is light, and ye shall find rest to your souls." At one time he speaks in the language of terror, and says, "fear not them who after that they have killed the body, have no more that they can do; but fear Him who is able to cast both soul and body into hell, yea, I say into you, fear him." But at another time, the awful admonisher breaks out into the pathetic exclamation, "Oh! Jerusalem, Jerusalem! how often would I have gathered your children, even as a hen gathereth her brood under her wings, but ye would not."

If I might be permitted now, to add a suggestion of an advisory nature, it would be in the language of an apostle; "let your *moderation* be known to all men." The true religion, the true excellence of character, requires that we should hold all the principles and affections of our nature in a due subordination and proportion to each other; that we should subdue all the clamoring voices of passion and desire, of fear and hope, of joy and sorrow, to complete harmony; that we should regard and cultivate our nature *as a whole*. Almost all error is some truth, carried to excess, or diminished from its proper magnitude. Almost all evil is some good or useful principle, suffered to be immoderate and ungovernable, or suppressed and denied its proper influence and action. Let, then, moderation be a leading trait of our virtue and piety. This is not dullness. Nothing is farther from dullness. And nothing, surely, is more beautiful in character, or more touching, than to see a lively and intense sensibility controlled by the judgment; strong passions subdued and softened by reflection; and on the other hand, to find a vigorous, clear and manly understanding, quickened by a genuine fervor and enthusiasm. Nothing is more wise or more admirable in *action,* than to be resolute and yet calm, earnest and yet self-possessed, decided and yet modest; to contend for truth and right with meekness and charity; to go forward in a good cause without pretension, to retire with dignity; to give without pride, and to withhold without meanness; to rejoice with moderation, and to suffer with patience. And nothing, I may add, was more remarkable in the character of our Saviour, than this perfect sobriety, consistency, self-control.

This, therefore, is the perfection of character. This will always be found, I believe, to be a late stage in the progress of religious worth from its first beginnings. It is comparatively easy to be one thing and that alone; to be all zeal, or all reasoning; all faith or all action; all rapture, or all chilling and captions fault-finding. Here novices begin. Thus far they may easily go. Thus far men may go, whose character is the result of temperament and not of culture; of headlong propensity, and not of careful and conscientious discipline. It is easy for the bruised reed to be broken. It is easy for the smoking flax to be quenched. It is easy to deal harshly and rudely with the matters of religious and virtuous experience: to make a hasty effort, to have a paroxysm of emotion, to give way to a feverish and transient feeling, and then to smother and quench all the rising purposes of a better life. But true religion comes to us with a wiser and more considerate adaptation,—to sustain and strengthen the bruised reed of human weakness; to fan the rising flame of virtuous and holy purposes: it comes to revive our failing courage, to restrain our wayward passions.

It will not suffer us to go on with our fluctuations and our fancies; with our transient excitements, and momentary struggles. It will exert a more abiding, a more rational influence. It will make us more faithful and persevering. It will lay its hand on the very energies of our nature, and will take the lead and control, the forming and perfecting of them. May we find its real and gracious power! May it lead us in the true, the brightening path of the just, till it brings us to the perfect day!

Oh! my brethren, we sin against our own peace, we have no mercy upon ourselves, when we neglect such a religion as this. It is the only wisdom, the only soundness, the only consistency and harmony of character, the only peace and blessedness of mind. We should not have our distressing doubts and fears; we should not be so subject as we are to the distracting influences of passion, or of the world without us, if we had yielded our hearts wholly to the spirit and religion of Jesus. It is a religion adapted to us all. To every affection, to every state of mind, troubled or joyous, to every period of life, it would impart the very influence that we need. How surely would it guide our youth, and how would it temper, and soften, and sanctify all the fervors of youthful affection! How well would it support our age, making it youthful again with the fervent hope of immortality! How would it lead us, too, in all the paths of earthly care and business and labour, turning the brief and weary courses of worldly toil into the ways that are everlasting! How faithfully and how calmly would it conduct us to the everlasting abodes! And how well, in fine, does he, of whom it was prophesied that he should not break the bruised reed nor quench the smoking flax; how well does he meet that gracious character, when he says,—shall we not listen to him?—"Come unto me all ye that labour and are heavy laden, and I will give you rest: take my yoke which is easy, and my burden, which is light; learn of me, for I am meek and lowly in heart, and ye shall find rest unto your souls."

V.

THE APPEAL OF RELIGION TO HUMAN NATURE.

UNTO YOU, O MEN, I CALL; AND MY VOICE IS TO THE SONS OF MEN.—Prov. viii. 4.

The appeal of religion to human nature, the deep wisdom of its instructions to the human heart, the language of power and of cheering with which it is fitted to address the inmost soul of man, is never to be understood, perhaps, till our nature is exalted far beyond its present measure. When the voice of wisdom and purity shall find an inward wisdom and purity to which it can speak, it will be received with a welcome and gladness, with a joy beyond all other joy, such as no tongue of eloquence has ever expressed, nor the heart of worldly sensibility ever yet conceived. It is, therefore, with the most unfeigned diffidence, with the most distinct conciousness that my present labour must be incipient and imperfect, that I enter upon this great theme—the appeal of religion to human nature.

What ought it to be? What has it been? These are the inquiries which I shall pursue. Nor shall I attempt to keep them altogether separate in the discussion; since, both the defects and the duties of religious instruction may often be best exhibited under the same head of discourse. Neither shall I labour to speak of religion under that abstract and figurative character with which wisdom is personified in the context, though that may be occasionally convenient; but whether it be the language of individual reason, or conscience; whether it be the voice of the parent, or of the preacher; whether it be the language of forms or of institutions, I would consider how religion has appealed, and how it ought to have appealed, to human nature.

The topics of discourse, under which I shall pursue these inquiries, are the following; in *what character* should religion address us? To *what* in us should it speak? And *how* should it deliver its message? That is to say, the substance, the subject, and the spirit of the appeal, are the topics of our inquiry. I cannot, of course, pursue these inquiries beyond the point to which the immediate object of my discourse, will carry them; and I am willing to designate that point, at once, by saying, that the questions are, whether the character in which religion is to appeal to us, be moral or not; whether that in us to which it chiefly appeals, should be the noblest or the basest part of our nature; and finally, whether the manner and spirit of its appeal should be that of confidence or distrust, of friendship or hatred.

I. And with regard to the first question, the answer, of course, is, that the character in which religion should address us, is purely moral. As a moral principle, as a principle of rectitude, it must speak to us. Institutions, rites, commands, threatenings, promises— all forms of appeal must contain this essence; they must be moral; they must be holy.

It may be thought strange that I should insist upon a point so obvious, but let me crave your patience. What is the most comprehensive form of morality, holiness, gratitude, religion? It is love; it is goodness. The character of the Supreme Perfection is set forth in this one attribute: "God is love." This is the very glory of God. For when an ancient servant desired to "see his glory," the answer to the prayer was, that "he caused all his goodness to pass before him."

The character, then, in which religion should appeal to human nature, is that of *simple* and *essential goodness.* This, the moral nature of man is made to understand and to feel; and nothing else but this. This character, doubtless, has various expressions. Sometimes it takes the forms of command and threatening; but still these must speak, in the name of goodness. If command and threatening stand up to speak for themselves, alone—dissociated from that love which gives them all their moral character—then, I say, that the moral nature of man cannot receive their message. A brute can receive that; a dog or a horse can yield to mere command or menace. But the moral nature can yield to nothing which is not moral; and that which gives morality to every precept and warning is the goodness which is breathed into them. Divest them of this, and they are not even religious. Nor are those persons religious, who pay obedience to command, as command, and without any consideration of its moral nature, of the intrinsic and essential sanction which goodness bestows on the command

The voice of religion, then, must be as the voice of goodness. Conceive of every thing good and lovely, of every thing morally excellent and admirable, of every thing glorious and godlike; and when these speak to you, know that religion speaks to you. Whether that voice comes from the page of genius, or from the record of heroic and heavenly virtue, or from its living presence and example, or from the bosom of silent reverie, the innermost sanctuary of meditation; whatever of the holy and beautiful speaks to you, and through what medium soever it comes, it is the voice of religion. All excellence, in other words, is religion.

But here we meet with what seems to me—and so must I denominate it, in justice to my own apprehensions,—a stupendous error; an error, prevalent I believe, and yet fatal, so far as it goes, to all religious emotion. All excellence, I said, is religion. But the great error is, that in the popular apprehension, these things are not identified. In other words, religion and goodness are not identified in the general mind: they are not held by most men to be the same thing. This error, I say, if it exists, is fatal to genuine religious emotion; because men cannot heartily love, as a moral quality, any thing which is not, to them, goodness. Or, to state this position as a simple truism, they cannot love any thing which is not, to them, loveliness.

Now I am willing, nay I earnestly wish, that with regard to the real nature of religion, there should be the utmost discrimination; and I will soon speak to that point. But I say for the present—I say, again, that religion is made, intrinsically and altogether a different thing, from what is commonly regarded as loveliness of character, and therefore that it speaks to men, speaks to human nature, not as goodness but as some other thing.

For proof of this, I ask you first to look at that phraseology by which religion is commonly described, and to compare it with the language by which men express those lovely qualities that they most admire. See, then, how they express their admiration. You hear them speak of one who is amiable, lovely, fascinating; of one who is honourable, upright, generous. You hear them speak of a good parent, of an affectionate child, of a worthy citizen, of an obliging neighbour, of a kind and faithful friend, of a man whom they emphatically call "a noble man;" and you observe a fervour of language and a glow of pleasure while these things are said; a kindling animation in the tone and the countenance, which inspires you with a kindred sympathy and delight. But mark now, in how different a language and manner, the qualities of religion are described. The votary of religion is said to be very "serious," perhaps, but with a look and tone as if a much worse thing were stated; or you hear it said of him that he is "a pious man," or, he is "a very experienced person," or he is "a Christian, if ever there was one;" but it seems even when the religious themselves say all this, as if it were an extorted and cold homage; as if religion were something very proper indeed, very safe perhaps, but not very agreeable certainly; there is no glow, there is no animation, and there is generally no sympathy.

In further proof that religion is not identified with the beautiful and admirable in character, I might turn from the language in common use, to actual experience. *Is* religion, I ask—not the religion of poetry, but that which exists in the actual conceptions of men, the religion of professors, the religion that is commonly taught from our pulpits—is it usually regarded as the loveliest attribute of the human character? When your minds glow with the love of excellence, when you weep over the examples of goodness, is this excellence, is this goodness which you admire, religion? Consult the books of fiction, open the pages of history, resort to the stores of our classical literature, and say, if the religious man of our times appears in them at all; or if, when he does appear in them, it is he that chiefly draws your affection? Say, rather, if it is not some personage, whether of a real or fictitious tale, that is destitute of every distinctive quality of the popular religion, who kindles your enthusiasm? So true is this, that many who have held the prevailing ideas of religion, have regarded, and on their principles, have justly regarded, the literature of taste and of fiction, as one of the most insidious temptations that could befall them. No, I repeat, the images of loveliness that dwell in the general mind, whether of writers or readers, have not been the images of religion. And thus it has happened, that the men of taste, and of a lively and ardent sensibility, have, by no means yielded their proportion of votaries to religion. The dull, the gloomy, the sick, the aged, have been religious; not—i. e. not to the same extent—the young and the joyous in their first admiration and their first love; not the intellectual and refined in the enthusiasm of their feelings and in the glory of their imaginations.

But let me appeal once more to experience. I ask then; do you love religion? I ask you, I ask any one, who will entertain the question; do you love religion? Does the very word carry a sound that is agreeable, delightful to you? Does it stand for something attractive and lovely? Are the terms that describe religion—grace, holiness, repentance, faith, godliness—are they invested with a charm to your heart, to your imagination, to your whole mind? Now, to this question, I am sure, that many would answer freely and decidedly, "No, religion is not a thing that we love. We cannot say that we take that sort of interest in it. We do not professs to be religious, and—honestly—we do not wish to be." What! I might answer in return: do you love nothing that is good? Is there nothing in character, nothing in attribute, no abstract charm that you love? "Far otherwise;" would be the reply.

"There are many persons that we love: there are many characters in history, in biography, in romance, that are delightful to us; they are so noble, so beautiful."

How different then—do we not see—are the ideas of religion, from the images of loveliness that dwell in many minds! They are actually the *same* in principle. All excellence has the same foundation. There are not, and cannot be, two different and opposite kinds of rectitude. The moral nature of man, deranged though it be, is not deranged so far as to admit this; and yet how evident is it, that religion is not identified with the excellence that men love!

But I hear it said, " the images of loveliness which dwell in the general mind, are *not* indeed the images of religion, and ought not to be; for they are false, and would utterly mislead us." Grant, now, for the sake of argument, that this were true, and whom would the admission benefit? What would follow from the admission? Why, this clearly; that of being religious, no power or possibility is within human reach. For men must love that which seems to them to be lovely. If that which seems to them to be lovely is not religion; if religion is something else, and something altogether different; religion, it is clear they cannot love. That is to say, on this hypothesis, they cannot be religious; they cannot, by any possibility, but that in which all things are possible with God; they cannot by any possibility that comes within the range of the powers and affections, that God has given them.

But it is not true that men's prevailing and constitutional perceptions of moral beauty are false. It is not true, that is to say, that their sense of right and wrong is false; that their conscience is a treacherous and deceitful guide. It is not true; and yet, doubtless, there is a discrimination to be made. Their perceptions may be, and undoubtedly often are low and inadequate, and marred with error. And therefore when we use the words, excellent, admirable, lovely, there is danger that to many, they will not mean all that they ought to mean; that men's ideas of these qualities will not be as deep and thorough and strict, as they ought to be: while, if we confine ourselves to such terms for religious qualities, as serious, holy, godly, the danger is that they will be just as erroneous, besides being technical, barren, and uninteresting.

There is a difficulty on this account attending the language of the pulpit, which every reflecting man, in the use of it, must have felt. But the truth, amidst all these discriminations, I hold to be this; that the universal and constitutional perceptions of moral loveliness which mankind entertain, are *radically* just. And therefore the only right doctrine and the only rational direction to be addressed to men, on this subject is to the following effect; "Whatever your conscience dictates; whatever your mind clothes with moral beauty; that to you, is right; be that to you, religion. Nothing else can be, if you think rationally; and therefore let that be to you the religion that you love; and let it be your endeavour, continually to elevate and purify your conceptions of all virtue and goodness." Nay, if I knew a man whose ideas of excellence were ever so low, I should still say to him, Revere those ideas; they are all that you can revere. The very apprehensions you entertain of the glory of God, cannot go beyond your ideas of excellence. All that you can worship then, is the most perfect excellence you can conceive of. Be that, therefore, the object of your reverence. However low, however imperfect it is, still be that to you the image of the Divinity. On that scale of your actual ideas, however humble, let your thoughts rise to higher and higher perfection."

I say, however low. And grant now that the moral conceptions of a man are very low; yet if they are the highest he has, is there any thing higher that he can follow? Will it be said there are the Scriptures? But the aid of the Scriptures is already presupposed in the case. They *contribute* to form the very perceptions in question. They are a light to man, only as they kindle a light within him. They do not, and they cannot mean more to any man, than he understands, than he perceives them to mean. His perceptions of their intent then, he must follow. He cannot follow the light, any farther than he sees it.

But it may be said that many of the ignorant and debased see very little light; that their perceptions are *very* low; that they admire qualities and actions of a very questionable character. What then? You must begin with them where they are! But let us not grant too much of this. Go to the most degraded being you know, and tell him some story of noble disinterestedness, or touching charity; tell him the story of Howard, or Swartz, or Oberlin; and will he not approve; will he not admire? Then tell him, I say—as the summing up of this head of my discourse—tell him that this is religion. Tell him that this is a faint shadow, to the infinite brightness of divine love; a feeble and marred image, compared with the infinite benignity and goodness of God!

II. My next observation is, on the principles to be addressed. And, on this point, I say in general, that religion should appeal to the good in man against the bad. That there *is* good in man, not fixed goodness; but that there is something good in man is evident from the fact that he has an idea of goodness. For if the matter be strictly and philosophically traced, it will be found that the idea of goodness can spring from nothing else but experience, but the inward sense of it.

But not to dwell on this; my principal object under this head of discourse is to maintain, that religion should appeal *chiefly*, not to the lowest, but to the highest of our moral sentiments.

There are sentiments in our nature to which powerful appeal can be made, and they are emphatically, its high and honourable sentiments. If you wished to speak in tones that should thrill through the very heart of the world, you would speak to these before all others. Almost all the richest poetry, the most admirable, the fine arts, the most popular and powerful eloquence in the world, have addressed these moral and generous sentiments of human nature. And I have observed it as quite remarkable indeed, because it is an exception to the general language of the pulpit, that all the most eloquent preachers have made great use of these very sentiments; they have appealed to the sense of beauty, to generosity and tenderness, to the natural conscience, the natural sense of right and wrong, of honour and shame.

To these, then, if you would move the human heart, you would apply yourself. You would appeal to the indignation at wrong, at oppression, or treachery, or meanness, or to the natural admiration which men feel for virtuous and noble deeds. If you would touch the most tender feelings of the human heart, you would still make your appeal to these sentiments. You would represent innocence borne down and crushed by the arm of power; you would describe patriotism labouring and dying for its country: or you would describe a parent's love with all its cares and anxieties and its self-sacrificing devotion: or you would portray filial affection, watching over infirmity and relieving pain and striving to pay back something of the mighty debt of filial gratitude. Look abroad in the world, or look back upon the history of ages past, and ask for those on whom the enthusiasm and pride and affection of men love to dwell. Evoke from the shadows of the times gone by, their majestic, their cherished forms, around which the halo of everlasting admiration dwells: and what are they? Behold the names of the generous, the philanthropic, and the good; behold, the voice of martyred blood on the altars of cruelty, or on the hills of freedom for ever rising from the earth—eternal testimonies to the right and noble sentiments of mankind.

To these, then, religion ought to have appealed. In these sentiments, it ought to have laid its foundation, and on these it ought to have built up its power. But has it done so? *Could* it do so, while it held human nature to be utterly depraved?

But there is a farther question. *Can any* religion, Christian or heathen, in fact, entirely discard human nature? Certainly not. Must not every religion that speaks to man, speak to *something* human? Undoubtedly, it must. What then is the end of all this zeal against human nature? Has it not been, I ask, to address the worst parts of it? There has been no scruple, about appealing to fear and anxiety. But of the sentiments of admiration, of the sense of beauty in the human heart, of the deep love for friends and kindred that lingers there, religion has been afraid. Grant indeed, that these sentiments and affections have been too low. It was the very business of religion to elevate them. But while it has failed to do this, in the degree it ought, how often has it spread a rack of torture for our fear and solicitude! How often has it been an engine of superstition, an inflicter of penance, a minister of despondency and gloom; an instrument effective, as if it were framed on purpose, to keep down all natural buoyancy. generosity and liberal aspiration! How often has religion frowned upon the nature that it came to save; and instead of winning its confidence and love, has incurred its hatred and scorn; and instead of having drawn it into the blessed path of peace and trust, has driven it to indifference, infidelity or desperation!

And how lamentable is this! Here is a world of beings, filled with enthusiasm, filled with a thousand warm and kindling affections; the breasts of millions are fired with admiration for generous and heroic virtues; and when the living representative of these virtues appears among us—a Washington, or some illustrious compeer in excellence—crowded cities go forth to meet him, and nations lift up the voice of gratitude. How remarkable in the human character is this moral admiration! What quickening thoughts does it awaken in solitude! What tears does it call forth, when we think of the prisons, the hospitals, the desolate dwellings, visited and cheered by the humane and merciful! With what ecstacy does it swell the human breast, when the vision of the patriotic, the patiently suffering, the magnanimous and the good, passes before us! In all this the inferior race has no share. They can fear; but esteem, veneration, the sense of moral loveliness, they know not. These are the prerogatives of man, the gifts of nature to him, the gifts of God. But how little, alas! have they been called into the service of his religion! How little have their energies been enlisted in that which is the great concern of man!

And all this is the more to be lamented, because those who are most susceptible of feeling and of enthusiasm, most need the power and support of religion. The dull, the earthly, the children of sense, the mere plodders in business, the mere votaries of gain, may do, or may think they can do, without it. But how many beings are there, how many spirits of a finer mould, and of a loftier bearing, and of more intellectual wants, who, when the novelty of life is worn off, when the enthusiasm of youth has been freely lavished, when changes come on, when friends die, and there is care and weariness, and solitude to press upon the heart—how many are there, then, that sigh bitterly after some better thing, after something greater, and more permanent, and more satisfying! And how do they need to be told that religion is that better thing; that it is not a stranger to their wants and sorrows; that its voice is speaking and pleading within them, in the cry of their lamentation, and in the felt burthen of their necessity; that religion is the home of their far-wandering desires; the rest, the heaven, of their long-troubled affections! How do they need to hear the voice that says, "Unto you, O men—men of care, and fear, and importunate desire—do I call; and my voice is to the sons of men—to the children of frailty, and trouble, and sorrow!"

III. Let us now proceed to consider, in the third place and finally, from the relation between the power that speaks and the principle addressed, in what manner the one should appeal to the other.

The relation then between them, I say, is a relation of amity. But let me explain. I do not say, of course, that there is amity between right and wrong. I do not say, that there is amity between pure goodness, and what is evil in man. But that which is wrong and evil in man, is the perversion of something that is good and right. To that good and right, I contend that religion should speak. To that it must speak, for there is nothing else to hear it. We do not appeal to abstractions of evil in man, because there are no such things in him; but we appeal to affections; to affections in which there is a mixture of good and evil. To the good, then, I say, we must appeal, *against* the evil. And every preacher of righteousness, may boldly and fearlessly approach the human heart, in the confidence that however it may defend itself against him, however high it may build its battlements of habit and its towers of pride, he has friends in the very citadel.

I say, then, that religion should address the true moral nature of man, as its friend, and not as its enemy; as its lawful subject, and not as an alien or a traitor; and should address it, therefore, with generous and hopeful confidence, and not with cold and repulsive distrust. What *is* it, in this nature to which religion speaks? To reason, to conscience, to the love of happiness, to the sense of the infinite and the beautiful, to aspirations after immortal good; to natural sensibility, also, to the love of kindred and country and home. All these are in this nature, and they are all fitted to render obedience to religion. In this obedience they are satisfied, and indeed they can never be satisfied without it.

Admit, now, that these powers are ever so sadly perverted and corrupted; still, no one maintains that they are destroyed. Neither is their testimony to what is right ever, in any case, utterly silenced. Should they not then, be appealed to in a tone of confidence?

Suppose, for instance, to illustrate our observation, that simple reason were appealed to on any subject *not* religious; and suppose, to make the case parallel, that the reason of the man on that subject were very much perverted, that he was very much prejudiced and misled. Yet would not the argument be directed to his reason, as a principle actually existing in him, and as a principle to be confided in and to be recovered from its error? Would not every tone of the argument and of the expostulation show confidence in the principle addressed?

Oh! what power might religion have had, if it had breathed this tone of confidence; if it had gone down into the deep and silent places of the heart as the voice of friendship; if it had known what precious treasures of love and hope and joy are there, ready to be made celestial by its touch; if it had spoken to man as the most affectionate parent would speak to his most beloved, though sadly erring child; if it had said in the emphatic language of the text, "Unto you, O *men*, I call, and my voice is to the sons of men;" lo! I have set my love upon you; upon you, men of the strong and affectionate nature, of the aspiring and heaven-needing soul; not upon inferior creatures, not upon the beasts of the field, but upon you have I set my love; give entrance to me, not with fear and mistrust, but with good hope and with gladness; give entrance to me, and I will make my abode with you, and I will build up all that is within you, in glory, and beauty, and ineffable brightness." Alas! for our erring and sinful, but also misguided and ill-used nature; bad enough indeed we have made it or suffered it to be made; but if a better lot had befallen it, if kindlier influences had breathed upon it; if the parent's and the preacher's voice, inspired with every tone of hallowed feeling, had won it to piety; if the train of social life, with every attractive charm of goodness, had led it in the consecrated way, we had ere this known, what now, alas! we so poorly know—we had known what it is to be children of God, and heirs of heaven.

My friends, let religion speak to us in its own true character, with all its mighty power, and winning candour and tenderness. It is the principle of infinite wisdom that speaks. From that unknown period before the world was created—so saith the holy record; from the depth of eternity, from the centre of infinity, from the heart of the universe, from "the bosom of God;" its voice has come forth, and spoken to us, to us, men, in our lowly habitations. What a ministration is it! It is the infinite communing with the finite; it is might communing with frailty; it is mercy stretching out its arms to the guilty. It is goodness taking part with all that is good in us, against all that is evil. So full, so overflowing, so all-pervading is it, that all things give it utterance. It speaks to us in every thing lowly, and in every thing lofty. It speaks to us in every whispered accent of human affection; and in every revelation that is sounded out from the spreading heavens. It speaks to us from this lowly seat at which we bow down in prayer; from this humble shrine veiled with the shadows of mortal infirmity; and it speaks to us alike, from those altar-fires, that blaze in the heights of the firmament. It speaks where the seven thunders utter their voices; and it sends forth its voice—of pity more than human, of agony more than mortal—from the silent summit of Calvary.

Can a principle so sublime and so benignant as religion, speak to us but for our good? Can infinity, can omnipotence, can boundless love, speak to us, but in the spirit of infinite generosity, and candour, and tenderness? No; it may be the infirmity of man to use a harsh tone, and to heap upon us bitter and cruel upbraidings; but so speaks not religion. It says—and I trace an accent of tenderness and entreaty in every word—"Unto you, O men, I call; and my voice—my voice is to the children of men."

O man! whosoever thou art, hear that voice of wisdom. Hear it, thou sacred conscience! and give not way to evil; touch no bribe; touch not dishonest gain; touch not the sparkling cup of unlawful pleasure. Hear it, ye better affections! dear and holy! and turn not your purity to pollution, and your sweetness to bitterness, and your hope to shame. Hear it, poor, wearied, broken, prostrate, human nature! and rise to penitence, to sanctity, to glory, to heaven. Rise now; lest soon, it be for ever too late. Rise, at this entreaty of wisdom, for wisdom can utter no more. Rise,—arise at this voice; for the universe is exhausted of all its revelations—infinity, omnipotence, boundless love have lavished their uttermost resources in this one provision, this one call, this one Gospel, of mercy!

VI.

THE CALL OF HUMANITY AND THE ANSWER TO IT.

OH! THAT I KNEW WHERE I MIGHT FIND HIM; THAT I MIGHT COME EVEN TO HIS SEAT! I WOULD ORDER MY CAUSE BEFORE HIM, AND FILL MY MOUTH WITH ARGUMENTS. I WOULD KNOW THE WORDS WHICH HE WOULD ANSWER ME, AND UNDERSTAND WHAT HE WOULD SAY TO ME.—Job xxiii. 3, 4 and 5 vs.

It is striking to observe, how large a part of the book of Job, and especially of Job's own meditation, is occupied with a consideration of the nature and character of the Supreme being. The subject-matter of the book, is human calamity. The point proposed for solution, is the interpretation of that calamity. The immediate question—of very little interest now, perhaps, but one of urgent difficulty in a darker age—is, whether calamity is retributive; whether, in proportion as a man is afflicted, he is to be accounted a bad man. Job contends against this principle, and the controversy with his friends turns upon this point. But as I have already remarked, it is striking to observe how often his mind rises apparently quite above the controversy, to a sublime meditation on God. As if feeling, that provided he could fix his trust there, he should be strong and triumphant, thither he continually resorts. With these loftier soarings, are mingled, it is true, passionate complaint and sad despondency and bitter reproaches against his friends, and painful questionings about the whole order of providence. It is indeed a touching picture of a mind in distress; with its sad fluctuations; its words of grief and haste bursting into the midst of its words of prayer; its soarings and sinkings; its passionate and familiar adjurations of heaven and earth to help it; and with the world of dark and undefined thoughts, which roll through it like waves of chaos: in short, it is a picture, whose truth can be realized only by experience.

But I was about to observe that this tendency of Job's mind in the Supreme, though it may seem to carry him, at times, up quite out of sight of the question in hand, is really a natural tendency, and that it naturally sprung from the circumstances in which he was placed. The human condition is throughout, allied to a divine power; and the strong feeling of what this condition is, always leads us to that Power. The positive good and evil of this condition, therefore, have especially this tendency. This is implied in the proem or preface of the book of Job; which gives an account after the dramatic manner which characterizes the whole book, of the circumstances that lead to Job's trial. After a brief prefatory statement informing the reader who Job was, and what were his possessions, the scene is represented as opening in heaven. Among the sons of God, Satan presents himself, the Accuser, the Adversary. And when Job's virtue is the theme of commendation, the Accuser says, "Doth Job fear God for naught? A grand Emir of the East; cradled in luxury; loaded with the benefits of heaven: doth he fear God for naught? Put forth thine hand now, and touch all that he hath, and he will curse thee to thy face!" It is done; and Job is stripped of his possessions, servants, children—all. And Job falls down upon the ground and worships; and says, "The Lord gave, the Lord hath taken away; blessed be the name of the Lord."

But again the Accuser says; thou hast not laid thine hand yet upon his person. Come yet nearer; "put forth thine hand now, and touch his bone, and his flesh, and he will curse thee to thy face." Again it is done; and Job is smitten and overwhelmed with disease; and he sits down in ashes and scrapes himself with a potsherd; a pitiable and loathsome object. The faith of his wife too, gives way, of her who, above all, should have supported him then; but who, from the reverence and love which she felt for her husband, is least able to bear the sight of his misery. She *cannot* bear it: and partaking of the prevalent feelings of the age about outward prosperity, as the very measure and test of the Divine favour, she says, "dost thou still retain thine integrity? Curse God and die!" "Give up the strife; you have been a good man; you have helped and comforted many; and now you are reduced to this. Give up the strife; curse God and die!" And Job answered, "thou speakest as one of the foolish women speaketh!" What nature! We seem to *hear* that fireside conversation. What nature! and what delicacy, mingled with reproof! "Thou speakest not as my wife, but as one of the foolish, prating women speaketh. What! shall we receive good at the hand of the Lord, and shall we not receive evil? In all this did not Job sin with his lips."

Then the three friends of Job came to him; and it is a beautiful trait of delicacy for those ancient times, that these friends, according to the representation, "sat down upon the ground with him seven days and seven nights, and *spake not a word unto him;* for they saw that his grief was great." When we recollect that all over the East, loud wailings and lamentations were the usual modes of testifying sympathy, we are led to ask, whence came—whence, but from inspiration, this finer conception, befitting the utmost culture and delicacy of later times? "Seven days and seven nights they sat with him, and none of them spake a word to him." Of course, we are not to take this too literally. According to the Hebrew custom, they mourned with him seven days: that is, they were in his house, and they came, doubtless, and sat with him from time to time; but they entered into no large discourse with him; they saw that it was not the time for many words; they mourned in silence.

This I have said is a beautiful conception of what belongs to the most delicate and touching sympathy. There comes a time to speak, and so the friends of Job judged; though their speech proved less delicate and judicious than their silence. There comes a time to speak; there are circumstances which may make it desirable; there are easy and unforced modes of address which may make it grateful; there are cases where a thoughtful man may help his neighbour with his wisdom, or an affectionate man may comfort him, with sympathy; "a word fitly spoken," says the sacred proverbialist, "is like apples of gold in pictures of silver."

And yet after all, it seems to me that words can go but a little way into the depths of affliction. The thoughts that struggle there in silence; that go out into the silence of infinitude, into the silence of eternity, have no emblems. Thoughts enough, God knoweth, come there; such as no tongue ever uttered. And those thoughts do not so much want human sympathy as they want higher help. I deny not the sweetness of that balm; but I say that something higher is wanted. The sympathy of all good friends, too, we know that we have, without a word spoken. And moreover, the sympathy of all the world, though grateful, would not lighten the load, one feather's weight. Something else the mind wants, something to rest upon. There is a loneliness in deep sorrow, to which God only can draw near. Its prayer is emphatically "the prayer of a lonely heart." Alone, the mind is wrestling with the great problem of calamity; and the solution, it asks from the infinite providence of heaven. Did I not rightly say, then, that calamity directly leads us to God; and that the tendency, so apparent in the mind of Job, to lift itself up to that exalted theme of contemplation, was natural? And it is natural too that the one book of affliction given us in the holy record, the one book wholly devoted to that subject, is, throughout and almost entirely, a meditation on God.

I wish to speak, in the present season of meditation, of this tendency of the mind, amidst the trials and distresses of life, to things superior to itself, and especially to the Supreme Being. It is not affliction of which I am to speak, but of that to which it leads. My theme is, the natural aspiration of humanity to things above and beyond it, and the revealings from above to that aspiration; it is in other words, the call of humanity and the answer to it. "I would order my cause before him," says Job, "I would know the words he would answer me."

There are many things in us, of which we are not distinctly conscious; and it is one office of every great ministration to human nature, whether its vehicle be the pen, the pencil, or the tongue, to waken that slumbering consciousness into life. And so do I think, that it is one office of the pulpit. That inmost consciousness, were it called forth from the dim cells in the soul, where it sleeps; how instantly would it turn to a waking and spiritual reality, that life, which is now to many, a state so dull and worldly, so uninteresting and unprofitable!

How it should be such to any, seems to me, I confess, a thing almost inconceivable. It may be because my life is, as I may say, professionally a meditation upon themes of the most spiritual and quickening interest. Certainly I do not lay any claim to superior purity, for seeming to myself to see things as they are. But surely, this life, instead of being anything negative or indifferent, instead of being anything dull and trivial, seems to me I was ready to say, as if it were bound up with mystery, and agony, and rapture. Yes, rapture as well as agony; the rapture of love, of reciprocated affection, of hope, of joy, of prayer; and the agony of pain, of loss, of bereavement; and over all their strugglings, the dark cloud of mystery. If any one is unconscious of the intensity and awfulness of this life within him, I believe it is because he does not know what he is all the while feeling. Health and sickness, joy and sorrow, success and disappointment, life and death, are familiar words upon his lips, and he does not know to what depths they point within him. It is just as a man may live unconscious that there is anything unusual about him, in this age of unprecedented excitement; in this very crisis of the world's story.

Indeed a man seems never to know what any thing means, till he has lost it; and this, I suppose, is the reason why losses, vanishings away of things, are among the teachings of this world of shadows. The substance indeed teacheth; but the vacuity whence it has disappeared, yet more. Many an organ, many a nerve and fibre in our bodily frame, performs its silent part for years, and leaves us almost or quite unconscious of its value. But let there be the smallest injury, the slightest cut of a knife, which touches that organ or severs the fibre ; and then we find, though it be the point of our finger, that we want it continually ; then we discover its value ; then we learn, that the fine and invisible nerves that spread themselves all over this wonderful frame, are a significant hand-writing of divine wisdom. And thus it is, with the universal frame of things in life. One would think that the blessings of this world were sufficiently valued ; but after all, the full significancy of those words, property, ease, health ; the wealth of meaning that lies in the fond epithets, parent, child, friend, we never know till they are taken away ; till in place of the bright, visible being, comes the awful and desolate shadow where nothing is ; where we stretch out our hands in vain, and strain our eyes upon dark and dismal vacuity. Still, in that vacuity we do not *lose* the object that we loved ; it only becomes more real to us. Thus do blessings not only brighten when they depart, but are fixed in enduring reality ; and friendship itself receives its everlasting seal, beneath the cold impress of death.

I have said thus much for the sake of illustration, of suggestion ; to show you that the imprint of things may be upon us, which we scarcely know ; to intimate to you—what I believe—that a dim consciousness of infinite mystery and grandeur, lies beneath all this common place of life ; yes, and to arouse even the most irreligious worldliness, by the awfulness and majesty that are around it. As I have seen a rude peasant from the Appenines, falling asleep at the foot of a pillar in one of the majestic Roman churches ; doubtless the choral symphonies yet fell soft upon his ear, and the gilded arches were yet dimly seen through the half slumbering eye-lids; so, I think, it is often, with the repose and the very stupor of worldliness. It cannot quite lose the sense of where it is, and of what is above and around it.

The scene of its actual engagements may be small; the paths of its steps, beaten and familiar; the objects it handles easily spanned, and quite worn out with daily uses. So it may be, and amidst such things, that we all live. So we live our little life; but heaven is above us; and eternity is before us, and behind us; and suns and stars are silent witnesses and watchers over us. Not to speak fancifully, of what is matter of fact; do you not always feel that you are enfolded by infinity? Infinite powers, infinite spaces; do they not lie all around you? Is not the dread arch of mystery, spread over you; and no voice ever pierced it? Is not eternity enthroned amidst yonder starry heights; and no utterance, no word ever came from those far-lying and silent spaces? Oh! it is strange—to think of that awful majesty above, and then to think of what is beneath it; this little struggle of life; this poor day's conflict; this busy ant-hill of a city. Shut down the dome of heaven close upon it; let it crush and confine every thought to the present spot, to the present instant; and such *would* a city be. But now, how is it? Ascend the lonely watch-tower of evening meditation, and look forth and listen; and lo! the talk of the streets, the sounds of music and revelling, the stir and tread of a multitude, go up into the silent and all-surrounding infinitude!

But is it the audible sound only that goeth up? Oh! no; but amidst the stir and noise of visible life, from the inmost bosom of the visible man, there goeth up a call, a cry, an asking, unuttered, unutterable; an asking for revelation, saying in almost speechless agony; "Oh! break, dread arch of mystery! tell us, ye stars, that roll above the waves of mortal trouble; speak! enthroned majesty of those awful heights; bow down you mysterious and reserved heavens and come near; tell us, what ye only know; tell us of the loved and lost; tell us what we are, and whither we are going!"

Is not man such an one? Is he not encompassed with a dome of incomprehensible wonders? Is there not that, in him and about him which should fill his life with majesty and sacredness? Is there not something of sublimity and sanctity thus born down from heaven, into the heart of every man? Where is the being so base and abandoned but he hath some traits of that sacredness left upon him; something so much in discordance perhaps with his general repute, that he hides it from all around him; some sanctuary in his soul, where no one may enter; some sacred enclosure—where the memory of a child is, or the image of a venerated parent, or the echo of some sweet word of kindness that was once spoken to him; an echo, that shall never die away?

Would man awake to the higher and better things that are in him, he would no longer feel, I repeat, that life to him is a negative, or superficial, or worldly existence. Evermore are his steps haunted with thoughts, far beyond their own range; which some have regarded, as the reminiscences of a pre-existent state. As a man who passeth a season in the sad and pleasant land of Italy, feels a majestic presence of sublime ages and histories with him, which, he does not always distinctly recognize, but which lend an indescribable interest to every field, and mountain, and mouldering wall, and make life to be, all the while, more than mere life; so it is with us all, in the beaten and worn track of this worldly pilgrimage. There is more here, than the world we live in; " it is not all of life to live." An unseen and infinite presence is here; a sense of something greater than we possess; a seeking, through all the void waste of life, for a good beyond it; a crying out of the heart for interpretation; a memory of the dead, which touches, ever and anon, some vibrating thread in this great tissue of mystery.

I cannot help thinking, that we all, not only have better intimations, but are capable of better things than we know; that the pressure of some great emergency would develope in us powers, beyond the worldly bias of our spirits; and that, so heaven dealeth with us, from time to time, as to call forth those better things. Perhaps there is not a family so selfish in the world, but that if one in it were doomed to die; if tyranny demanded a victim, it would be utterly impossible for its members, parents and children, to choose out that victim; but that all and each one would say, "I will die, but I cannot choose." Nay, in how many families, if that dire extremity had come, would one and another step forth, freed from the vile meshes of ordinary selfishness, and say, like the Roman father and son, "let the blow fall on me!" There are greater and better things in us all, than the world takes account of, or than *we* take note of, would we find them out. And it is one part of our spiritual culture to *find* these traits of greatness and power, to revive these faded impressions of generosity and goodness; the almost squandered bequests of God's love and kindness to our souls; and to yield ourselves to their guidance and control.

I am sensible that my discoursing now, has been somewhat desultory and vague. Perhaps, though I delight not in such discoursing generally, it has not been, in this instance, without a purpose. For the conciousness which I wish to address, is doubtless itself something, too shadowy and vague. But it is real, though indistinct. An unsatisfied asking is for ever in all human hearts. We know that the material crust of this earth does not limit our thoughts; that the common-place of life does not suffice us; that there are things in us, which go far beyond the range of our ordinary, earthly pursuits. Depraved as we may be, these things are true. They are indeed signs that we are fallen; but they are signs too that all is not lost. They are significant revelations; and they are admonitions no less powerful.

But now when our minds go out beyond the range of their visible action, what do they find? We have spoken of the great call of humanity; what is the answer?

The first answer comes from the mind itself. When we descend into the depths of our own being, we find desires which nothing less than the infinite can satisfy, powers fitted for everlasting expansion; powers whose unfolding at every step, only awakens new and vaster cravings; and sorrows, which all the accumulated wealth and pleasure of the world can never, never soothe. If a man's life consisted in that which he possesseth, how intolerable would it be! To be confined to what we have and what we are, is to be shut up in a dungeon, where we cannot breathe! Is not this whole nature then itself a stupendous argument for something greater to come? Is not this very conciousness deep in our souls, itself an answer? When you look at the embryo bird in the shell, you know that it is made to burst that little prison. You see feet that are made to run, and wings to fly. And as it pecks at the imprisoning shell, you see in that very impulse, the prophetic certainty that it is to come forth to light and air. And is the noblest being on earth alone to be for ever imprisoned, to perish in his prison; for ever to feel himself imprisoned; for ever to press against the barriers of his present knowledge and existence; and never to go forth? Are *man's* embryo powers alone—are *his* cravings and aspirations after something higher, to be accounted no revealings, no prophecies of a loftier destiny?

And again; when we lift up our thoughts to the vast infinitude, what do we find? Order, holding its sublime reign among the countless revolving suns and systems; and light, fair and beautiful, covering all as with a garment. Look up to the height of heaven in some bright and smiling summer's day; behold the etherial softness, the meteor of beauty that hangs over us; and does it not seem as if it were an enfolding gentleness; a silent, hushed breathing of unutterable love? Was ever a mother's eye bent on her child, more sweet and gentle? Was ever a loving countenance, more full of ineffable meaning? "Oh! you sweet heavens!" hath many a poet said; and can he who made those heavens, sublime and beautiful, wish us any harm? Were *you* made lord of those heavens, could you hurl down unrecking sorrow and disaster upon the poor tremblers beneath you? God, who hath breathed that pitying and generous thought into your heart, will not belie it in himself. My heart is to me a revelation, and heaven is to me a revelation of God's benignity. And when the voices of human want and sorrow go upward—as one has touchingly said, "like inarticulate cries, and sobbings of a dumb creature, which in the ear of heaven, are prayers"—I can no more doubt that they find gracious consideration and pity above, than if a voice of unearthly tenderness breathed from the sky, saying, "Poor frail beings! borne on the bosom of imperfection, and laid upon the lap of sorrow; be patient **and** hopeful; ye are not neglected nor forgotten; **the** heaven above you, holds itself in majestic reserve, because ye cannot bear what it has to tell you—holds you in solemn suspense, which death only may break; be faithful unto death; be trustful for a while; and all your lofty asking shall have answer, and all your patient sorrow shall find issue, in everlasting peace."

But, once more, there is more than a voice; there is a *revelation* in nature, and especially in the mission of Jesus Christ, more touching than words.

I have said that there is no uttered speech, from all around us; and yet have maintained that there is expression as clear and emphatic as speech; and I now say, it is much more expressive than speech. Let me observe here, that we are liable to lay quite an undue stress upon this mode of communication, upon speech; simply because speech is the ordained and ordinary vehicle of converse between man and man. If men had communicated with one another by pantomime; if forms, and not utterances had been the grand instrument of impression; if human love had always been expressed only by a brighter glow of the countenance, and pity only by a softer shadowing upon its beauty, then had we better understood perhaps, the grand communication of nature. Then had the bright sky in the day-time, and the soft veil of evening, and all the shows of things, around the whole dome of heaven and amidst the splendour and beauty of the world—all these, I say, in the majesty of silence, had been a revelation, not only the clearest, but the most impressive that was possible. I say in the majesty of silence. For accustomed as we are to speech; how much more powerful in some things is silence! How intolerable would it have been, if every day when it came had audibly said, "God is good;" and every evening when it stole upon us, had said, "God is good;"

and every cloud when it rose, and every tree as it blossomed, and every plant as it sprung from the earth, had audibly said, "God is good!" No, the silence of nature is more impressive, would we understand it, than any speech could be; it expresses what no speech can utter. No bare word can tell what that bright sky meaneth; what the wealth of nature meaneth; what is the heart's own deep assurance, that God is good.

But yet more; in the express revelation that is given us, it is not the bare word spoken, that is most powerful; it is the character of interposing mercy that is spread all over the volume. It is the miracle—that causes nature to break the secret of an all-controlling power, in that awful pause and silence. It is the loving and living excellence of Jesus; that miracle of his life, more than all. The word is but an attestation to something done. Had it been done in silence; could all generations have *seen* Jesus living, Jesus suffering; and heaven opened; it had been enough. Words are but the testimony, that hath gone forth to all generations and all ages, of what hath been *done*. God *is* ever *doing* for us, what—be it said reverently—what he cannot speak. As a dear friend, can look the love, which he cannot utter; so do I read the face of nature; so do I read the record of God's interposing mercy. I feel myself embraced with a kindness, too tender and strong for utterance. It cannot *tell* me how dear to the Infinite love, my welfare, my purity, is. Only by means and ministrations, by blessings and trials, by dealings and pressures of its gracious hand upon me, can it make me know. So do I read the volume of life and nature; and so do I read the volume of revelation. I see in Jesus living, in Jesus suffering; I see in the deep heart of his pain and patience, and love and pity, what no words can utter. I learn this not from any excellency of speech, but from the excellency of his living and suffering. Even in the human breast the deepest things, are things which it can never utter. So it was in the heart of Jesus. So it is—I speak it reverently—in the nature of God, "For no ear hath ever heard, the things which God hath prepared for them that love him. But God hath revealed them to us by his spirit; for the spirit, and the spirit alone, searcheth all things, yea, the deep things of God."

VII.

HUMAN NATURE CONSIDERED AS A GROUND FOR THANKSGIVING

KNOW YE THAT THE LORD HE IS GOD; IT IS HE THAT HATH MADE US, AND NOT WE OURSELVES; WE ARE HIS PEOPLE AND THE SHEEP OF HIS PASTURE. ENTER INTO HIS GATES WITH THANKSGIVING, AND INTO HIS COURTS WITH PRAISE; BE THANKFUL UNTO HIM AND BLESS HIS NAME.—Psalm c. 3—4.

THE theme of gratitude which is here presented to us, is, our existence, our nature. "It is He that hath *made* us, and not we ourselves: we are his people and the sheep of his pasture." It is not what we possess or enjoy, but what we *are;* or it is what we possess and enjoy in relation to what we are, that I would make the subject of grateful commemoration in our present meditations.

In truth, every call to praise, is but an echo of this. For if it be duly considered, will it not be found, that all possible blessings,—all that *can* be the occasions of thanksgiving,—must be referred back, when we trace them, to the blessing which is conferred upon us in a nature capable of enjoying them. The bounty and the beauty of the world, were nothing but for the seeing eye and the sensitive frame; the wisdom which all things teach were nothing, but for the perceiving mind; the blessed relations of our social existence would be all a barren waste, if we had not a heart to feel them; and all the tendencies and conditions of our life and being, all our labours and pleasures, all our joys and sorrows, would be but one dark struggle or darker despair, if we had not a moral soul and will, to bring good out of evil, imperishable virtue out of perishable circumstance, and immortal victory out of the ever-pressing strife of human existence.

Every blessing, then, hath the essential condition that makes it such, in my very humanity. I am called upon to be thankful, for food and raiment, for the bounties and gratuities of nature, for green fields and whitening harvests, for peace and freedom and government; and for those blessings that are beyond and above all—the immeasurable and eternal blessings of religion. I am called upon to be thankful for all these things, and I am so. But still I must say, and must so answer, that I *cannot* be thankful for one of these blessings, without being first, and last, and throughout, thankful that I am a man.

The advantage of *being a man*, therefore, is what I propose now to consider; the blessing bestowed in our very humanity; that indeed without which we had not the power of gratitude.

I am thankful, then, that I am a man. This is the central fact, around which all things range themselves in clusters of blessings.

I am thankful that I am human. I am thankful that I am not a clod; that I am not a brute. Nay, nor do I ask to be an angel. I am glad that I am human. My very humanity, despite of all that is said against it, is a blessing and a gladness to me. Although it may sound strangely—to the thoughtless man on one account, and to the theologian on another; yet will I say, that I accept this humanity thankfully—with all its imperfections, with all its weaknesses, with all its exposures to error and sin. None but a high moral nature *could* be so exposed. Although I stand amidst a multitude, where the infirmities of this nature meet me on every side, in many a shaded brow and pale check, in many a countenance where grief and gladness are strangely mingled, where joy itself is touched with sadness; yet still I say, that with all the joy and sadness of this nature, included, interwoven, and making up one momentous, mysterious and touching experience, I accept, I embrace, I cherish it with gratitude: I rejoice that it is mine.

I do not wish, I repeat, to be something else. I do not wish that I were an angel; and I do not wish that I were like the inhabitant of some distant star. I do not *know* what he is. But this humanity that throbs in my bosom—I know what *this* is; it is near me, it is dear unto me; I rejoice that I am a man.

And upon this I insist, and am going to insist, because there is, I fear, a commonly prevailing disparagement of our humanity, which leaves no proper, no grateful sense of what it is. There is a feeling in many minds, as if it were a misery, a misfortune, almost a disgrace to be a man. I am not speaking merely of the theological disparagement—the dull fiction of oriental philosophy and of scholastic darkness— though that, doubtless, has helped to create the common impression, that it is but a poor advantage, but a doubtful good, to be a man. I am not speaking alone of that scorn and desecration, by theology, of the very humanity which it ought to have loved and helped. There are other causes that have tended to the same result: human pride, misanthropy, discontent, anger with our kind, anger with our lot; and the natural sense too, of human ills and errors. It is curious to see how almost all our higher literature betrays its trust to the very humanity which it celebrates,—denies in general what it teaches in detail—heaps satire and scorn upon mankind, and yet makes *men* its heroes. It is wonderful to see how, not authors only, but men generally, can berate and vilify the very being that they are. Humanity—man—these are not contrasted, but correlative things; you cannot eulogize the former, and desecrate the latter; the former is the ideal, the latter the real; the one is the picture, the other, the original. What man *is*, must furnish the elements from which we draw out the idea of what man should be; what you think, what you feel, is human, and *that* tells what humanity should be. There is doubtless a struggle between these conceptions, of the actual humanity and the ideal humanity; and for this very struggle too, I admire the human being. It could not agitate inferior natures. That man can separate the good from the evil, and set it up as a model; that he can sigh over the evil, is a praise and a glory to him. Ay, and that he can satirize, scorn and execrate the evil, and can do it with such uncompromising heartiness that he goes too far, seems to me not a disreputable tendency of his nature. There is something right then, something respectable in the leaning to darker views. In this respect, there is something right in theology, in literature, and in common opinion. But for the sake of justice and of gratitude, for man's sake, and for God's sake, if I may reverently say so, let not all this go too far; let it not spread the shadow over all, lest it hide from us, both man and God. I must therefore resist this tendency: because it is wrong, and especially at present, because it hinders a just gratitude to the Almighty Creator, for the nature he has given us.

For this—what we are—is, I repeat, the central truth around which all other truths that appeal to gratitude, do range themselves: it is the sun in the system of God's mercies—their common bond and enlightener. It will not do to set up that antagonism which is commonly taught, between man and God ; to say that God indeed is altogether good, but that man is altogether bad ; that God is glorious, but that man is altogether mean ; that it is proper indeed to celebrate God's goodness and glory, but that this is especially to be done by discrediting all worth and value in man. Who is it, after all, that celebrates the goodness of God? It is no other than man. The worshipper, the adorer, the singer of praises in this world, is none other than man. If his nature is all contrast to the divine, what is the value of his praise, of his judgment? Nay, how came the divine to be known? Man, I say, is the worshipper. And what more is the angel, unless that he is so in a higher measure, or with a purer intent. There must then be a beauty in human as well as in angelic nature, or all the beauty of the creation and of its Maker, could avail nothing—were nothing, to us. I know not what eyes look out from yonder bright orbs of heaven ; but I know that eye is not, nor soul there, that can see any thing brighter, lovelier, more majestic, more divine, than the glory of Him that made us: that made the earth so fair, and the heavens so beautiful and sublime. I claim kindred with those dwellers on high. I bow with them in adoration. I join my voice to their lofty anthem. Shall I think lightly of this glorious affinity?

No, I am thankful that I am a man. Boldly do I say it: that I rejoice, that I delight in my nature. I rejoice that God has made me, and made me such an one—a sensitive, social, religious being—one of the seers, one of the worshippers, one of the immortals. Mourn I well may, that I have failed so far, so lamentably far, from what he has made me for. But still I must be none the less thankful for the wonderful signatures that he has set upon my being.

Does any one critically ask, why, with such repetition, I insist upon this? I answer, because I would make, on this point, a distinct and decided impression of what I mean to say. I mean to resist that ingratitude which holds it to be a misfortune or a mischance to be a man. I mean, if I can, to roll off that burden of darkness and desolation, with which our *humanity* is thought to overshadow the world. It is the light in the world, and not the darkness. It is the eye that sees, and not the cloud that obscures. Or if there be cloud and darkness in it, as well as over it; in it too, and in it alone on earth, is the power of vision that can, and does, and will see through all. If it be not, then, I repeat, there is nothing in this world that can see; and all, without and within, is darkness; darkness as the shadow of death—as the gloom of the grave. No, it is a good thing to be a man, or else there is no good in this world. Let no one's heart sink within him, when that name, dear, and holy—the name of MAN, is uttered. Let no one give himself to dull, sighing, sorrowing, complaining, disconsolate thoughts of his humanity. It is a high and glorious gift.

I exist. What a blessing and a wonder is that! A few years ago, and I was not; no spot in the fair universe, held *me*. From dark and void nothingness, I am called to the glad precincts of being; into the living and loving bosom of nature; into communion with the things that are; myself—chiefest blessing!—myself among the things that are. And do I ask to whom I owe this blessing? Whence came I—do I ask? What one among the mysterious powers of heaven gave me this wonderful being? Reason answers, and Holy Writ answers, there is but One who creates. And the Psalmist teaches us, and says, "it is He that hath made us, and not we ourselves." It is He, God, that hath called me into being; to stand beneath these shining heavens; to look around upon the loveliness of earth; to breathe the air of verdant fields and see the light of rising and setting suns; to behold the moulded beauty of sloping vallies and swelling mountains, and the flashing light of streams and ocean waves. Every body *says* that this is the darkest world in the universe. Who knows it? Who knows that there is any one among all the spheres of heaven more beautiful than this? The old Greek sages thought not thus—who used the same word, κοσμος, for beauty and for the world. Other kind of beauty there may be, but who shall dare to say that any creation has proceeded from God, that is not all beautiful? I do not like that phrase—"this dark world." Poetry may use it, and in some relations and in some moods, there may be a propriety in its use. But what I complain of, is, that the feeling has sunk down into the common heart; the unadmiring, unholy, unthankful feeling, that this is a dark world; the darkest of all worlds. I complain that the casual shade of poetry has settled into a fixed, opaque incrustation over the general mind; that it is common to feel as if this were a coarse, ungenial, ungrateful, almost an ill-made world; as if it were the rough-hewn penitentiary of the creation, frowning upon us, from its granite walls, and its dark and dingy arches. And therefore I say, who knows it? Who knows that there is any thing in the far-lying fields of heaven, more beautiful, of more entrancing loveliness, than the world we dwell in? I say, who knows it? But I might say rather, shame on the superstitious weakness, the uncultivated thought, the unkindled apathy, that finds nothing here but a prison wall, surrounding a convict's yard! Shame on the eye that cannot see and on the heart that cannot feel, the **wonders** and beauties of this fair and lovely creation around us! No poetry, hath it? Nay, nor no piety—none at least that is a fit offering to the glorious Creator!

And as man stands amidst the fair creation, with what a wonderful apparatus is he provided for communication with it; with a perception for every element; for the sweets of every bounty in nature, for the fragrance of every field, for the soft, embracing air, for the sounds that come from every hill and mountain and murmuring stream and ocean wave; for the light that beams from the far distant stars. We look upon the lately invented electro-magnetic telegraph, as a wonder; and it is so. But man's whole sensitive frame is a more wonderful telegraph. He wakes from sleep; and all nature around becomes a living presence; life streams in through every pore of the quick-feeling vesture with which he is clothed. He listens; and into the polished and waxen chambers of the ear, comes the hum of cities, the bleating of flocks upon the hills, the sound of the woodman's axe in the deep forest—comes the echoing of the wide welkin above him—comes above all, the music of human speech. He opens his eye, and stars that rise upon the infinite seas of space, are telegraphed to his vision.

We are proverbially insensible to the value of that which we have always possessed; of which we cannot go back in our conscious thought, to the origin. If seeing were an invention, how should we admire it! We admire the telescope—itself the product of a reasoning power which God has given us, and which will doubtless discover yet greater things.

But suppose that the eye had at first been formed to **see** only this world; and all beyond had been a wall of darkness; and that then, at some given era, there had been superadded to that organ, the telescopic power, and upon the human eye had burst the wonders of heaven: how dark on the page of human history, would have lain the ages before; and how would that era be forever celebrated, almost as the beginning of human existence! And what *is* the telescope compared with this!—built at much expense; a cumbrous weight to be carried from place to place; and constructed with elaborate mechanism to turn its axis one way and another; while in the beggar's eye, as he lifts it to heaven, and turns it unconsciously from point to point, is an instrument, which all the skill of science, aided by the wealth of empires, could never construct.

Say you not, then, even considering man in this light, only as endowed with senses, that it is good to be a man? And yet considering him thus, we have only placed him upon the stage of his life's great action, and given him the materials and the instruments with which he is to work.

Standing on this theatre, he sees, he hears, he observes, indeed; and this is wonderful. But how much more wonderful is that transmutation, by which observation becomes knowledge; sight, perception; and hearing, oracular wisdom! The *world* stands in its majesty and beauty; but it is transformed into another kind of majesty and beauty by the labours of science and art. The result—the actual state of human knowledge, it seems to me, is worthy of more consideration than it always receives. I cannot think that an angel, if he were to visit this world, would look upon this structure of its labouring wisdom with disparaging scorn. The world has done its work—done some work, surely. Behold the fabric of science it has raised; with its vast and ranged collections of objects from all nature; from fields and forests, from mountains and mines, from woods and waters; with its curious and world-interpreting laboratories; with its million-volumed libraries, stored with the wisdom of ages; with its illumined chambers of philosophy, and its dome, the grand observatory of the skies, swelling up to heaven;—and then see how man takes from the majestic halls of science, the principles and results which he applies to the advancement of his comfort, civilization and welfare; how he is making nature every day more and more his helper and his friend; how he takes the swift lightning and makes it his telegraphic messenger; how he chains to his fiery car on the land and on the sea that elemental power which he had known before only in the whirlwind and the storm. Nay, look at that system of practical wisdom which he has wrought out from the daily experience of life—the system of common sense—that which instructs him in the knowledge of men and the uses of things; that aptitude and adjustment of his faculties to every exigency; that which, if a man utterly lacks, he ceases to be a man, and is pronounced a fool. Because it is called *common* sense, it is considered as something ordinary and indifferent. We will never learn that the greatest things are common; the greatest gifts, universal. Not the philosopher alone is wise. Nay, every man is wiser as a man than any man is, merely as a learned man. All the wisdom there is in books, is not equal to the wisdom that floats in the common air about us; the wisdom of life; the wisdom from which books draw all their life; the wisdom that is gained, not in the study nor the cloister, but in the great school which God has built—the school of life. Consider it, proud philosopher! or self-complacent man of rank or of wealth! Suppose yourself deprived of that light of common sense in which the multitude walks: what then, would your libraries or your palaces, or your thrones, avail you? *Avail* you? They had not *been.* They had not been written, nor built, nor lifted up. And what would *you* be without the common food of unwritten reason? A starveling, an idiot, a fool. Yes, though you sat upon a throne, you would be sent out, like Nebuchadnezzar, to eat grass with the ox.

When I think of all that man, as an intellectual being, has acquired and achieved, it amazes me that any body can speak of this world as the abode of a poor, toiling, drudging, ignorant, contemptible race. I would beat down every aristocracy whether of birth or learning, or wealth, that says this. I think the world has done very well—done much, though not all that it might. I think this a very respectable race—respectable?—why, a wonderful race. Do not answer me, now, with a satirical thought of the poor, dwarfed, ignorant creatures that you sometimes see around you. Do not cast their faults upon the whole family. It is a serious matter that we are considering. It is a serious thing to defame and belie a whole world. It is a thing you could not do at all, but for the vagueness of your contemplation. You could not so discredit your family, your family circle, your village, your city, your country. Oh! no, this is too near you. Nay, and let another speak ill of your city or your country, not to say your family, and he will hear your indignant defence. But when you speak of the great world, you seem to think that its shoulders are broad enough to bear any thing. It is as if you shot an arrow into the great, circumambient air; it can neither hit nor hurt any body. Or it is the world in past ages that you speak of; a dead world that cannot answer; it lies before you, quite a passive theme, and you seem to think it a fine thing, to write cold history or scornful satire upon it, as a wretched and worthless world. I cannot agree with this unbrotherly scorn, because the *world* is its object.

Nay, and there is one yet more serious aspect of this subject; that in which it presents a providence. It seems to me a poor business for philosophy, first to make the world as mean and base as it can, and then to turn about and try to explain why it was made at all; how its existence can be, in any way, reconciled with the goodness of providence. A hard problem it is then for the philosopher; too hard for him; and he worries himself with it in vain. It gives but little satisfaction in the case, to say that, although men have been fools, they might have been wiser if they would. The truth is, they have been wiser than the cynical philosopher admits. The case is not so hard as he makes it. And he must make it better, or he can never solve his problem. None but a more considerate and fraternal philosophy ever will solve it. On the side of this fraternal philosophy I take my place; and in the spirit of it, I say again, that considering myself as an intellectual being, and pretending to be no wiser than the average of men, I do not think it a misfortune to be a man; I am thankful that I am a man.

And what think you, my friends, of society; that living mechanism of human relationships that spreads itself over the world; that finer essence within it, which as truly moves it as any power, heavy or expansive, moves your sounding manufactories or swift-flying cars? The man-machine hurries to and fro upon the earth, moves this way and that, stretches out its hands on every side, to toil, to barter, to unnumbered labours and enterprises; and almost ever the motive, that which moves it, is something that takes hold of the comforts, affections, and hopes of social existence. It is true that the mechanism often works with difficulty, drags heavily, grates and screams with harsh collision. And it is true, that the essence of finer motive, becoming intermixed with baser, with coarser ingredients, often clogs, obstructs, jars and deranges the free and noble action of social life. But surely he is not wise, and will not be duly grateful, who turns the eye of the cynic upon all this, and loses the blessed sense of social good in its perversions. That I can be a *friend*, that I can *have* a friend, though it were but one in the world; that fact, that blessedness I will set against all the sufferings of my social nature. That there is such a place on earth as a *home;* that resort, that sanctuary of in-walled and shielded joy, I will set against all the surrounding desolations of life. That I can be a true, social man; that I can speak my true thought, amidst all the janglings of controversy and the warring of opinions; that fact from within, outweighs all facts from without.

The truth is, that in the visible aspect and action of society, often repulsive and annoying, we are apt to lose the due sense of its invisible blessings. As in the frame of nature, it is not the coarse and palpable, not soils and rains, not even fields and flowers, that are so beautiful, as the invisible spirit of wisdom and beauty that pervades it; so in the frame of society, it is the invisible, and therefore unobserved, that is most beauttful. And yet in the visible, I have often thought there is more beauty than is often acknowledged. The human countenance, I am wont to think, is more beautiful than it is usually considered. I speak not here of what is commonly called beauty; that which arises from symmetry of feature and delicacy of complexion. There is a beauty in almost every countenance

—the wonderful beauty and power of expression—that far surpasses all that these too much lauded charms can bestow upon any. An artist once said to me, when I spoke of the common faces he had to paint; "no, there is a beauty in the human countenance that I can never paint; what I meet with, every day in the street —the plainest that I meet—I can never paint its beauty." I felt at once rebuked, and obliged too, as one that receives a wiser thought than his own. Yes, it is true, and I see it every day. There are expressions of ingenuousness and modesty, of love and pity, breaking out from the plainest and the roughest features; there are evanescent shadings of thought and feeling flitting over every countenance, that never were transferred to the canvass. Worldly fashion may set up its laws and its idols; but it were a more wisely-instructed eye that should see loveliness every where.

Let not this be thought too trivial for this place; I speak of the out-shining of the secret soul, through "the human face divine." And indeed, how much is secret and unseen in the frame of society! What an invisible law is that—an invisible law of God it is— that reigns over the relationship of sex! The delicacy of that relation is stronger than any human government; a graceful veil, and yet a linked chain. It is like the at once attractive and repelling electric forces, which, unchained, would explode with crash and ruin, and yet are ever held fast by an invisible hand! Or will you go down to the rougher paths of life? What nerves the arm of toil? If man minded himself alone, he would fling down the spade and the ax, and rush to the wilderness, or roam through the world as a wilderness; and he would make the world a desert. His home, which he sees not, perhaps, but once or twice in a day; that home is the invisible bond of the world.

And what is it that gives the loftiest character to business, to trade and commerce? What but the good, strong and noble faith that men put in one another? Fraud there is; but it is the exception, in the goings on of business; honesty is the rule, and all the frauds in the world cannot, cannot tear the great bond of human confidence. If they could, commerce would furl its sail on all seas, and all the cities of the world would crumble to ruins. *There* stands a man on the other side of the world!—whom you never saw, whom you never will see; and yet that man's bare character, do you hold good for a bond of thousands. And what is the most striking feature of the political state? Not governments, not constitutions, not laws, not enactments, not police—but the universal will of the people to be governed by the common weal. Take off that restraint, and no government on earth can stand for an hour.

We have now considered our being as sensitive, intellectual, and social, and as furnishing, in each one of these characters, signal occasions for gratitude to its Author. There is one higher character presenting still stronger claims, and yet demanding still higher faith for its recognition; I mean, of course, the moral, the spiritual, the divine nature that man possesses. For here it is precisely—in this region where the moral will puts forth its power, that it encounters such difficulty and is guilty of such failure, that it seems, no doubt, at times, as if the world were overshadowed with sins and sorrows.

Of the actual attainments of this spiritual nature, it is true, we must entertain but a moderate and humbling estimate. And yet I must say, that the nature **has** done more and better than it always has credit for. 1 must confess that I am led at times to wonder, **not** that the world is so bad as it is, but to wonder that it is not worse. Human nature has been so badly treated by those who should have known it better, that its virtues sometimes more surprise me than its vices. We hear indeed of horrible atrocities at which society stands aghast; but when I think of the undisciplined strength of passion, the untamed anger that boils in the human breast, the unschooled propensities that rage in the human frame, I wonder rather at the limits that are set to their range.

> There's a Divinity that shapes our ends,
> Rough hew them how we will.

How few men are as bad as they might be; as bad as they are tempted to be! How many checks are there in the moral system of our being and life! How many painful emotions beset the evil course; how many admonitory voices are there of sin-inflicted suffering, disease and sorrow, that warn and almost compel man to be wise! That which divines have called "restraining grace"—that restraint indeed of the Great Will that reigns over us—what a marvellous feature is it in the moral economy!

And that I can suffer when I sin, that I can sorrow for the wrong that is in me, that I can sigh and struggle to be free from it—I am glad of that. Were it not for this moral nature, this conscience, all were wrecked; but it exists, it is strong, it works mightily in the human heart. I know not *who* makes it suffer and sorrow and struggle as it does, but God. It seems to me that all institutions, all preachings, all machinery of human device, are weak, compared with this all-pervading power of God that works within us. And indeed all other means are nothing but as they take hold of that power.

And if by that power I can, and do, rise to virtue, if I gain the victory over temptation, if I attain to a true and solid peace, to an inward sufficiency, to the supreme and absorbing love of goodness and of God, then indeed are my feet set upon a rock, and a new song is put into my mouth; and it is a song of thanksgiving. Nothing on earth or in heaven, can ever be such a cause of thankfulness with me, as this.

What an interest belongs to the very strifes and trials that may lead to this? A man who makes a fortune on the burning soil of India, is thankful to that country—with all its heat and dust and languor and disease, he is thankful to it. A man who stands here at home, with energy and opportunity to repair his broken fortunes, blesses that opportunity and that energy. So do we stand in the field of the world. We may have failed to a certain extent, or we may have failed altogether, to secure the great interest of life. But still the opportunity for better efforts is given; time is lengthened out; the day and the means of grace are ours; conscience is in our hearts, and the Bible is in our hands, and prayer may be on our lips; all is not lost; the time past may be redeemed, the erring steps retrieved; our very errors may teach us; our sad experience may teach us—blessed be its sadness then!—and we may rise to sanctity, to blessedness and to heaven. And if, I say again, we can and do thus succeed; if, from this often-deceiving, and ever-changing and fleeting world, we may draw and fix within us, one thing which is sure and steadfast and immovable and always abounding, one feeling that is assurance and **sufficiency** and victory, a happiness in wisdom, **in** love and in God, which is, we know, in its very nature everlasting, which, we feel, will never desert us, will never let us be unhappy, go where on earth, go where in heaven, we will; what a prize, to bear away from a struggling life and from the battling world, is this? Who does not say, "thanks be to God?" And who that understands the great, comforting and redeeming ministration of the Gospel to this end, does not say— "thanks be to God through our Lord Jesus Christ?" Yes, my brethren, through Jesus Christ, above all. We have not been left to struggle alone. One has come to us, bearing the image of God, bearing the mission of God; One, all compassion and tenderness, all truth and loveliness, has come to us and taught us, and helped us, and prayed for us, and died for us: and to him, under God, do we owe the prize. And when it is gained and borne away to heaven, then and there shall we say, "blessing and honour and glory and power, be unto Him that sitteth on the throne, and to the Lamb forever and ever!"

And in fine, my friends, that we shall *bear away* this prize from earth to heaven—is that to be lamented? Shall that thought check and chill all our gladness and thanksgiving?

I rejoice that I am a man—a sensitive, intellectual, social, moral being: above all, that I am a moral being. I rejoice that I have a conscience, and a knowledge of God. I rejoice that I am a being subject to a great, moral trial. I lament that I have fallen, but all the more am I thankful that I can rise. I thank God that I can spiritually sorrow and struggle, and spiritually can gain the victory. But now shall I surprise you— shall I seem to say too much if I say, I thank God that **I am** mortal. I thank God that he has put a limit to this earthly probation. Not with grieving but with hope, do I recognise the solemn truth that one day—what day I know not, and for that too am I thankful—that one day, appointed in God's wisdom, I shall die!—yes, that I shall die!—that I shall lay aside this body for another form of being! I would not live always. I would not always feel the burdens and barriers with which mortality has surrounded and overlaid me. Some time or other, I would part hence; some time or other I would that my friends should part hence. Oh! could we go in families! But that too, I see, would not be well. For then how bound up in our families should we be—how selfish and how reserved and exclusive! No, I take the great dispensation as it is, and I am thankful for it. All its strong bonds, all its urgent tasks, all its disciplinary trials—I accept all, and accept all with gratitude. Sweet, angel visits of peace are these also; thrilling pleasures in my sensitive frame; lofty towerings and triumphs of intellect; blessed bonds and joys of society; the glorious vision of the infinite perfection; I am thankful for them all. I am thankful that every age of life has its character, task and hope; that childhood comes forth upon the stream of life, in its frail but fairy and gay vessel—with its guardian angel by its side—the banks covered with flowers, and the vermilion tints of morning upon the hills; that youth stands amidst the bright landscape, stretching its eye and its arm to the cloud-castle of honour and hope; that manhood struggles amidst the descending storm, with resignation, with courage, with an eye fixed on heaven; and that although shapes of wrath and terror are amidst the elements, the guardian angel too is there, holding its bright station in the clouds; and that when age at last comes, life's struggle over, life's voyage completed—that light from heaven streams down upon the darkness and desolation of earth, and the good angel is by its side, and pointing upward says, "thither—thither shalt thou go"!*

* The allusion here, is to that admirable series of paintings, by Mr Cole, entitled "The Stream of Life."

ON HUMAN LIFE.

VIII.

THE MORAL SIGNIFICANCE OF LIFE.

NOW A THING WAS SECRETLY BROUGHT TO ME, AND MINE EAR RECEIVED A LITTLE THEREOF. IN THOUGHTS FROM THE VISIONS OF THE NIGHT, WHEN DEEP SLEEP FALLETH ON MEN; FEAR CAME UPON ME, AND TREMBLING WHICH MADE ALL MY BONES TO SHAKE. THEN A SPIRIT PASSED BEFORE MY FACE, AND THE HAIR OF MY FLESH STOOD UP. IT STOOD STILL; BUT I COULD NOT DISCERN THE FORM THEREOF; AN IMAGE WAS BEFORE MINE EYES; THERE WAS SILENCE; AND I HEARD A VOICE.—Job iv. 12—16.

HUMAN life to many, is like the vision of Eliphaz. Dim and shadowy vails hang round its awful revelations. Teachings there are to man, in solemn and silent hours, in thoughts from the visions of the night, in vague impressions and unshaped reveries; but, on this very account, they fail to be interpreted and understood. There is much teaching; but there is also much unbelief.

There is a scepticism, indeed, about the entire moral significance of life, which I propose, in this discourse, to examine. It is a scepticism, sometimes taking the form of philosophy, sometimes of misanthrophy and scorn, and sometimes of heavy and hardbound worldliness, which denies that life has any lofty, spiritual import: which resolves all into a series of toils and trifles and vanities, or of gross and palpable pursuits and acquisitions. It is a scepticism, not about creeds, not about Christianity; it lies farther back—lies far deeper; it is a scepticism about the very meaning and intent of our whole existence.

This scepticism I propose to meet; and for this purpose, I propose to see what argument can be extracted out of the very grounds on which it founds itself.

The pertinency of my text to my purpose, as I have already intimated, lies in this; there is much of deep import in this life, like that which Eliphaz saw in the visions of the night—not clear, not palpable, or at least not usually recognised and made familiar; but it cometh, as it were in the night, when deep sleep falleth on men; it cometh in the still and solitary hours; it cometh in the time of meditation or of sorrow, or of some awful and overshadowing crisis of life. It is secretly brought to the soul, and the ear receiveth a little thereof. It is as a spirit that passeth before us, and vanisheth into the night shadow; or it standeth still, but we cannot discern the form thereof; there is an undefined image of truth; there is silence; and at length there is a voice.

It is of these unrecognised revelations of our present being, that I would endeavour to give the interpretation; I would attempt to give them a voice.

But let us spread out a little in the first place, the sceptic's argument. It says; "What is there in human existence that accords with your lofty, Christian theory? You may talk about the grandeur of a human life, the sublime wants and aspirations of the human soul, the solemn consciousness, amidst all life's cares and toils, of an immortal destiny; it is all a beautiful dream! Look over the world's history, and say—what intimations does it furnish of that majestic design, the world's salvation? Look at any company of toiling and plodding men in the country around you; and what are they thinking of, but acres and crops, of labour and the instruments of labour? Go into the noisy and crowded manufactory, and what is there, but *machinery*—animate or inanimate; the mind as truly girded and harnessed to the work, as the turning-lathe or the banded wheel? Gaze upon the thronged streets, or upon holiday crowds, mixing the oaths of the profane with the draughts of the intemperate; and where is the spiritual soul that you talk of? Or look at human life in a large view of it, and of what is it made up? "Trouble and weariness"—you see that it is the cynic's complaint—"trouble and weariness; the disappointment of inexperience or the dulness of familiarity; the frivolity of the gay or the unprofitable sadness of melancholy; the heavy ennui of the idle or the plodding care of the busy; the suffering of disease or the wasted energy of health; frailty, its lot and its doom, death; a world of things wasted, worn out, perishing in the use, tending to nothing, and accomplishing nothing; so complete the frivolity of life with many, that they actually think more of the fine apparel they shall wear, than of the inward spirit, which you say is to inherit the immortal ages!"

All this, alas! is too true; but it is not true to the extent nor in the exclusive sense, alleged. That but few meditate on their lot as they ought, is perfectly true; but there are impressions and convictions that come into the mind through other channels than those of meditation. They come perhaps, like the shadowy vision of Eliphaz, in darkness and silence—vague, indistinct, mysterious, awful; or they come in the form of certain, but neglected and forgotten truths. And they come, too, from those very scenes, in which the eye of the objector can see nothing but material grossness or thoughtless levity. This is what I shall especially attempt to show. I shall not undertake, in this discourse, to go farther; but I believe that I shall not perform a useless service to the true faith of our being, if I may be able, in some measure, to unveil and bring to light, those secret intimations which are often smothered, indeed, but which from time to time, are flashing out from the cloud of human cares and pursuits.

"Man," it is said, "is bound up in materialism, imprisoned by the senses, limited to the gross and palpable; far-reaching thoughts, soaring aspirations are found in essays and speculations about him rather than in his own experience; they are in books, rather than in brick-yards and ploughed fields and tumultuous marts."

What stupendous revelations are cloaked and almost hidden by familiarity! This very category of scepticism; what is it, but the blind admission of the sublimest truth? A *man* is recognized as standing amidst this palpable cloud of care and labour; enclosed, it is said, shut up in sense and matter; but still a *man!* A dungeon is this world, if you please so to represent it; but in this dungeon, is a prisoner—moaning, sorrowing, sighing to be free. A wilderness world it is, in the thought of many; but *one* is struggling through this wilderness, who imparts to it a loftier grandeur than its own; his articulate voice, his breathed prayer, or his shout amidst the dim solitudes—nay, the very sound of his axe in the forest depths—is sublimer than all the solemn symphonies of autumn winds sweeping through its majestic aisles.

Grant that matter and sense are man's teachers; and consider these teachings in their very humblest form, in their very lowest grade—what they teach *perforce*, and in spite of man's will. What are they? Materialism itself suggests to man the thought of an immaterial principle. The senses awaken within him the consciousness of a soul. Of a soul, I say; and what is that? Oh! the very word, soul, is itself soiled by a common use, till we know not what it means. So that this universal endowment of humanity, this dread endowment, by which infinity, eternity, nay and divinity, belong to its innate and inmost conceptions, can be at once admitted and almost overlooked, in the account of human existence.

In man the humblest instruments reveal the loftiest energies. This is not enthusiasm, but philosophy. Modern philosophy has distinctly unfolded this principle; that all our mental conceptions suggest their opposites; the finite, the infinite; the seen, the unseen; time, eternity; creation, a God. The child that has tried his eye upon surrounding objects, soon learns to send his thought through the boundless air, and to embrace the idea of infinite space. The being that is conscious of having lived a certain time, comes to entertain as correlative to that consciousness, the conception of eternity. These are among the fundamental facts of all human experience. Such, to a man in distinction from an animal, is the instrumentality of his very senses. As with a small telescope, a few feet in length and breadth, man learns to survey heavens beyond heavens, almost infinite; so with the aid of limited senses and faculties does he rise to the conception of what is beyond all visible heavens, beyond all conceivable time, beyond all imagined power, beauty and glory. Such is a human life. Man stands before us, visibly confined within the narrowest compass; and yet from this humble frame, stream out on every side the rays of thought, to infinity, to eternity, to omnipotence, to boundless grandeur and goodness. Let him who will, account this existence to be nothing but vanity and dust. I must be allowed on better grounds, to look upon it as that, in whose presence all the visible majesty of worlds and suns and systems sink to nothing. Systems and suns and worlds are all comprehended in a single thought of this being, whom we do not yet know.

But let us pass from these primary convictions which are suggested by matter and sense, to those spheres of human life, where many can see nothing but weary labour, or trifling pleasure, or heavy ennui.

Labour, then—what is it, and what doth it mean? Its fervid brow, its toiling hand, its weary step; what do they mean? It was in the power of God to provide for us, as he has provided for the beasts of the field and the fowls of heaven: so that human hands should neither toil nor spin. He who appointed the high hills as a refuge for the wild goats, and the rocks for the conies, might as easily have caused marble cities and hamlets of enduring granite, to have been productions of nature's grand masonry. In secret forges and by eternal fires, might every instrument of convenience and elegance have been fashioned; the winds might have woven soft fabrics upon every tree, and a table of abundance might have been spread in every wilderness and by every seashore. For the animal races it *is* spread. Why is it not for man? Why is it especially ordained as the lot of man, that in the sweat of his brow he shall eat his bread? Be ye sure that it hath a meaning. The curse, so much dreaded in the primeval of innocence and freedom of nature, falls not causeless on the earth. Labour is a more beneficent ministration than man's ignorance comprehends, or his complainings will admit. It is *not* mere blind drudgery, even when its end is hidden from him. It is all a training, it is all a discipline; a development of energies, a nurse of virtues, a school of improvement. From the poor boy that gathers a few sticks for his mother's hearth, to the strong man who fells the forest oak, every human toiler, with every weary step and every urgent task, is obeying a wisdom far above his own wisdom, and is fulfilling a design far beyond his own design—his own supply and support or another's wealth, luxury or splendour.

But now let us turn to an opposite scene of life. I mean that of pleasure and dissipation. Is this all mere frivolity, a scene that suggests no meaning beyond its superficial aspects? Nay, my friends, what significance is there in unsatisfying pleasure? What a serious thing is the reckless gaiety of a bad man? What a picture, almost to move our awe, does vice present to us? The desperate attempt to escape from the ennui of an unfurnished and unsatisfied mind; the blind and headlong impulse of the soul, to quench its maddening thirst for happiness in the burning draughts of pleasure; the deep consciousness which soon arises of guilt and infamy; the sad adieu to honour and good fame; the shedding of silent and bitter tears; the flush of the heart's agony over the pale and haggard brow; the last determined and dread sacrifice of the soul and of heaven, to one demoniac passion; what serious things are these? What signatures upon the soul, to show its higher nature? What a fearful hand-writing upon the walls that surround the deeds of darkness, duplicity and sensual crime? The holy altar of religion hath no seriousness about it, deeper, or I had almost said, more awful than that which settles down upon the gaming table, or broods oftentimes over the haunts of corrupting indulgence. At that altar, indeed, is teaching; words, words are uttered *here;* instruction, cold instruction, alas! it may be, is delivered in consecrated walls; but if the haunts of evil could be unveiled, if the covering could be taken off from guilty hearts, if every sharp pang and every lingering regret of the vitiated mind, could send forth its moanings and sighs into the great hearing of the world; the *world* would stand aghast at that dread teaching.

But besides the weariness of toil and the frivolity of pleasure, there is another state of life that is thought to teach nothing; and that is ennui; a state of leisure, attended with moody reveries. The hurry of pursuit is over, for the time; the illusions of pleasure have vanished; and the man sits down in the solitariness of meditation; and "weary, flat, stale and unprofitable appear to him all the uses of this life." It seems to him, as I once heard it touchingly expressed even by a child, "as if every thing was nothing." This has been the occasional mood of many lofty minds, and has often been expressed in our literature.

> " Life's little stage, (says one) is a small eminence,
> Inch high above the grave; that home of man,
> Where dwells the multitude; we gaze around;
> We read their monuments; we sigh; and while
> We sigh, we sink and are what we deplored;
> Lamenting, or lamented all our lot!"
> "To morrow," says our great dramatist,
> " and to-morrow, and to-morrow,
> Creeps in this petty pace from day to day,
> To the last syllable of recorded time;
> And all our yesterdays have lighted fools
> The way to dusty death. * * * * * *
> Life's but a walking shadow; a poor player,
> That struts and frets his hour upon the stage,
> And then is heard no more; it is a tale
> Told by an idiot, full of sound and fury,
> Signifying nothing."

But bound up with this poor, frail life, is the mighty thought that spurns the narrow span of all visible existence. Out of this nothing, springs a something—a significant intimation, a dread revelation of the awful powers that lie wrapped up in human existence. Nothing more reveals the majestic import of life than this ennui, this heart-sinking sense of the vanity of all present acquisitions and attainments. "Man's misery," it has been well said, "comes of his greatness." The sphere of life appears small, the ordinary circle of its avocations, narrow and confined, the common routine of its cares insipid and unsatisfactory; why? Because he who walks therein demands a boundless range of objects. Why does the body seem to imprison the soul? Because the soul asks for freedom; because it looks forth from the narrow and grated windows of sense upon the wide and immeasurable creation; because it knows that around and beyond it, he outstretched the infinite and the everlasting paths.

I have now considered some of those views of life which are brought forward as objections against our Christian theory of its greatness. My purpose in this discourse is not to penetrate into the wisdom of its deeper relations, but to confine myself to its humblest aspects, and to things that are known and acknowledged to be matters of fact.

With this view, I proceed to observe in the last place, that *every thing* in this life bears traits that may well stir our minds to admiration and wonder.

How mysterious is the connection of mind with matter; of the act of my will with the motion of my hand; this wonderful telegraphic communication between the brain and every part of the body! We talk of nerves; but how knoweth the nerve in my finger, of the will that moves it? We talk of the will: but what is it, and how does its commanding act originate? It is all mystery. Within this folding veil of flesh, within these dark channels, every instant's action is a history of miracles. Every familiar step is more than a story in a land of enchantment. Were the marble statue before us, suddenly endowed with that self-moving power, it would not be intrinsically more wonderful than is the action of every being around us.

The human face is itself a wonder. I do not mean in its beauty, nor in its power of expression; but in its variety and its individuality. What is the problem that is here solved? Suppose it were stated thus: given, a space nine inches long and six inches broad; the form essentially the same, the features the same, the colours the same; required, unnumbered hundreds of millions of countenances so entirely different, as, with some rare exceptions, to be completely and easily distinguishable. Would not the whole mechanical ingenuity of the world be thrown into utter despair of approaching any way towards such a result? And yet it is completely achieved in the human countenance. Yes, the familiar faces that are around us, bear mysteries and marvels in every look.

Again, the house thou dwellest in, that familiar abode, what holds it together, and secures it on its firm foundation? Joint to joint, beam to beam, every post to its socket, is swathed and fastened by the mighty bands that hold ten thousand worlds in their orbits. This is no phantasm of the imagination; it is the philosophical fact. All actual motion, and all seeming rest, are determined by unnumbered, most nicely balanced, and at the same time, immeasurable influences and attractions. Universal harmony springs from infinite complication. And therefore, every step thou takest in thy dwelling—still I only repeat what philosophers have proved—the momentum of every step, I say, contributes its part to the order of the universe.

What then is a life, conscious of these stupendous relations, and what are its humblest dwellings? If you lived in a palace that covered a hundred miles of territory, and if the stamping of your foot could convey an order to its farthest limits; you would feel that that, indeed, was power and grandeur. But you live in a system of things, you dwell in a palace, whose dome is spread out in the boundless skies; whose lights are hung in the wide arches of heaven; whose foundations are longer far than the earth and broader far than the sea; and you are connected by ties of thought, and even of matter, with its whole boundless extent. If your earthly dwelling, your house of life, were lifted up and borne visibly among the stars, guarded with power and clothed with light; you would feel that that was a sublime fortune for any being to enjoy. To ride in a royal chariot would be a small thing compared with that. But you *are* borne onward among the celestial spheres; rolling worlds are around you; bright, starry abodes fill all the coasts and skies of heaven; you *are* borne and kept by powers, silent and unperceived indeed, but real and boundless as the immeasurable universe.

The infinite, we allow is mysterious; but not less so, in truth, is the finite and the small. It is said that man cannot comprehend infinity. It is true, and yet it is falsely said in one respect. The declaration that we cannot understand infinity, usually conveys the implication that we can comprehend that which is the opposite of infinity; that is, the little scene around us. But the humblest object beneath our eye, as completely defies our scrutiny, as the economy of the most distant world. Every spire of grass, of which the scythe mows down millions in an hour, holds within it secrets, which no human penetration ever fathomed. Examine it with the microscope, and you shall find a beautiful organization; channels for the vital juices to flow in; some to nourish the stalk; others to provide for the flower and prepare the seed; other instruments still, to secrete the nutriment that flows up from the soil, and to deposite and incorporate it with the plant; and altogether, a mechanism more curious than any, perhaps, ever formed by the ingenuity of man. And yet there are questions here, which the profoundest philosopher cannot answer. What is the principle of life,—without which, though the whole organization remains, the plant dies? And what is that wonderful power of secretion? No man can tell. There are inscrutable *mysteries*, wrapped up in the foldings of that humble spire of grass.

Sit down now, and take thy pen, and spread out thine account, as some writers have done, of the insignificance of human life. But wilt thou pause a little and tell me first, how that pen was formed wherewith thou art writing, and that table whereon thy tablets are laid? Thou canst tell neither. *Wilt* thou not pause then, when the very instruments thou art using, should startle thee into astonishment? Lay thine hand where thou wilt, and thou layest it on the hiding bosom of mystery. Step where thou wilt, and thou dost tread upon a land of wonder. No fabled land of enchantment ever was filled with such startling tokens. So fraught are all things with this moral significance, that nothing can refuse its behest. The furrows of the field, the clods of the valley, the dull beaten path, the insensible rock, are traced over and in every direction, with this handwriting, more significant and sublime than all the beetling ruins and all the buried cities, that past generations have left upon the earth. It is the handwriting of the Almighty!

In fine, the history of the humblest human life is a

tale of marvels. There is no dull or unmeaning thing in existence, did we but understand it; there is not one of our employments, no, nor one of our states of mind, but is, could we interpret it, as significant—not as instructive, but as significant, as holy writ. Experience, sensation, feeling, suffering, rejoicing; what a world of meaning and of wonder lies in the modes and changes and strugglings and soarings of the life in which these are bound up. If it were but new, if we had been cast upon " this shore of being " without those intervening steps of childhood that have now made it familiar ground; how had we been rapt in astonishment at every thing around, and every thing within us!

I have endeavoured in the present discourse—perhaps in vain—to touch this sense of wonder: to arouse attention to the startling and awful intimations, to the striking and monitory lessons and warnings of our present existence. And if some of the topics and suggestions of my discourse have been vague and shadowy, yet I am ready to say; better to be startled by the shadows of truth, than to sleep beneath its noontide ray: better to be aroused by the visions of a dream, than to slumber on in profound unconsciousness of all the signs and wonders of our being. Oh! that I could tear off this dreadful common-place of life, and show you what it is. There would be no want then, of entertainment or excitement; no need of journeys or shows or tales to interest us; the every-day world would be more than theatres or spectacles; and life all-piercing, all-spiritual, would be more than the most vivid dream of romance; how much more than the most eager pursuit of pleasure or profit!

My Brethren, there is a vision like that of Eliphaz, stealing upon us, if we would mark it, through the vails of every evening's shadows, or coming in the morning with the mysterious revival of thought and consciousness; there is a message whispering in the stirred leaves, or starting beneath the clods of the field, in the life that is everywhere bursting from its bosom. Every thing around us images a spiritual life; all forms, modes, processes, changes, though we discern them not. Our great business with life is so to read the book of its teaching; to find that life is not the doing of drudgeries, but the hearing of oracles! The old mythology is but a leaf in that book, for it peopled the world with spiritual natures. Many-leaved science still spreads before us the same tale of wonder. Spiritual meditation, interpreting experience, and above all, the life of Jesus, will lead us still farther into the heart and soul and the innermost life of all things. It is but a child's life, to pause and rest upon outward things, though we call them wealth and splendour. It is to feed ourselves with husks, instead of sustaining food. It is to grasp the semblance, and to lose the secret and soul of existence. It is as if a pupil should gaze all day upon the covers of his book, and open it not, and learn nothing. It is indeed that awful alternative which is put by Jesus himself; to gain the world—though it be the whole world—and to lose our own soul.

IX.

THAT EVERY THING IN LIFE IS MORAL.

WHAT IS MAN THAT THOU SHOULDST MAGNIFY HIM, AND SET THINE HEART UPON HIM; AND THAT THOU SHOULDST VISIT HIM EVERY MORNING, AND TRY HIM EVERY MOMENT?—Job vii. 17—18.

THAT we are "tried every moment,"—is the clause of the text, to which I wish in this discourse, to direct your meditation. By which, in the sense of the passage before us, is not meant that we are continually afflicted, but that we are constantly proved and put to the test; that every thing which befalls us, in the course of life and of every day, bears upon us, in the character of a spiritual discipline, a trial of our temper and disposition; that every thing developes in us feelings that are either right or wrong. I have spoken in my last discourse of the moral significance of life. I propose to speak in this, of the possible moral use and of the inevitable moral effect of every thing in life. My theme, in short, is this; that every thing in life is moral, or spiritual.

There is no conviction which is at once more rare, and more needful for our improvement, than this. If the language of Job's discontent and despair in the chapter from which our text is taken, is not familiar to many, yet to very many, life appears at least mechanical and dull. It *is* not such, in fact, but it appears such. It appears to be mere labour, mere business, mere activity. Or it is mere pain or pleasure, mere gain or loss, mere success or disappointment. These things, if not mechanical, have at least, to many minds, nothing spiritual in them. And not a few pass through the most important transactions, through the most momentous eras of their lives, and never think of them in their highest and most interesting character. The pervading morality, the grand spiritual import of this earthly scene, seldom strikes their minds, or touches their hearts. And if they think of ever becoming religious, they expect to be so only through retirement from this scene, or, at least, through teachings and influences and processes far removed from the course of their daily lives.

But now I say, in contradiction to this, that *every thing in life,* is spiritual. What is man, says Job, that thou visitest him every morning? This question, presents us, at the opening of every day, with that view of life, which I propose to illustrate. That conscious existence which, in the morning, you recover from the embraces of sleep; what a testimony is it to the power and beneficence of God? What a teacher is it, of all devout and reverent thoughts? You laid yourself down and slept. You lay, unconscious, helpless, dead to all the purposes of life, and unable by any power of your own ever to awake. From that sleep, from that unconsciousness, from that image of death, God has called you to a new life; he has restored to you the gift of existence. And now what meets you on this threshold of renewed life? Not bright sunbeams alone, but God's mercies visit you in every beaming ray and every beaming thought, and call for gratitude; and you can neither acknowledge nor resist the call without a moral result. That result may come upon you, sooner than you expect. If you rise from your bed, with a mind undevout, ungrateful, self-indulgent, selfish—something in your very preparations for the day, something that may happen in a matter slight as that of the toilet, may disturb your serenity and cloud your day at the beginning. You may have thought that it was only the *prayer* of the morning that had any religion, any thing spiritual in it. But I say that there is not an article in your wardrobe, there is not an instrument of daily convenience to you, however minute or otherwise indifferent, but it has a power so far moral, that a little disarray or disorder in it, may produce in you a temper of mind, ay, a *moral* state, of the most serious character. You may not be conscious of this; that is, you may not be distinctly sensible of it, and yet it may be none the less true. We are told that the earth, and every substance around us, is full of the electric fluid; but we do not constantly perceive it. A little friction, however, developes it, and it sends out a hasty spark. And so in the moral world—a slight chafing, a single turn of some wheel in the social machinery—and there comes, like the electric spark, a flashing glance of the eye, a hasty word, perhaps a muttered oath—that sounds ominous and awful as the tone of distant thunder! What is it that the little machinery of the electrical operator develops? It is the same power, that gathering its tremendous forces, rolls through the firmament, and rends the mountains in its might. And just as true is it, that the little round of our daily cares and occupations, the humble mechanism of daily life, bears witness to that moral power, which, only extended, exalted, enthroned above, is the dread and awful Majesty of the heavens.

But let us return to our proposition. *Every thing is moral,* and therefore, as we have said, great and majestic; but let us for a few moments confine ourselves to the simple consideration, that every thing in its bearings and influences is moral.

All times and seasons are moral; the serene and bright morning, we have said; that wakening of all nature to life; that silence of the early dawn, as it were the silence of expectation! that freshening glow, that new inspiration of life, as if it came from the breath of heaven; but the holy eventide also, its cooling breeze, its falling shade, its hushed and sober hour; the sultry noontide, too, and the solemn midnight; and spring-time and chastening autumn; and summer that unbars our gates and carries us forth amidst the ever-renewed wonders of the world; and winter that gathers us around the evening hearth: all these as they pass, touch by turns the springs of the spiritual life in us, and are conducting that life to good or evil. The very passing of time, without any reference now to its seasons, developes in us much that is moral. For what is the passing of time, swifter or slower; what are its lingering and its hasting, but indications, but expressions often, of the state of our own minds; it hastes often, because we are wisely and well employed; it lingers, it hangs heavily upon us, because our minds are unfurnished, unenlightened, unoccupied with good thoughts, with the fruitful themes of virtue; or because we have lost almost all virtue in unreasonable and outrageous impatience. Yes, the idle watch-hand often points to something within us; the very dial-shadow falls upon the conscience!

The course of time on earth is marked by changes of heat and cold, storm and sunshine; all this too is moral. The weather, dull theme of comment as it is often found, is to be regarded with no indifference as a moral cause. For, does it not produce unreasonable anxieties, or absolutely sinful complainings? Have none who hear me ever had reason to be shocked to find themselves *angry* with the elements; vexed with chafing heat, or piercing cold, or the buffeting storm; and ready when encountering nature's resistance, almost to return buffet for buffet?

But let us turn from the course of inanimate nature to matters in which our own agency is more distinct and visible.

Go with me to any farm-house in the land, and let us see what is passing there, and what is the lofty and spiritual import of its humble history. It is the theatre of strenuous toils and beseting cares. Within doors is work to be done; that work which is proverbially "never *done:*" and without, the soil is to be tilled, the weeds and brambles are to be rooted up, fences are to be builded—of wood or stone—and to be kept in repair; and all this is to be done with tools and instruments that are not perfect, but must be continually mended; the axe and the scythe grow dull with use; the plough and the harrow are sometimes broken; the animals which man brings in to assist his labours, have no instincts to make them do the very thing he wishes; they must be trained to the yoke and the collar; with much pains and some danger.

Now the evil in all this, is not the task that is to be performed, but the grand mistake that is made about the spiritual purpose and character of that task. Most men look upon such a state of life as mere labour, if not vexation; and many regard it as a state of inferiority and almost of degradation. They *must work*, in order to obtain sustenance, and that's all they know about this great dispensation of labour. But why did not the Almighty cast man's lot beneath the quiet shades and amid embosoming groves and hills, with no such task to perform; with nothing to do but to rise up and eat, and to lie down and rest? Why did he ordain that *work* should be done, in all the dwellings of life, and upon every productive field, and in every busy city and on every ocean wave? Because, to go back to the original reason—it pleased God to give man a nature destined to higher ends than indolent repose and irresponsible indulgence. And because, in the next place, for developing the energies of such a nature, *work* was the proper element. I am but repeating perhaps, what I have said before to you, but I feel that in taking this position, I am standing upon one of the great moral landmarks which ought to guide the course of all mankind; but on which, seen through a mist or not seen at all, the moral fortunes of millions are fatally wrecked. Could the toiling world but see that the scene of their daily life is all spiritual, that the very implements of their toil, or the fabrics they weave, or the merchandize they barter, were all designed for spiritual ends; what a sphere for the noblest improvement might their daily lot then be? What a revolution might this single truth produce in the condition and character of the whole world? But now, for a man to gird himself for spiritual improvement; what is it? Why, with most men, it is to cast off the soiled and dusty garments of toil, the slough of mere worldly drudgery as they are called; and to put on the Sunday suit and go to church, or to sit down and read a book. Good employments are these, but one special design of them is, to prepare the mind for the action of life. We are to hear and read, we are to meditate and pray, partly at least, for this end—that we may act well. The action of life is the great field for spiritual improvement. There is not one task of industry or business, whether in field or forest, on the wharf or the exchange, but it has spiritual ends. There is not one of the cares or crosses of our daily labour, but it **was** especially ordained, to nurture in us patience, calmness, gentleness, disinterestedness, magnanimity. Nor is there one tool or implement of toil, but it is a part of the great spiritual instrumentality.

Every thing in life, then, I repeat, is essentially spiritual. Every *relation* in life is so. The relations of parent, child, brother, sister, friend, associate, husband, wife, are throughout every living tie and thrilling nerve that binds them together, *moral*. They cannot subsist a day nor an hour, without putting the mind to a trial of its truth, fidelity, forbearance, disinterestedness.

But let us take the case of the parent; of the young mother, for instance. She may have passed her youth in much thoughtlessness; in a round of fashionable engagements that have left her little time to think, even when approaching the most solemn relationships of life; and she may have become a wife and mother, before she has settled, or even meditated, any reasonable plan or principle of life and of duty. Now, I am not about to say that the new charge committed to her hands, brings with it many obvious duties and strong obligations; but I desire you to observe how, what is moral in the case, is thrust upon her; as if a hand were suddenly stretched forth into her path, with movement and gesture that bade her pause and consider. For *what* is in that path? It is a being, though but a little child, in whom is suddenly revealed that awful attribute, the indomitable will. That will, perhaps, utters itself in a scream of passion; it stamps upon the ground in a fury of anger; it vents itself in tears; or flashes in lightning from the eye. Yes, the being that a few days before was an unconscious and helpless infant in her arms, has all at once put on the terrific attribute of will; and its astonished guardian stands aghast, as if an uncaged lion had broken upon her path. *What*, then, is in that path? I answer, it is what nothing but moral firmness can fairly meet, and nothing but the gentleness and patience of piety and prayer can ever successfully and wisely manage, control and subdue! And I say again, that if moral action, if religious consideration was never before awakened, that very epoch, that very hour, might reasonably be the commencement with her, of a complete and spiritual regeneration! For nothing less than actual regeneration from a thoughtless, self-indulgent life, ever did, or ever can, prepare any one thoroughly and faithfully to discharge the duties of a parent.

Again, every thing in the *condition* of life is moral; wealth, the means of lavish expense, or the argument for avaricious hoarding; poverty, the task-master that exacts labour, or inflicts self-denial; mediocrity of means, the necessity, the vexatious necessity, as some will consider it, of attending to the little items of expense, or the mortifying inferiority to others, in the splendour of equipages and establishments; trade, the splendid success, the fortunate speculation, the disappointed hope, the satisfactory endorsement, the dishonoured note, the sharp bargain—all moral; the professions and callings of life, some making their incumbents unreasonably proud, others making their equally useful agents, unreasonably humble. When we look upon things in this light, how moral is every thing around us! This great city is one extended scene of moral action. There is not a blow struck in it, but has a purpose, and a purpose ultimately good or bad, and therefore moral. There is not an action performed but it has a motive; and motives are the very sphere of morality. These equipages in our streets, these houses and their furniture; what symbols are they of what is moral, and how are they, in a thousand ways, ministering to right or wrong feeling? You may have thought that you were to receive the teachings of morality and religion only by resorting to church; but take your seat in your well-furnished, perhaps, splendid apartment, and there is not an object around you but may minister to the good or bad state of your mind. It is a little empire of which your mind is the creator. From many a trade and occupation and art in life, you have gathered contributions to its comfort or splendour. The forest, the field, the ore-bed, the ocean; all elements, fire, water, earth, air, have yielded their supplies to form this dwelling-place, this palace of your thoughts. Furniture, whose materials came from beyond the sea; polished marbles wrought from the quarries of Italy; carpets from the looms of England; the luxurious couch, and the shaded evening lamp; of what are all these the symbols? What emotions do they awaken in you? Be they emotions of pride, or be they emotions of gratitude; be they thoughts of self-indulgence only, or thoughts, merciful thoughts, of the thousands who are destitute of all the comforts of life; what a moral complexion do they bear?

Nay, and this spiritual dispensation of life may press down upon a man in a way he little thinks of. For how possible is it, that amidst boundless wealth, in its most gorgeous mansion, and surrounded by every thing that can minister to pleasure, a family may be more miserable than the poorest family in the land!—the children, spoiled by indulgence, made vain and proud by their over-estimated advantages, made peevish, impatient and imbecile, by perpetual dependence on others, and not half so happy even, as thousands of children who are half clad and unshod, and who never knew what it was to give a command; their elders, injured or ruined in constitution by luxuries, enfeebled and dulled in mind by the hard tasks that are imposed on the functions of the body, and yet absurdly puffed up with pride that they can live splendidly and fare sumptuously every day; how possible is it, I repeat, that coarse fare and a pallet of straw, may turn out to be better than the bed of down, and the loaded table, and the cellar of choice wines! Ay, the loaded table, what a long moral account, accumulating day by day, through years, may have been written upon that table; and payment, perchance, must be made on the couch of agony!

Again, *society* is, throughout, a moral scene. I cannot enlarge upon this point as it would be easy to do, but must content myself with one or two observations. Conversation, for instance, is full of inward trials and exigencies. It is impossible that imperfect minds should commune together without a constant trial of their tempers and virtues. Though of the most friendly and kindred spirit, they will have different opinions, or varying moods; one will be quicker or slower of apprehension than the other on some point; one will think the other wrong, and the other will feel as if it were unkindly or uncharitably construed; and there will be dispute, and pertinacity, and implication, and retort, and defence, and complaint; and well, if there are not sarcasm and anger. And well, if these harsh sounds do not invade the sanctuary of home! Well, if they do not bring disturbance to the social board, and discord amidst the voices of music and song!

Is not every thing, then, in social life, moral?— really a matter of religion, a trial of conscience? You enter your dwelling. The first thing that you see, and it may be a very slight thing, may call upon you for an act of self-command. The thing may not be as it should be; but that is not the most material consideration; that is not what most concerns you. The material consideration is, that your mind may be put out of its proper place, that you may not be as you should be. You go from your door. The sight of the first man you behold, may call for a trial of all your virtues. You enter into the throng of society. Every turn of your eye, may present an occasion for the exercise of your self-respect, your calmness, your modesty, your candour, your forgetfulness of self, your love of others. You visit the sick, or necessitous. Every step may be one of ostentation, or at least of self-applause; or it may be one of true generosity and goodness. You stand amidst the throng of men; and your position has many relations; you are higher or lower than others, or you are an equal and a competitor; and none of these relations can be wisely sustained without the aid of strong religious considerations. Or, your position is fixed and unalterable. You are a parent; and you give a command or make a request. A thoughtful observer will perceive the very tone of it to be moral: and a friend may know that it has cost twenty years of self-discipline to form that gentle tone! Or you are a child; and you obey or disobey; and let me tell you that the act, nay, the very manner of your act, is so vitally good or bad, that it may send a thrill of gladness, or a pang, sharp as a sword, to the heart of your parent. Or you are a pupil; and can any act or look be indifferent, which by its levity, or negligence, or ill-humour, adds to the already trying task of those who spend anxious days and nights for you?

But I must leave those specifications, which I find

indeed cannot well be carried into the requisite detail in the pulpit; but I must leave them also for the sake of presenting in close, one or two general reflections on the whole subject.

I observe then, that the consideration of every thing in our life as moral, as spiritual, would impart an unequalled interest and dignity to life.

First, an unequalled interest.

It is often said that the poet or the man of genius, is alive to a world around him, to aspects of nature and life, which others do not perceive. This is not strictly true; for when he describes his impressions he finds a responsive feeling in the breasts of his readers. The truth is, and herein lies much of his power and greatness, that he is vividly and distinctly conscious of those things which other men feel indeed, but feel so vaguely, that they are scarcely aware, till told of them. So it is in spiritual things. A world of spiritual objects and influences, and relations, lies around us all. We all vaguely deem it to be so; but what a charmed life; how like to that of genius or poetic inspiration, is his, who communes with the spiritual scene around him; who hears the voice of the spirit in every sound; who sees its signs in every passing form of things, and feels its impulse, in all action, passion, being!

"The kingdom of heaven," says our Saviour, "is like a treasure hid in a field." There is a treasure in the field of life, richer than all its visible wealth; which whoso finds, shall be happier than if he had discovered a mine of gold. It is related that the mine of Potosi was unveiled, simply by tearing a bush from the mountain side. Thus near to us lie the mines of wisdom; thus unsuspected they lie all around us. 'The word," saith Moses, speaking of this very wisdom, "is very nigh thee." There is a secret in the simplest things, a wonder in the plainest, a charm in the dullest. The veil that hides all this requires but a hand stretched out to draw it aside.

We are all naturally seekers of wonders; we travel far to see sights, to look upon the mountain height or the rush of waters, to gaze upon galleries of art or the majesty of old ruins; and yet a greater than all these is here. The world-wonder is all around us; the wonder of setting suns and evening stars; the wonder of the magic spring time, of tufted bank and blossoming tree; the wonder of the Infinite Divinity, and of his boundless revelation. As I stood yesterday and looked upon a tree, I observed little jets as of smoke, darting from one and another of its bursting buds. Oh! that the secrets of nature might thus burst forth before us; that the secret wisdom of the world might thus be revealed to us! Is there any splendour to be found in distant travels, beyond that which sets its morning throne in the golden East; any dome sublimer than that of heaven; any beauty fairer than that of the verdant and blossoming earth; any place, though invested with all the sanctities of old time, like that home which is hushed and folded within the embrace of the humblest wall and roof? And yet all these—this is the point at which I aim—all these are but the symbols of things far greater and higher. All this is but the spirit's clothing. In this vesture of time is wrapped the immortal nature; m this brave show of circumstance and form, stands revealed the stupendous reality. Break forth, earth-bound spirit! and *be* that thou art, a living soul; communing with thyself, communing with God; and thou shalt find thy vision, eternity; thine abode, infinity; thy home, in the bosom of all-embracing love!

"So build we up the being that we are;
Thus deeply drinking in the soul of things,
We shall be wise perforce.
                    Whate'er we see,
Whate'er we feel, by agency direct
Or indirect, shall tend to feed and nurse
Our faculties, shall fix in calmer seats
Of moral strength, and raise to loftier heights
Of love divine, our intellectual soul."

And thus, in the next place, shall we find that all the real dignity and importance that belong to human life, belong to every human life ; i. e. to life in every condition. It is the right mind, the right apprehension of things only that is wanting, to make the peasant's cottage as interesting, as intrinsically glorious, as the prince's palace. I wish that this view of life might be taken by us ; not only because it is the right view, but because it would tend effectually to promote human happiness, and especially contentment. Most men look upon their employments and abodes as common-place and almost as mean. The familiar objects around them, appear to them almost as vulgar. They feel as if there could be no dignity nor charm in acting and living as they are compelled to do. The plastered wall, and the plain deal boards, the humble table, spread with earthen, or wooden dishes ; how poor does it all seem to them ! Oh ! could they live in palaces of marble, clothed with silken tapestries, and filled with gorgeous furniture, and canopies of state—it were something. But now, to the spiritual vision, what is it all ? The great problem of humanity is wrought out in the humblest abodes ; no more than this is done in the highest. A human heart throbs beneath the beggar's gabardine ; it is no more than this, that stirs with its beating, the prince's mantle. What is it, I say, that makes life to be life indeed—makes all its grandeur and power? The beauty of love, the charm of friendship, the sacredness of sorrow, the heroism of patience, the soul-exalting prayer, the noble self-sacrifice; these are the priceless treasures and glories of humanity; and are these *things of condition?* On the contrary, are not all places, all scenes, alike clothed with the grandeur and charm of virtues like these? And compared with these, what are the gildings, the gauds and shows of wealth and splendour? Nay, compared with every man's abode—his sky-dome and earth-dwelling—what can any man's abode be? Thou livest in a world of beauty and grandeur. Who liveth in a fairer, a more magnificent world than thou? It is a dwelling which God hath made for thee; does that consideration deprive it of all its goodliness? And suppose thou wast rich, and wast surrounded with all the gayety and grandeur of wealth: how might they hide from thee, alas! all the spiritual meanings of thy condition! How might the stately wall and the rich ceiling hide heaven from thy sight! Let thine eye be opened to the vision of life; and what state then, what mere visible grandeur, can be compared to thine? It is all but a child's bauble, to the divine uses of things, the glorious associations, the beatific visions that are opened to thee! God hath thus "magnified," and to use the strong and figurative language of our text, "set his heart" upon the humblest fortunes of humanity.

There are those who, with a kind of noble but mistaken aspiration, are asking for a life which shall in its form and outward course, be more spiritual and divine than that which they are obliged to live. They think that if they could devote themselves entirely to what are called labours of philanthropy, to visiting the poor and sick, *that* would be well and worthy; and so it would be. They think that if it could be inscribed on their tomb-stone, that they had visited a million of couches of disease, and carried balm and soothing to them, *that* would be a glorious record ; and so it would be. But let me tell you, that the million occasions will come, ay, and in the ordinary paths of life, in your homes and by your fire-sides—wherein you may act as nobly, as if all your life long, you visited beds of sickness and pain. Yes, I say, the million occasions will come, varying every hour, in which you may restrain your passions, subdue your hearts to gentleness and patience, resign your own interest for another's advantage, speak words of kindness and wisdom, raise the fallen and cheer the fainting and sick in spirit, and soften and assuage the weariness and bitterness of the mortal lot. These cannot indeed be written on your tombs, for they are not one series of specific actions, like those of what is technically denominated philanthropy. But in them, I say, you may discharge offices, not less gracious to others, nor less glorious for yourselves than the self-denials of the far-famed sisters of charity, than the labours of Howard or Oberlin, or than the sufferings of the martyred host of God's elect. They shall not be written on your tombs ; but they are written deep in the hearts of men—of friends, of children, of kindred all around you : they are written in the book of the great account!

How divine a life would this be! For want of this spiritual insight, the earth is desolate, and the heavens are but a sparkling vault or celestial mechanism. Nothing but this spirit of God in us, can " create that new heavens and new earth, wherein dwelleth righteousness." For want of this, life is to many, dull and barren, or trifling, uninteresting, unsatisfactory—without sentiment, without poetry and philosophy alike, without interpretation or meaning or lofty motive.

Whirled about by incessant change, making an oracle of circumstance and an end of vanity, such persons know not why they live. For want of this spiritual insight, man degrades himself to the worship of condition, and loses the sense of what he is. He passes by a grand house, or a blazoned equipage, and bows his whole lofty being before them—forgetting that he himself is greater than a house, greater than an equipage, greater than the world. Oh! to think, that this walking majesty of earth should so forget itself; that this spiritual power in man should be frittered away, and dissipated upon trifles and vanities; how lamentable is it! There is no Gospel for such a being; for the Gospel lays its foundations in the spiritual nature. There is nothing for man, but what lies in his spirit, in spiritual insight, in spiritual interpretation. Without this, not only is heaven nothing, but the world is nothing. The great Apostle has resolved it all in few words: "There is no condemnation to them who are in Christ Jesus, who walk not after the flesh, but after the spirit; but to all others there is condemnation,—sorrow, pain, vanity, death. For to be carnally minded is death; but to be spiritually minded is life and peace."

X.

LIFE CONSIDERED AS AN ARGUMENT FOR FAITH AND VIRTUE.

BUT HE ANSWERED AND SAID, IT IS WRITTEN THAT MAN SHALL NOT LIVE BY BREAD ALONE, BUT BY EVERY WORD THAT PROCEEDETH OUT OF THE MOUTH OF GOD.—Matthew iv. 4.

THE necessity to man of something above all the resources of physical life, is the subject to which, in this discourse, I shall invite your attention.

In two previous discourses on human life which I have addressed to you, I have endeavoured to show, in the first place and in general, that this life possesses a deep moral significance, notwithstanding all that is said of it, as a series of toils, trifles and vanities; and in the next place, and in pursuance of the same thought, that every thing in life is positively moral; not merely that it is morally significant, but that it has a positive moral efficiency for good or for evil. And now I say in the third place, that the argument for the moral purpose is clenched by the *necessity* of that purpose, to the well being of life itself. "Man," says our Saviour, with solemn authority, "shall not live by bread alone, but"—by what? how few seem to believe in it!—"by every word that proceedeth out of the mouth of God."

How few seem to believe in it; how few do believe this, in the highest sense; and yet how true is it! Into how large a part even of the most ordinary life, enters a certain kind and degree of spirituality! You cannot do business, without some faith in man; that is, in the spiritual part of man. You cannot dig in the earth, without a reliance on the unseen result. You cannot step or think or reason, without confiding in the inward, the spiritual principles of your nature. All the affections and bonds, and hopes and interests of life, centre in the spiritual. Break that central bond, and you know that the world would rush to chaos.

But something higher than this indirect recognition is demanded in our argument. Let us proceed to take it up in form.

There are two principles then, involved in the moral aim and embracing its whole scope, whose necessity I propose now to consider. They are faith and virtue; the convictions, that is to say, on which virtue reposes, and the virtue itself. Something above a man's physical life must there be to help it—something above it in its faith—something beyond it, in its attainment.

In speaking of faith as necessary to human life, I need not here undertake to define its nature! This will sufficiently appear as we proceed. What I wish to speak of, is, in general, a faith in religion; in God, in spiritual truth and hopes. What I maintain in general, is the indispensableness to human life, of this religious faith. My present purpose is, to offer some distinct and independent considerations in support of this faith; and these considerations I find based, imbedded, deep-founded in human life. To illustrate the general character of the view which I wish to present, let us make a comparison. Let it be admitted then, and believed, on the one hand, that there is a God; let the teachings of Jesus, also, be received; that this God is our father; that he has a paternal interest in our welfare and improvement; that he has provided the way and the means of our salvation from sin and ruin; that he hears our prayers and will help our endeavours; that he has destined us, if faithful, to a future and blessed and endless life; and then, how evident is it that upon this system of faith, we can live calmly, endure patiently, labour resolutely, deny ourselves cheerfully, hope steadfastly, and "be conquerors," in the great struggle of life, "yea, and more than conquerors, through Christ who has loved us!" But take away any one of these principles; and where are we? Say that there is no God, or that there is no way opened for hope and prayer, and pardon and triumph, or that there is no heaven to come, no rest for the weary, no blessed land for the sojourner and the pilgrim; and where are we? And what are we? What are we, indeed, but the sport of chance, and the victims of despair? What are we, but hapless wanderers upon the face of the desolate and forsaken earth; surrounded by darkness, struggling with obstacles, distracted with doubts, misled by false lights; not merely wanderers who have lost their way, but wanderers, alas! who have no way, no prospect, no home? What are we but doomed, deserted voyagers upon the dark and stormy sea, thrown amidst the baffling waves without a compass, without a course, with no blessed haven in the distance to invite us to its welcome rest?

What now is the conclusion from this comparison? It is, that religious faith is indispensable to the attainment of the great ends of life. But that which is necessary to life, must have been designed to be a part of it. When you study the structure of an animal, when you examine its parts, you say, "This was designed for food; there must be food for this being, somewhere; neither growth nor life is possible without it." And when you examine the structure of a human mind and understand its powers and wants, you say with equal confidence, " This being was made for faith; there must be something, somewhere, for him to believe in; he cannot healthfully grow, he connot happily live without it."

The argument which I now urge for faith, let me distinctly say, is not that which is suggested by worldly prudence; that religion is a good thing for the State, useful to society, necessary for the security of property; and therefore to be received and supported. The concession that the great interests of the world cannot be sustained without religion, and therefore that religion is necessary, is considered by many, I fear, as yielding not to reasoning fairly, but to policy. This was the view of religion, doubtless, which pervaded the ancient systems of polytheism. It was a powerful state engine; a useful social economy; and hence, with multitudes, it was little more than a splendid ritual. It was not a personal thing. It was not received as true, but only as expedient. Now that which I maintain is this; not that religion is necessary, and therefore respectable; not that religion is necessary, and therefore to be supported in order that the people may be restrained and managed, and held in check; but my argument is, that religion is necessary, and therefore *true*. The indispensableness of religion, I hold, is not merely a reason for its being supported, but a reason for its being believed in.

The point maintained, let me now more distinctly observe, is this: that in every kind of existence, in every system of things, there are certain primary elements or powers, which are essential to its just order and true well-being; and that under a wise Providence, these elements must be regarded as bearing the stamp of divine appointment and authority. Find that which is necessary to any being or thing, and you find that which was designed to be a part of that being or thing. Find that which, in the long run, injures, hurts or hinders; find that which is fatal to the growth, progress or perfection of any being or thing, and you find that which does not properly belong to it. He who would cultivate a tree, knows that a soil, and a certain internal structure, are necessary to that end. And if he should, with that end in view, set himself to deprive it of those essential elements of growth, his act would be one of perfect fatuity.

Let us dwell upon this point and the illustration of it, a little longer.

In the human body, we say, food is necessary. Stint it, and the body languishes; cut off the supply, and it ceases to exist. So in the human body, the circulation of the blood is necessary. Interrupt it, and the body is diseased; stop it, and the body dies. How truly has our Saviour denominated his doctrine, the very food and life-blood of the soul! "Verily, verily, I say unto you, except ye eat the flesh and drink the blood of the Son of Man, ye have no life in you; whoso eateth my flesh and drinketh my blood hath eternal life;" meaning, according to a figurative and well-known use of language at that time, his spirit and doctrine. And how manifestly true is it! Cut off from any soul all the principles that Jesus taught, the faith in a God, in immortality, in virtue, in essential rectitude; and how inevitably will it sink into sin, misery, darkness and ruin! Nay, cut off all sense of these truths, and the man sinks at once to the grade of the animal.

Again, in the system of the universe, there is one principle that is essential to its order; the principle of gravitation. Sever this bond that holds all worlds and systems together, and they would instantly fly into wild and boundless chaos. But society, in its great relations, is as much the creation of heaven, as the system of the universe. Sever, then, all the moral bonds that hold it together; cut off from it every conviction of truth and integrity, of an authority above it, and of a conscience within it; and society would immediately rush to disorder, anarchy and ruin. If, then, to hold society together and to bind it in happy order, religion be as necessary as gravitation is to hold together the frame of nature, it follows that religion is as really a principle of things as gravitation; it is as certain and true.

Once more; animal life has its law, instinct. And when we look at the races of animals, and see how indispensable this law is to their welfare; when we see that without this principle, they would inevitably fall into misery and destruction, we have no doubt that instinct is a heaven-ordained law. Equally necessary to *man*, is some law. What is it? He has appetites, propensities, passions, like the animal; but he has no instincts to control them and keep them safe. What law then must *he* have? Will it be said that prudence, the love of himself, the love of happiness, is sufficient to guide him? That will depend upon his idea of happiness. If it is purely sensual, then he is left to the impulses of sense; and that too without the guardianship of instinct, and with all the additional peril, in which the infinite cravings of his soul put him, and against which, indeed, no barrier of instinct or prudence could ever defend him. But if his idea of happiness includes a spiritual good, that implies a faith in the spiritual; and this is the very faith for which I contend. And I contend, too, that this faith, faith in moral principles, faith in virtue and in God, is as necessary for the guidance of a man, as instinct is for the guidance of an animal. This, I believe, will not be denied. I believe that every man must be conscious that to be given up to his sensual impulses, without any faith in virtue or in God, would be as certain ruin to him, as it would be to an animal to be sent into the world without the control of instinct. And if it be so, then has the one principle, a place as truly appointed, a mission as truly authentic in God's providence, as the other.

But further; man and animal too, need more than safety. They need some positive good, something that satisfies. The animal has it, in the pleasures of sensation. But will these suffice for a man? It would be an insult to any one, feeling as a man, formally to answer the question. But if higher pleasures are demanded, these must be the pleasures of the soul. And these pleasures must depend on certain principles; they must recognise a soul; that is, they must recognise the properties and responsibilities of a soul; they must recognise a conscience and the sense of an authority above us; and these are the principles of faith.

Moreover, the soul on earth is placed in fearful straits of affliction and temptation. This too, it would be but an insult to human feeling formally to prove. And in this view, I maintain, and I only maintain what every reflecting man must feel to be true, that no tolerable scheme of life, no tolerable scheme of a rational, tried, suffering, and yet improving and happy existence, can be formed, which leaves out the religious principle, the principle of faith. I do not ask you to receive this as what is said in the pulpit, or, is wont to be laid down in religious discourse; but I desire you to see that it stands, and stands eternally, in the very truth of things. A man *cannot* suffer and be patient; he *cannot* struggle and conquer; he *cannot* improve and be happy, without conscience, without hope, without God in the world. Necessity is laid upon us to embrace the great truths of religion and to live by them, to live happily; and can the language of this necessity be mistaken? Can it be, that while there is one thing, above all others, necessary to support, strengthen, guide and comfort us; that one thing—upon which, moreover, the hearts of the wise and good have ever rested,—should be, of all things in the world, the thing most false, treacherous, and delusive?

It would be strange indeed, if it were so; and strange would be the assertion even to the point of incredibility. What!—we should say,—has every thing in the universe certain laws and principles for its action; the star in its orbit, the animal in its activity, the human body in its functions; and has the human soul nothing to guide it? Nay, man as a physical being, has strong and sure supports. Has he none as a spiritual being? He knows how to feed and nourish his body; there are laws for that. Must his soul die, for want of aliment; for want of guidance? For his physical action too, he has laws of art. The builder, the sower, the toiler at the oar and the anvil, has certain principles to go by. Has the MAN none at all? Nay more, the wants of *animal* sense are regarded. In every hedge, and water-pool, and mountain top, there is supply. For the rational soul is there no provision? From the lofty pine, rocked in the darkening tempest, the cry of the young raven is heard. And for the cry and the call of all that want and sorrow and agony that overshadow and rive the human heart, is there no answer?

But I cannot argue the point any farther; and I

need not; it is too plain. The total rejection of all moral and religious belief, strikes out a principle from human nature as essential to it, as gravitation is to inanimate nature, as instinct is to animal life, or as the circulation of the blood to the human body.

It is on this principle that it is said, "he that believeth not, shall be damned." This is apt to be regarded as a harsh declaration; but the truth is, it is only the assertion of a simple fact; and of a fact which every thoughtful and feeling mind knows to be true. The Bible speaks, as we should speak to the famished man, saying "eat—drink; or die!" Its words, "death" and "damnation," mean nothing else but that unavoidable misery which must spring from boundless wants unsatisfied; boundless wants which nothing but boundless objects, the objects of faith, can satisfy.

I have now considered life as an argument, and an independent argument for faith. It would be easy to spread this view of life, over the whole ground of that preliminary discussion, which introduces the evidences of Christianity; and to show that the presumption of reason and experience, and the whole weight of that presumption, instead of being, as is commonly supposed, against the believer, is, in fact, in his favour. But the space which I designed to give to this topic, is already taken up by the few hints which I have laid before you; and I must now pass to the other branch of my discourse, and occupy the time that remains to me, with the consideration of life as an argument for accomplishing its moral design; in other words, as a motive to virtue. This too, as well as the former, I propose to consider as an independent topic.

Thus, then, I state it. Let what will be true, or be false; admit ever so little into your creed, reject ever so much; nay, go to the uttermost limits of skepticism;

deny revelation; deny the "elder Scripture" written in the heart; deny the very being of a God!—what then? I will now express no horror nor wonder, though I might do so; I will speak to you as a calm reasoner: and I say, what then? Why here you are, a living being; there can be no skepticism about that; here you are, a living being, alive to happiness, alive to misery; here you are in vicissitude, in uncertainty, in all the accidents of a mingled lot, in conditions and relations that touch all the secret springs of the soul; here you are, amidst a frail life, and daily approaching to certain death; and if you say you have no concern nor care for the end of all this, then have you forfeited all claim to the attributes of a reasonable nature, and are not to be addressed as a reasonable creature.

But no one says this. No one refuses to come within the range of those considerations that bind him to fulfil his destiny, to accomplish the legitimate objects of his being, to be upright, virtuous, and pure. No one rejects this bond in theory, however he may resist it in practice.

Let us see, then, how strong this bond is. Let us look at life, as a social, and as an individual lot.

God has ordained that life shall be a social condition. We are members of a civil community. The life, the more than life of that community, depends upon its moral condition. Public spirit, intelligence, uprightness, temperance, kindness, domestic purity, will make it a happy community. Prevailing selfishness, dishonesty, intemperance, libertinism, crime, will make it a miserable community. Look then at this life which a whole people is living. Look at the heavings of its mighty heart, at the throbbings of the universal pulse of existence. Look at the stream of life, as it flows, with ten thousand intermingled branches and channels, through all the homes of human love. Listen to that sound as of many waters, that rapturous jubilee, or that mournful sighing, that comes up from the congregated dwellings of a whole nation.

I know that to many, the Public is a kind of vague abstraction: and that what is done against the Public, the public interest, law, or virtue, presses lightly on the conscience. Yet what is this Public, but a vast expansion of individual life?—an ocean of tears, an atmosphere of sighs; or a surrounding world of joy and gladness? It suffers with the suffering of millions. It rejoices with the joy of millions. Who then art thou—private man or public man, agent or contractor, senator or magistrate, cabinet secretary or lofty president—who art thou that darest, with indignity and wrong, to strike the bosom of the public welfare? Who art thou, that with vices, like the daggers of a parricide, darest to pierce that mighty heart, in which the ocean of existence is flowing?

But have we, in this general view, presented all that belongs to social life? No; there are other relations. You are a parent or a child, a brother or a sister, a husband, wife, friend, or associate. What an unequalled interest lies in the virtue of every one whom thou lovest? Ay, in his virtue, nowhere but in his virtue, is garnered up the incomparable treasure. Thy brother, thy husband, thy friend; what carest thou for, compared with what thou carest for his honour, his fidelity, his kindness? Thy parent; how venerable is his rectitude! how sacred his reputation! and what blight is there to thee, like his dishonour! Thy child—ay, thy child!—be thou heathen or Christian, thou would'st have him do well: thou hast poured ou all the fulness of parental love in the one desire, that he may do well;

that he may be worthy of thy cares and thy freely bestowed gains; that he may walk in the way of honour and happiness. And yet he cannot walk one step in that way without virtue. Such, yes, such is life in its relationships. A thousand clasping ties embrace it; each one sensitive and thrilling to the touch; each one like the strings of a delicate instrument, capable of sweet melodies and pleasures; but each one, wounded, lacerated, broken, by rudeness, by anger, and by guilty indulgence.

But that life, my friends, whose springs of powerful action are felt in every department and relationship of society; whose impulses are abroad everywhere, like waves upon the boundless sea; that life gathers up and concentrates all its energies upon the individual mind and heart. To that individual experience—to mine, to yours—I would last appeal.

The personal experience of life, I say; by what strange fatality is it, that it can escape the calls which religion and virtue make upon it? Oh, if it were something else; if it were something duller than it is; if it *could*, by any process, be made insensible to pain and pleasure; if the human heart were but made a thing as hard as adamant, then were the case a different one; then might avarice, ambition, sensuality channel out their paths in it, and make it their beaten way, and none might wonder at it, or protest against it. If we *could* but be patient under the load of a worldly life; if we could—Oh! Heaven! how impossible!—if we could bear the burthen, as beasts of burthen bear it; then as beasts might we bend all our thoughts to the earth; and no call from the great heavens above us, might startle us from our plodding and earthly course.

But to what a being, to what a nature, am I permitted in the name of truth and religion to speak? If I might use the freedom with which one would speak to a son, who was casting off all holy bonds, I should say " you are not a stone; you are not an earth-clod; you are not an insensible brute; yet, you ought to be such, to refuse the call of reason and conscience. Your body should be incapable of pain and your soul of remorse. But such you are not, and cannot make yourself." When the great dispensation of life presses down upon you, my friend, how is it with you? You weep; you suffer and sorrow. I hold every human being to that. Think what we will; speculate as wildly, doubt as rashly as we can; yet here is a matter of fact. Cold, dead, earthly, or philosophic, as we may be, yet we are beings that weep, that suffer and sorrow. What! sorrow and agony—can they dwell in the same heart with worldliness and irreligion, and desire no other companionship? Tell me not of the recklessness of melancholy and disappointment, or the desperation of vice. Say not, *young* man, that you care nothing what befalls in this miserable and worthless life. Recklessness, with its scornful lip and its smothered anger; desperation, with its knitted brow and its glaring eye; I have seen it; and what is it? What is it, but agony —agony which almost chokes the voice that is all the while striving to tell us how calm and indifferent it is?

But let us look at the matter coolly; coolly, as if it were a matter of the most deliberate calculation. You are a toiler in the field of life. You would not consent to labour, for a week, nor for a day; no, and you will not lift one burthen from the earth, without a recompense. Are you willing to bear those burthens of the heart, fear, anxiety, disappointment, trouble—compared with which the severest toil is a pleasure and a pastime; and all this without any object or use? You are a lover of pleasure. And you would not voluntarily forego an hour's pleasure without some object to be gained by it, the preservation of health, or the prospect of future, compensatory enjoyments. Are you willing then to suffer; to be sick or afflicted—for so, from time to time, does the dispensation of life press upon you—are you willing to have days and months lost to comfort and joy, overshadowed with calamity and grief, without any advantage, any compensation? You are a dealer in the merchandise of this world. And you would not, without a return, barter away the most trifling article of that merchandise. Will you thus barter away the dearest treasures of your heart, the very sufferings of your heart? Will you sell the very life-blood from your failing frame and fading cheek, will you sell tears of bitterness and groans of anguish, for nothing? Can human nature, frail, feeling, sensitive, sorrowing human nature, afford to suffer for nothing?

I have touched now upon the darker colouring of human experience; but that experience, whether bright or dark, is all vivid; it is all, according to the measure of every one's power, earnest and affecting; it is all in its indications, solemn and sublime; it is all moving and monitory. In youth, in age, it is so; in mature vigour, in failing and declining strength; in health and in sickness; in joy and in sorrow; in the musings of solitude, and amidst the throng of men; in privacy and amidst the anxieties and intrigues of public station; in the bosom of domestic quietude, and alike in the press and shock of battle; every where, human life is a great and solemn dispensation. Man, suffering, enjoying, loving, hating, hoping, fearing; now soaring to heaven, and now sinking to the grave; man is ever the creature of a high and stupendous destiny. In his bosom is wrapped up, a momentous, an all-comprehending experience, whose unfolding is to be, in ages and worlds unknown. Around this great action of existence, the curtains of time are drawn, but there are openings through them, to the visions of eternity. God from on high looks down upon this scene of human probation; Jesus hath interposed for it, with his teachings and his blood; heaven above waits with expectation; hell from beneath is moved at the fearful crisis; every thing, every thing that exists around us, every movement in nature, every counsel of providence, every interposition of heavenly grace, centres upon one point—upon one point—*the fidelity of man!*

Will he not be faithful? Will he not be thoughtful? Will he not do the work, that is given him to do? To his lot—such a lot; to his wants, weighing upon him like mountains; to his sufferings, lacerating his bosom with agony; to his joys, offering foretastes of heaven; to all this tried and teaching life, will he not be faithful? Will not you? Shall not I, my brother? If not, what remains—what can remain, to be done for us? If we will not hear these things, neither should we believe, though one rose from the dead. No; though the ghosts of the departed and the remembered, should come at midnight through the barred doors of our dwellings; though the sheeted dead should stalk through the very aisles of our churches; they could not more powerfully teach us than the dread realities of life; nay more, and those memories of misspent years too, those ghosts of departed opportunities, that point to our consciences and point to eternity, saying, "work while the day lasts, for the night of death cometh in which no man can work!"

XI.

LIFE IS WHAT WE MAKE IT.

UNTO THE PURE ARE ALL THINGS PURE.—Epistle of Paul to Titus i. 15.

And to expand the same sentiment a little; all things bear to us, a character corresponding with the state of our own minds. Life is what we make it; and the world is what we make it.

I can conceive that to some who hear me, this may appear to be a very singular, if not extravagant statement. You look upon this life and upon this world, and you derive from them, it may be, a very different impression. You see the earth perhaps, only as a collection of blind, obdurate, inexorable elements and powers. You look upon the mountains that stand fast for ever; you look upon the seas, that roll upon every shore their ceaseless tides; you walk through the annual round of the seasons; all things seem to be fixed, summer and winter, seed-time and harvest, growth and decay; and so they are. But does not the mind, after all, spread its own hue over all these scenes? Does not the cheerful man make a cheerful world? Does not the sorrowing man make a gloomy world? Does not every mind make its own world? Does it not, as if indeed a portion of the Divinity were imparted to it; does it not almost *create* the scene around it? Its power, in fact, scarcely falls short of the theory of those philosophers, who have supposed that the world had no existence at all, but in our own minds. So again with regard to human life: it seems to many, probably, unconscious as they are of the mental and moral powers which control it, as if it were made up of fixed conditions, and of immense and impassable distinctions. But upon all conditions presses down one impartial law. To all situations, to all fortunes high or low, the *mind* gives their character. They are in effect, not what they are in themselves, but what they are to the feeling of their possessors. The king upon his throne and amidst his court may be a mean, degraded, miserable man; a slave to ambition, to voluptuousness, to fear, to every low passion. The peasant in his cottage, may be the real monarch; the moral master of his fate; the free and lofty being, more than a prince in happiness, more than a king in honour. And shall the mere names which these men bear, blind us to the actual positions which they occupy amidst God's creation? No; beneath the all-powerful law of the heart, the master, is often a slave; and the slave—is master.

It has been maintained, I know, in opposition to the view which we take of life, that man is the creature of circumstances. But what is there in the circumstances of the slave to make him free in spirit, or of the monarch to make him timid and time-serving? This doctrine of fate—that man is but a bubble upon the sea of his fortunes, that he is borne a helpless and irresponsible being upon the tide of events,—is no new doctrine, as some of its modern advocates seem to suppose; it has always formed a leading part of the creed of Atheism. But I ask if the reverse of this doctrine is not obviously true? Do not different men bring out of the same circumstances totally different results? Does not that very difficulty, distress, poverty or misfortune, which breaks down one man, build up another and make him strong? It is the very attribute, the glory of a man; it is the very power and mastery of that will which constitutes one of his chief distinctions from the brute, that he *can* bend the circumstances of his condition to the intellectual and moral purposes of his nature.

But it may be said, that the mind itself, is the offspring of culture; that is to say, the creature of circumstances. This is true, indeed, of early childhood. But the moment that the faculty of moral will is developed, a new element is introduced, which changes the whole complexion of the argument. Then a new power is brought upon the scene, and it is a ruling power. It is delegated power from heaven. There never was a being sunk so low, but God has thus given him the power to rise. God commands him to rise, and therefore, it is certain, that he can rise. Every man has the power and every man should use it, to make all situation, all trials and temptations, conspire to the promotion of his virtue and happiness. In this, then, the only intelligible sense, man, so far from being the creature of circumstances, creates them, controls them, makes them, that is to say, to be all they are of evil or good to him as a moral being.

Life then is what we make it, and the world is what we make it. Even our temporary moods of mind, and much more, our permanent character, whether social or religious, may be appealed to in illustration of this truth.

I. Observe, in the first place, the effect of our most casual moods of mind.

It is the same creation upon which the eyes of the cheerful and the melancholy man are fixed; yet how different are the aspects which it bears to them! To the one it is all beauty and gladness; "the waves of ocean roll in light, and the mountains are covered with day." It seems to him as if life went forth rejoicing upon every bright wave, and every shining bough, shaken in the breeze. It seems as if there were more than the eye seeth; a presence, a presence of deep joy, among the hills and the valleys, and upon the bright waters. But now the gloomy man, stricken and sad at heart, stands idly or mournfully gazing at the same scene, and what is it? What is it, to him? The very light,—"Bright effluence of bright essence increate,"—yet the very light seems to him as a leaden pall thrown over the face of nature. All things wear to his eye a dull, dim, and sickly aspect. The great train of the seasons is passing before him, but he sighs and turns away, as if it were the train of a funeral procession; and he wonders within himself at the poetic representations and sentimental rhapsodies that are lavished upon a world so utterly miserable. Here then, are two different worlds in which these two classes of beings live; and they are formed and made what they are out of the very same scene, only by different states of mind in the beholders. The eye maketh that which it looks upon. The ear maketh its own melodies or discords. The world without reflects the world within.

II. Again, this life, this world is what we make it, by our social character; by our adaptation, or want of adaptation, to its social conditions, relationships and pursuits. To the selfish, to the cold and insensible, to the haughty and presuming, to the proud who demand more than they are likely to receive, to the jealous, who are always afraid they shall not receive enough, to the unreasonably sensitive about others' good or ill opinion, and in fine, to the violators of social laws, of all sorts, the rude, the violent, the dishonest and the sensual; to all these, the social condition, from its very nature will present annoyances, disappointments and pains, appropriate to their several characters. Every disposition and behaviour has a kind of magnetic attraction, by which it draws to it, its like. Selfishness will hardly be a central point around which the benevolent affections will revolve; the cold-hearted may expect to be treated with coldness, and the proud with haughtiness; the passionate with anger, and the violent with rudeness; and those who forget the rights of others, must not be surprised if their own are forgotten; and those who forget their dignity, who stoop to the lowest embraces of sense, must not wonder, if others are not concerned to find their prostrate honour, and to lift it up to the remembrance and respect of the world. Thus, the bad make the social world they live in. So, also, do the good. To the gentle, how many will be gentle; to the kind, how many will be kind! How many does a lovely example win to goodness! How many does meekness subdue to a like temper, when they come into its presence! How many does sanctity purify! How many does it command to put away all earthly defilements, when they step upon its holy ground! Yes, a good man, a really good man, will find that there is goodness in the world; and an honest man will find that there is honesty in the world; a man of principle will find principle; yes, a principle of religious integrity, in the hearts of others. I know that this is sometimes denied, and denied with much scorn and self-complacency. But when a man says that true religious virtue is all a pretence, though the charge is put forward in quite another guise, I confess that I most of all suspect the heart of the complainant. I suspect that it is a heart, itself estranged from truth and sanctity, that can find no truth nor sincerity in all the religious virtue that is around it. True, most true, most lamentably true it is; nothing is *so* lamentably true, as that there is too little religious fervour in the world; but still there is a feeling; there is some religious sensibility, the most precious deposite in the heart of society; there is some anxiety, on this great theme, holy and dear, to him whose mind is touched with that inexpressible emotion; and he whose mind is so touched, will as certainly find those deep tokens of the soul's life, as the kindling eye will find beauty amidst the creation, or as the attuned ear will find the sweet tone of music amidst the discords of nature. Thus it is, that the mind discovers social virtue and develops the social world around it. The corrupt mind elicits what is bad; and the pure mind brings out what is good.

But the pure mind makes its own social world, in another sense. It not only unfolds that world to itself, but all its relations to society are sanctified; the otherwise rough contracts of life are softened to it, and its way is graciously made smooth and easy. The general complaint is, that society is full of mistrust and embarrassment, of competitions, and misunderstandings, and unkind criticisms and unworthy jealousies. But let any one bear within him a humble mind; let him be too modest to make any unreasonable demands upon others, too mistrustful and tenderly solicitous about the keeping of his own heart, to be severe or censorious: let him simply be a good man, full of true and pure love to those around him, full of love to God, full of holy indifference to earthly vanities, full of the heavenward thought, that soars far beyond them; and what, now, has this man to do with worldly strifes and intrigues, with poor questions of precedence, and the small items of unsettled disputes and unsatisfied suspicions? An excellent simplicity that cannot understand them, a high aim that cannot bend its eye upon them, a generous feeling that cannot enter into them, a goodness that melts all difference into harmony; this is the wise man's protection and blessing.

III. I have spoken of the world of nature, and of the world of society. There is also a world of events, of temptations and trials and blessings; and this, too, is what we make it. It is what we make it by our religious character.

There are no blessings—and it is a stupendous truth that I utter—there are no blessings which the mind may not convert into the bitterest of evils; and there are no trials, which it may not transform into the most noble and divine of blessings. There are no temptations from which the virtue they assail, may not gain strength, instead of falling a sacrifice to them. I know that the virtue often falls. I know that the temptations have great power. But what is their power? It lies in the weakness of our virtue. Their power lies not in them, but in us, in the treason of our own hearts. To the pure, all things are pure. The proffer of dishonest gain, of guilty pleasure, makes them more pure; raises their virtue to the height of towering indignation. The fair occasion, the safe opportunity, the goodly chance of victory, with which sin approaches the heart to ensnare and conquer it, all are turned into defeat and disgrace for the tempter, and into the triumph and confirmation of virtue. But to the impure, to the dishonest, false-hearted, corrupt and sensual, occasions come every day, and in every scene, and through every avenue of thought and imagination. To the impure occasions come, did I say? rather do they make occasions; or if opportunities come **not,** evil *thoughts* come; no hallowed shrine, no holy temple, no sphere of life, though consecrated to purity and innocence, can keep them out. So speaketh the sacred text, and in this very striking language: "To the pure all things are pure; but to them that are defiled and unbelieving, nothing is pure; for even their mind and conscience is defiled."

Thus might we pass in survey all the circumstances of man's earthly condition, and bring from every state and pursuit of human life, the same conclusion. Upon the irreligious man, the material world has the effect to occupy him and estrange him from God; but to the devout man, the same scene is a constant ministration of high and holy thoughts. Thus also, the business of this world, while it absorbs, corrupts and degrades one mind, builds up another in the most noble independence, integrity and generosity. So too pleasure, which to some is a noxious poison, is to others, a healthful refreshment. The scene is the same. The same event happeneth to all. Life is substantially the same thing to all who partake of its lot. Yet some rise to virtue and glory; and others sink, from the same discipline, from the same privileges, to shame and perdition.

Life then, I repeat, is what we make it, and the world is what we make it. Life, that is to say, takes its colouring from our own minds; the world as the scene of our welfare or wo, is, so to speak, moulded in the bosom of human experience. The archetypes, the ideal forms of things without—if not as some philosophers have said, in a metaphysical sense, yet in a moral sense—they exist within us. The world is the mirror of the soul. Life is the history, not of outward events, not of outward events chiefly; but life, human life, is the history of a mind. To the pure, all things are pure. To the joyous, all things are joyous. To the gloomy, all things are gloomy. To the good, all things are good. To the bad, all things are bad. The world is nothing but a mass of materials, subject to a great moral experiment. The human breast is the laboratory. We work up those materials into what forms we please. This illustration too, if any one should take me too literally, will furnish the proper qualification. The materials, indeed, are not absolutely under our control. They obey the laws of a higher power. Those laws, too, are fixed laws. Yet the chemist in his laboratory, accomplishes all that he rationally desires to accomplish. The elements are enough under his command to answer all his purposes. Nay, if they did not furnish difficulties and require experiments, his science would not exist; his knowledge would be intuition. So with the moral experimenter. He has to overcome difficulties, to solve questions; still, within the range of rational wishes, and in submission to the power of God, he can work out what results he pleases; and if there were no difficulties, there would be no virtue, no moral science of life.

I am sensible that I have dwelt at considerable length upon the proofs of my doctrine; but I must beg your indulgence to some farther consideration of it, in application to two states of mind; I mean to complaint and discouragement. These states of mind have, indeed, the same leaning, but still they are very different. Complaint is bold and open-mouthed, and speaks like one injured and wronged. Discouragement is timid and silent: it does not consider whether it is wronged, but it knows that it is depressed, and at times, almost crushed to the earth. There are many minds to be found in one or other of these conditions. Indeed, I think that the largest amount of human suffering may be found in the form either of complaint or of discouragement; and if there be any thing in the doctrine of this discourse, to disarm the one, or to relieve the other, it well deserves a place in our meditations.

Our complaints of life, mainly proceed upon the ground, that for our unhappiness, something is in fault besides ourselves; and I maintain that this ground is not fairly taken. We complain of the world; we complain of our situation in the world.

Let us look a moment at this last point; what is called a situation in the world. In the first place, it is commonly what we make it, in a literal sense. We are high or low, rich or poor, honoured or disgraced, usually, just in proportion as we have been industrious or idle, studious or negligent, virtuous or vicious. But in the next place, suppose that without any fault of our own, our situation is a trying one. Doubtless it is so, in many instances. But then I say that the main point affecting our happiness in this case, is not our situation, but the spirit with which we meet it. In the humblest conditions, are found happy men; in the highest, unhappy men. And so little has mere condition to do with happiness, that a just observation, I am persuaded, will find about an equal proportion of it, among the poor and the rich, the high and the low. "But *my* relation to the persons or things around me," one may say, "is peculiarly trying; neither did I choose the relation; I would gladly escape from it." Still, I answer, a right spirit may bring from this very relation, the noblest virtue and the noblest enjoyment. "Ah! the right spirit!"—it may be said—"to obtain that is my greatest difficulty. Doubtless, if I had the spirit of an angel, or of an Apostle, I might get along very well. Then I should not be vexed, nor angered, nor depressed. But the very effort to gain that serene and patient mind, is painful, and often unsuccessful." Yes, and the ill success is the pain. It is not true, that thorough, faithful endeavour to improve is unhappy; that honest endeavour I mean, which is always successful. On the contrary, it is, this side heaven, the highest happiness. The misery of the effort is owing to its insufficiency. The misery then, is mainly our own fault.

On every account therefore, I must confess, that I am disposed to entertain a very ill opinion of misery. Whether regarded as proceeding from a man's condition or from his own mind, I cannot think well of it. I cannot look upon it with the favour which is accorded to it by much modern poetry and sentiment. These sentimental sighings over human misfortune which we hear, are fit only for children, or at least for the mind's childhood. You may say if you will, that the preacher's heart is hard when he avers this, or that he knows not trial or grief; but if you do, it will be because you do not understand the preacher's argument; no, nor his mind neither. What I say to you I say to myself; the mind's misery, is chiefly, its own fault. Sentimental sighings there may be in early youth, and in a youthful and immature poetry; but he who has come to the manhood of reason and experience, should know, what is true, that the mind's misery is chiefly its own fault; nay more, and is appointed, under the good providence of God, as the punisher and corrector of its fault. Trial is indeed a part of our lot; but suffering is not to be confounded with trial. Nay, amidst the severest trials, the mind's happiness may be the greatest that it ever knew. It has been so, in a body racked with pain; nay, and in a body consumed by the fire of the martyr's sacrifice. I am willing, however, to allow that some exceptions are to be made; as for instance, in the first burst of grief or in the pains of lingering disease. The mind must have time for reflection, and it must have strength left to do its work. But its very work, its very office of reflection, is to bring good out of evil, happiness out of trial. And when it is rigidly guided, this work it will do; to this result it will come. In the long run, it will be happy, just in proportion to its fidelity and wisdom. Life will be what it makes life to be, and the world will be what the mind makes it. With artificial wants, with ill-regulated desires, with selfish and sensitive feelings of its own cherishing, the mind must be miserable. And what then, is its misery? Hath it not planted in its own path the thorns that annoy it? And doth not the hand that planted grasp them? Is not the very loudness of the complaint, but the louder *confession*, on the part of him who makes it?

The complaint nevertheless with some, is very loud. "It is *not* a happy world," a man says, "but a very miserable world; those who consider themselves *saints* may talk about a kind Providence; *he* cannot see much of it; those who have all their wishes gratified may think it is very well; but he never *had his* wishes gratified; and nobody cares whether he is gratified or not; every body is proud and selfish," he says; "if there *is* so much goodness in the world, he wishes he could see some of it. This beautiful world! as some people call it; for his part he never saw any thing beautiful in it; but he has seen troubles and vexations, clouds and storms enough; and he has had long, tedious, weary days, and dark and dull nights; if he could sleep through his whole life, and never want any thing, it would be a comfort." Mistaken man! doubly mistaken; mistaken about the world, mistaken in thyself; the world thou complainest of, is not God's world, but thy world; it is not the world which God made, but it is the world which thou hast made for thyself. The fatal blight, the dreary dullness, the scene so distasteful and dismal, is all in thyself. The void, the blank, amidst the whole rich and full universe, is in thy heart. Fill thy heart with goodness, and thou wilt find that the world is full of good. Kindle a light within, and then the world will shine brightly around thee. But till then, though all the luminaries of heaven shed down their entire and concentrated radiance upon this world, it would be dark to thee. "The light that should be in thee, is darkness; and how great is that darkness!"

But I must turn in close, to address myself for a moment, to a very different state of mind, and that is discouragement. Complaint is to be blamed; but there is a heavy and uncomplaining discouragement pressing upon many minds, which demands a kinder consideration. They have tried and not succeeded; they have tried again, and failed—of the ends, the objects, which they sought; and they say, at length, " we give over; we can never *do* any thing in this world; ill fortune has taken the field against us, and we will battle with it no longer." Yet more to be pitied are those who have never had even the courage to strive; who, from their very cradle, have felt themselves depressed by untoward circumstances, by humble state or humble talents. Oftentimes the mind in such a case is, in culture and power, far beyond its own estimate; but it has no aptitude for worldly success; it has no power to cause itself to be appreciated by others; it has no charm of person or speech; it is neglected by society, where almost every one is too much occupied with his own advancement to think of pining merit; it is left to silent and solitary hours of discouragement and despondency. And in such hours—perhaps there are some here present who can bear me witness—the thoughts that sink deeply into the heart, though never it may be, breathed in words, are such as these: "*My* chance in this world, is a poor one; I have neither wealth, nor talents, nor family; I have nothing to give me importance; I have no friends to help me forward, or to introduce me favourably to the world; I have no path open to me; my succees is poor, even my expectation is poor. Let the fortunate be thankful, but I am not fortunate; the great prizes are not for me; despond I needs must, for hope I have none; I will sit down in silence, and eat the bread of a neglected lot; I will weep; but even that is useless; away then, hope! away tears!—I will bear my heart calmly, though sadly, in its way, through a cold, ungenial, unkind world."

And yet above this man is spread the sublimity of heaven, around him the beauty of earth; to this man is unfolded the vision of God; for this man Christ hath died, and to him, heaven is unveiled; before this man lies the page of wisdom and inspiration; and wisdom and sanctity, it is still given him to learn and gain; wisdom and sanctity, inward, all-sufficing and eternal. The universe is full and rich for him. The heaven of heavens invites him to its abode!

Oh! the intolerable worldliness of the world!—the worldliness of fashion and fashionable opinion! the worldliness of our eager throngs, and our gay watering-places, and our crowded cities, and our aspiring literature, and our busy commerce! Distinction! to be raised a little above the rest; to be talked of and pointed at, more than others; this hath blinded us to the infinite good that is offered to all men. And this distinction; what is it, after all? Suppose that you were the greatest of the great; one raised above kings; one to whom courts and powers and principalities paid homage, and around whom admiring crowds gathered at every step. I tell you that I would rather have arrived at one profound conclusion of the sage's meditation in his dim study, than to win that gaze of the multitude. I tell you that I had rather gain the friendship and love of one pure and lofty mind, than to gain that empty applause of a court or a kingdom. What then must it be to gain the approval, the friendship, the love of that ONE, infinitely great—infinitely dear to the whole pure and happy creation?

Before these awful and sublime realities of truth and sanctity, sink! all worldly distinction, and worldly imaginations! Discouragement and despondency! —for a creature to whom God hath offered the loftiest opportunity and hope in the universe? A humble, depressed, unfortunate lot!—for him, before whom are spread the boundless regions of truth, and wisdom, and joy? A poor chance!—for him who may gain heaven? Ah! sir, thy poverty, thy misfortune, is all in thyself. In the realm of God's beneficence, is an infinite fullness; and it all may be yours. Even to the despised and persecuted Christians of old the Apostle said this; and it is still, and for ever true, to all who can receive it. "Therefore," says he, in his lofty reasoning, "let no man glory in men; for all things are yours; whether the world, or life, or death, or things present or things to come; all are yours, and ye are Christ's, and Christ is God's!"

XII.

ON INEQUALITY IN THE LOT OF LIFE.

THE LORD IS GOOD TO ALL, AND HIS TENDER MERCIES ARE OVER ALL HIS WORKS.—Psalm cxlv. 9.

What I wish to suggest for your consideration from these words, is not the goodness of God only, but his goodness to all. I wish, in other words, to examine the prevailing opinion, that there is a great inequality in the distribution of the blessings of life. In opposition to this opinion, I take up the words of the text.

The Lord is good *to all*. It is not said merely that his tender mercies are over his works, but that they are over *all* his works. His providence is not only kind, but its kindness extends to every human being.

There is no general view of life, perhaps, with which the minds of men are more strongly impressed, than with the apparent inequalities of the human lot. It is probably the most prolific source of all secret repining and open complaint. Affliction of a severe kind, comes but seldom; but this inequality in the state of life is permanent. It is perfectly obvious too. Every one can see the difference between his situation in life, his dwelling, his equipage, and the observance which is paid to him; and those which belong to his more prosperous, wealthy or honoured neighbour. The distinctions of life, indeed, chiefly consist of the glare of outward things, and therefore more powerfully impress the senses.

Now if it can be made to appear that there is in fact, considerable deception in these estimates; that things are far more impartially balanced in the system of providence at large, than is commonly imagined; that inequality is not the rule of its operations, but only the exception to the rule; it would serve the important purpose of making us more contented with our lot; more happy in the opportunities and means of happiness that are given to us all; and more submissive and grateful, I would hope, to that Being who has so equally and so bountifully distributed them.

To this subject then, let me direct your thoughts this morning.

I. And in the first place you see, at once, an instance and an illustration of this impartiality of Divine Providence, in the inequalities caused by nature; in the allotments of climate, temperature, soil and scenery.

There is no one of us, perhaps, whose thoughts have not sometimes wandered to fairer climes than our own, to lands of richer productions and more luxuriant beauty; to those isles and shores of the classic East, where all the glory of man has faded indeed, where all the monuments of his power and art have fallen to decay, but where nature lives forever, and forever spreads its unfading charm; to the verdant and sunny vales of the South, regions of eternal Spring, where the circling seasons, as they pass, let fall no chill nor blight upon the fresh and fragrant bosom of the earth. But is there no counterpart to this scene? Where does the volcano lift up its subterraneous thunders, and pour forth its flaming deluge? It is in these very regions of eternal Spring. It is on the green and flowery mount, on the vine-clad hills; fast by the quiet fold of the shepherd, and amidst the rejoicings of the vintage. Whence comes the fearful rumour of the earthquake, that has whelmed a city in ruins? It comes from the land of the diamond and the cane; from the hills of Ophir; from groves of the palm and the olive; from valleys loaded with fruits, and fanned with aromatic gales; where if nature is more energetic to produce, she is also more energetic to destroy. Where does the dire pestilence walk in darkness, and the fell destruction waste at noon-day? Amidst groves of spices, and beneath bowers of luxuriance; and the beam that lights its victims to their tomb, is the brightest beam of heaven, and the scenes of which they take their last hasty leave, are the fairest that nature displays; as if life and death were intended to be set in the most visible and vivid contrast. And where, but there also, is that worse than plague and pestilence and earthquake, that degradation of the mind, that wide-spreading pestilence of the soul, that listless indolence, which only arouses, to deeds of passion! Let the millions of Southern Asia tell. Let Turkey, so often drenched with blood, answer. Let the wandering Arab, let the stupid Hottentot, let the slothful and sensual inhabitants of the fair isles of the Pacific, teach us. Who would not rather struggle with fiercer elements, than to sink an ignoble prey to the soft languors of pleasure and the besotting indulgences of passion? Who would not far prefer our wintry storm and "the hoarse sighings of the East wind," as it sweeps around us, if they will brace the mind to nobler attainments, and the heart to better duties?

There is one class of virtues that is fostered by the rigours of our climate, which deserves to be particularly noticed. I mean the *domestic* virtues. We are compelled, by the inclemency of our seasons, not only to have some permanent place of abode, but to resort to it. In milder regions, men live abroad; they are scarcely obliged to have any domicil. *We* are compelled to live at home; and we attach a meaning to the term, and we hallow it with feelings that were unknown to the polished Greek and the voluptuous Asiatic. It is the angry and lowering sky of winter, that lights up the cheerful fire in our dwellings, and draws around the friendly circle. It is the cheerlessness of every thing abroad, that leads us to find or make pleasures within; to resort to books and the interchange of thought; to multiply the sources of knowledge and strengthen the ties of affection. It is the frowning face of nature, like the dark cloud of adversity, that lends attraction to all the sympathies and joys of home.

II. But I come now in the second place to consider the impartiality of Divine Providence, in the condition of human life. Life—to borrow a comparison from the science of political economy—life, like nature, is a system of checks and balances. Every power of conferring happiness, is limited or else counteracted, by some other power either of good or evil. There is no blessing or benefit, but it has some drawback upon it; and there is no inconvenience nor calamity, but it enjoys some compensation. This results from the very nature of things. You cannot enjoy things incompatible. You cannot at once enjoy, for instance, the pleasures of the country and the town. You cannot mingle the quietude of obscurity with the emoluments and honours of office. You cannot have at the same time, the benefits of affliction and the joys of prosperity. If you would reach the loftiest virtue, you must sometimes endure sickness and pain, and you must, sometimes, be bowed down with sorrow. If you would have perpetual ease and indulgence, you must resign something of noble fortitude, holy patience, and of the blessed triumphs of faith.

The inequalities which appear in the condition of human life, relate chiefly to the possessions, the employments, or the distinctions of society. If we should examine these, we should probably find that they are of less importance to our happiness than is commonly imagined. Indeed, we know that they all depend chiefly on the use that is made of them; and their use depends upon the mind. Distinction and mediocrity, leisure and toil, wealth and poverty, have no intrinsic power of happiness or misery in their disposal. There is a principle *within*, that is to render them good or evil.

But, not at present to insist on this; these circumstances of inequality, in *themselves*, are less than they seem. It is common, I know, to hear of the prerogatives, the power, the independence, of the higher classes of society. But Divine Providence acknowledges no such nobility; no such exemption from the wants of the human lot. It teaches us very little about prerogative or independence, however the pride of man may flatter him. No tower of pride was ever high enough, to lift its possessor above the trials and fears and frailties of humanity. No human hand ever built the wall, nor ever shall, that will keep out affliction, pain and infirmity. Sickness, sorrow, trouble, death, are all-levelling dispensations. They know none high nor low. The chief wants of life, too, the great necessities of the human soul, give exemption to none. They make all poor, all weak. They put supplication in the mouth of every human being, as truly as in that of the meanest beggar.

Now consider society for one moment, in regard to

its employments. And there is not, perhaps, a greater infatuation in the world, than for a man of active and industrious habits, to look with envy or repining upon the ease and leisure of his neighbour. Employment, activity, is one of the fundamental laws of human happiness. Ah! the laborious indolence of him who has nothing to do; the preying weariness, the stagnant ennui of him who has nothing to obtain; the heavy hours which roll over him, like the waters of a Lethean sea, that has not yet quite drowned the senses in their oblivious stupor; the dull comfort of having finished a day; the dreariness in prospect of another to come; in one word, the terrible visitation of an avenging Providence to him that lives to himself!

But I need not dwell on a case so obvious, and proceed, at once, to mention the distinction of wealth and poverty.

It must not be denied that poverty, abject and desperate poverty, is a great evil; but this is not a common lot, and it still more rarely occurs in this country, without faults or vices, which should forbid all complaint. Neither shall it here be urged, on the other hand, that riches are acquired with many labours and kept with many cares and anxieties; for so also it may be said, and truly said, has poverty its toils and anxieties. The true answer to all difficulties on this subject, seems to be, that a "man's life consisteth not in the abundance of things which he possesseth." The answer, in short, may be reduced to a plain matter of fact. There is about as much cheerfulness among the poor as among the rich. And I suspect, about as much contentment too. For we might add, that a man's life, if it consist at all in his possessions, does not consist in what he possesses, but in what he *thinks* himself to possess. Wealth is a comparative term. The desire of property grows, and at the same time the estimate of it lessens, with its accumulation. And thus it may come to pass, that he who possesses thousands may less feel himself to be rich, and to all substantial purposes, may actually be less rich, than he who enjoys a sufficiency.

But not to urge this point, we say, that a man's life does not consist in these things. Happiness, enjoyment, the buoyant spirits of life, the joys of humanity, do not consist in them. They do not depend on this distinction, of being poor or rich. As it is with the earth, that there are living springs within it, which will burst forth somewhere, and that they are often most clear and healthful in tne most sterile and rugged spots; so it is with the human heart. There are fountains of gladness in it: and why should they not revive the weary? Why should they not cool the brow of labour, and the lips that are parched with toil? Why should they not refresh the poor man? Nay, but they do; and they refresh him the more, *because* he is poor and weary. Man may hew out to himself cisterns, and how often are they broken cisterns, which are scrupulously and proudly guarded from his poorer fellow-man: but the great fountains which God has opened are for all. This and that man may endeavour to appropriate them to himself; he may guide them to his reservoir; he may cause them to gush forth in artificial fountains and to fall in artificial showers in his gardens; but it is artificial still; and one draught of the pure well-spring of honest, homely happiness, is better than them all; and the shower which heaven sends, falls upon the rich and the poor, upon the high and the low alike; and with still more impartial favour, descends upon the good and the evil, upon the just and the unjust.

III. This impartiality will be still more manifest, if we reflect, in the third place, that far the greatest and most numerous of the divine favours are granted to all, without any discrimination.

Look, in the first place, at the natural gifts of Providence. The beauty of the earth, the glories of the sky; the vision of the sun and the stars; the beneficent laws of universal being; the frame of society and of government; protecting justice and Almighty providence; whose are these? What power of appropriation can say of any one of these, "this is mine and not another's?" And what one of these would you part with for the wealth of the Indies, or all the splendors of rank or office? Again, your eye-sight—that regal glance that commands in one act, the outspread and all-surrounding beauty of the fair universe—would you exchange it for a sceptre, or a crown? And the ear—that gathers unto its hidden chambers all music and gladness—would you give it for a kingdom? And that wonderful gift, speech—that breathes its mysterious accents into the listening soul of thy friend; that sends forth its viewless messages through the still air, and imprints them at once upon the ears of thousands; would you barter that gift for the renown of Plato or of Milton?

No, there are unappropriated blessings, blessings which none can appropriate, in every element of nature, in every region of existence, in every inspiration of life, which are infinitely better than all that can be hoarded in treasure, or borne on the breath of fame. All, of which any human being can say, "it is mine," is a toy, is a trifle, compared with what God has provided for the great family of his children! Is *he* poor to whom the great store-house of nature is opened, or does he think himself poor because it is God who has made him rich? Does *he* complain that he cannot have a magnificent palace to dwell in, who dwells in this splendid theatre of the universe; that he cannot behold swelling domes and painted walls, who beholds the "dread magnificence of heaven," and the pictured earth and sky? Do you regret the want of attendants, of a train of servants, to anticipate every wish and bring every comfort at your bidding? Yet how small a thing is it to be waited on, compared with the privilege of being yourself active; compared with the vigour of health and the free use of your limbs and senses? Is it a hardship that your table does not groan with luxuries? But how much better than all luxury, is simple appetite!

The very circumstances which gain for the distinctions of life such an undue and delusive estimation, are such as ought to make us cautious about the estimate we put upon them. They are distinctions, and therefore likely to be overrated; but is that a good and sound reason why we should affix to them an undue importance? Are the palaces of kings to be regarded with more interest, than the humbler roofs that shelter millions of human beings? What more is the marriage of a queen—to the individual mind—though surrounded with the splendor and state of a kingdom; though accompanied with shining troops and announced by roaring cannon; what more is it than that marriage of hearts, that is every day consummated beneath a thousand lowly roofs? The distinctions of life, too, are mostly factitious; the work of art, and man's device. They are man's gifts, rather than God's gifts; and for that reason I would esteem them less. They are fluctuating also, and therefore attract notice, but on that account too, are less valuable. They are palpable to the senses, attended with noise and show, and therefore likely to be over-estimated. While those vast benefits which all share and which are always the same, which come in the ordinary course of things, which do not disturb the ordinary and even tenor of life, pass by unheeded. The resounding chariot, as it rolls on with princely state and magnificence, is gazed upon with admiration and perhaps with envy. But morning comes forth in the east, and from his glorious chariot-wheels scatters light over the heavens and spreads life and beauty through the world: morning after morning comes, and noontide sets its throne in the southern sky, and the day finishes its splendid revolution in heaven, without exciting, perhaps, a comment or a reflection. The pageant of fashion passes, and has the notice of many an eye, perhaps, to which it is all in vain that the seasons pass by in their glory; that nature arrays herself in robes of light and beauty, and fills the earth with her train. To want what another possesses, to be outstripped in the race of honour or gain, to lose some of the nominal treasures of life, may be enough with some of us, to disturb and irritate us altogether; and such an one shall think little of it that he has life itself and that he enjoys it; it shall be nothing to him that he has quiet sleep in the night season, and that all the bounties of the day are spread before him; that he has friends and domestic joys, and the living fountain of cheerful spirits and affectionate pleasures within him.

Nor must we stop here in our estimate. There is an infinite sum of blessings which have not yet been included in the account; and these, like all the richest gifts of heaven, are open and free to all; I mean the gifts, the virtues, the blessings of religion.

It has already, indeed, sufficiently appeared, not only that the inequalities in the allotments of Providence, are attended with a system of compensations and drawbacks, which make them far less than they seem; and also on account of the vast blessings which are diffused every where and dispensed to all, that inequality, instead of being the rule of the Divine dealings, is only a slight exception to them. But we come now to a principle, that absorbs all other considerations; virtue, the only intrinsic, infinite, everlasting good, is accessible to all. If there were ever so strong and apparently just charges of partiality against the Divine Providence, this principle would be sufficient to vindicate it. "O God!" exclaims the Persian poet Sadi, "have pity on the wicked! for thou hast done every thing for the good, in having made them good."

How false and earthly are our notions of what is evil! How possible is it that all advantages besides religion, may prove the greatest calamities! How possible is it that distinction, that successful ambition, that popular applause, may be the most injurious, the most fatal evil that could befall us! How possible that wealth may be turned into the very worst of curses, by the self-indulgence, the dissipation, the vanity or hardness of heart that it may produce! And there is a judgment too, short of the judgment of heaven, that pronounces it to be so; the judgment of every right and noble sentiment, of all good sense, of all true friendship. There is a friend, not a flatterer, who, as he witnesses in some one, this sad dereliction, this poor exultation of vanity, this miserable bondage to flattery, or this direful success of some dark temptation—who, as he witnesses this, will say in his secret thoughts, with the Persian sage, "Oh! God, have pity on the wicked; have pity on my friend! would that he were poor and unnoticed, would that he were neglected or forsaken, rather than thus!" It is therefore a matter of doubt whether those things which we crave as blessings, would really be such to us. And then, as to the trials of life, their unequalled benefits are a sufficient answer to every objection that can be brought against their unequal distribution.

We hear it said that there is much evil in the world; and this or that scene of suffering is brought as an example of the partial dealings of heaven; and it is felt, if it is not said, perhaps, that "God's ways are unequal." But the strongest objector on this ground, I think, would yield, if he saw that the attendant and fruit of all this suffering, were a fortitude, a cheerfulness, a heavenliness, that shed brighter hues than those of earth, upon the dark scene of calamity and sorrow. I have seen suffering, sorrow, bereavement, all that is darkest in human fortunes, clothed with a virtue so bright and beautiful, that sympathy was almost lost in the feeling of congratulation and joy. I have heard more than one sufferer say, " I am thankful; God is good to me;" and when I heard that, I said, " it *is* good to be afflicted." There is, indeed, much evil in the world; but without it, there would not be much virtue. The poor, the sick and the afflicted, could be relieved from their trials at once, if it were best for them: but if they understood their own welfare, they would not desire exemption from their part in human trials. There might be a world of ease and indulgence and pleasure; but "it is a world," to use the language of another, " from which, if the option were given, a noble spirit would gladly hasten into that better world of difficulty and virtue and conscience, which is the scene of our present existence."

In fine, religion is a blessing so transcendent, as to make it of little consequence what else we have, or what else we want. It is enough for us, it is enough for us all; for him who is poor, for him who is neglected, for him who is disappointed and sorrowful; it is enough for him, though there were nothing else, that he may be good and happy forever. In comparison with this, to be rich, to be prosperous, and merely that, is the most trifling thing that can be imagined. *Is* it not enough for us, my brethren, that we may gain those precious treasures of the soul, which the world cannot give nor take away; that the joys and consolations and hopes of the Spirit and Gospel of Christ may be ours? Has not he a sufficiency; is not his heart full; is not his blessedness complete, who can say, " Whom have I in heaven but thee, and there is none upon earth that I desire besides thee: all things else may fail; my heart may lose its power, and my strength its firmness; but thou art the strength of my heart, and my portion forever."

The lesson, my friends, which these reflections lay before us, is this: to learn that we are all partakers of one lot, children of one Father; to learn in whatsoever state we are, therewith to be content, and therein to be grateful. If you are ever tempted to discontent and murmuring, ask yourself, ask the Spirit within you, formed for happiness, for glory and virtue, of what you shall complain. Ask the ten thousand mercies of your lives, of what you shall complain: or go and ask the bounties of nature; ask the sun that shines cheerfully upon you; ask the beneficent seasons as they roll, of what you shall complain; ask—ask—of your Maker; but God forbid that you or I should be guilty of the heinous ingratitude! No, my friends, let us fix our thoughts rather, upon the full and overflowing beneficence of heaven, upon the love of God. Let us fix our affections upon it, and then we shall have a sufficiency; then, though some may want and others may complain; though dissatisfaction may prey upon the worldly, and envy may corrode the hearts of the jealous and discontented; for us there shall be a sufficiency indeed; for us there shall be a treasure which the world cannot give, nor change, nor disturb; "an inheritance incorruptible and undefiled, and that fadeth not away."

XIII.

ON THE MISERIES OF LIFE.

FOR THE CREATURE [*that is man*] WAS MADE SUBJECT TO VANITY, [*that is to suffering*] NOT WILLINGLY, BUT BY REASON OF HIM [*or at the will of him*] WHO HATH SUBJECTED THE SAME IN HOPE.—Romans viii. 20

IN considering the spiritual philosophy of life, we cannot avoid the problem of human misery. The reality presses us on very side, and philosophy demands to sit in judgment on the fact.

I have often wondered that, with such themes as are presented to the pulpit, it could ever have been dull; still more that it should be proverbially dull. So practical are these themes, so profound, so intimate with all human experience, that I cannot conceive, what is to be understood, save through utter perversion, by a dull religion, a dull congregation, or a dull pulpit. If there were an invading army just landed upon our shores; if there were a conflagration or a pestilence sweeping through our city, and we were assembled here to consider what was to be done; in all seriousness and most advisedly do I say, that no questions could be raised, on such an occasion, more vital to our welfare, than those which present themselves to us here, on every Sunday. Take off the covering of outward form and demeanour from the heart of society, and what do we see? Is there not a struggle and a war going on; not upon our borders, but in the midst of us, in our dwellings, and in our very souls; a war, not for territory, nor for visible freedom; but for happiness, for virtue, for inward freedom? Are not misery and vice, as they were fire and pestilence, pressing, urging, threatening to sweep through this city, every day? Is not an interest involved in every day's action, thought, purpose, feeling, that is dearer than merchandise, pleasure, luxury, condition; dearer than life itself?

Does any one say, that religion is some abstract concern, some visionary matter, fit only for weak enthusiasts or doting fools; which has nothing to do with him nor with his real welfare; a thing indifferent, gone and given over to indifference, beyond all hope of recovery; in which he cannot, for his life, interest himself? Ay, proud philosopher! or vain worldling! sayest thou that? Is misery something abstract; with which thou canst not interest thyself? Is sin—that source of misery; is the wrong thought, the wrong deed, the deed folded, muffled in darkness, the thought shut up in the secret breast, which neither flashing eye nor flushed cheek may tell; is this, I say, something abstract and indifferent? And is the holy peace of conscience, the joy of virtue, a thing for which a human being need not, cannot care? Nay, these are the great, invisible, eternal realities of our life, of our very nature!

I have said that suffering, as the most stupendous fact in human experience, as the profoundest problem in our religious philosophy, presses us on every side. I will not mock you with formal proofs of its existence. And do not think either, that on this subject, I will go into detail or description. One may easily understand human experience, interpret the universal consciousness too well, to think *that* either needful or tolerable. I will not speak of sicknesses or disappointments or bereavements, many though they are. I will not speak of the minds, more in number than we think, that bear the one, solitary, deep-embosomed grief:

> One fatal remembrance, one sorrow that throws,
> In dark shade alike o'er their joys and their woes.
> To which life nothing brighter nor darker can bring,
> For which joy hath no balm, and affliction no sting.

I will not speak of the sighing that rises up from all the world, for a happiness unfound. But I point you to that which is seldom expressed, to that which lies deeper than all, that *eternal want;* which lies as a heavy residuum at the bottom of the cup of life; which albeit unperceived amidst the flowings and gushings of pleasure, yet when the waters are low, ever disturbs that fountain-head, that living cup of joy, with impatience, anxiety and blind up-heaving effort after something good. Yes, the creature, the human being is made subject to this. There is a wanting and a wanting, and an ever wanting, of what is never, never on earth, to be obtained! For let us be just here. Religion itself does not altogether assuage that feeling; "for even we ourselves," says the Apostle, "groan within ourselves." No; religion itself does not suppress that groan; though it does show, and therein is a most blessed visitation, that it can satisfy that feeling as nothing else can, and that it has in it, the elements for satisfying it fully and infinitely.

I dwell somewhat upon this point as a matter of fact, my brethren, because I conceive that it is one office of the preacher, as it is of the poet and philosopher, to unfold the human heart and nature, more fully to itself. Strange as the opinion may be thought, I do not believe that men generally know how unhappy, at any rate how far from happiness, they are. That stupendous fact, the soul's misery, is covered up with business, cares, pleasures and vanities. Were human life unveiled to its depths; were the soul, disrobed of all overlayings and debarred from all opiates, to come down, down to its own naked resources, it seems to me at times, that religion would need no other argument. With such apprehension at least as I have of this subject, I feel obliged to preach, as to some, and not a few, who not having taken the religious view of their existence, have come to look upon life with a dull and saddened eye. I believe there are not a few—it may be that they are of the more solitary in the world, and who have not as many stirring objects and prospects in life as others—who look upon the path that stretches before them as cheerless, and threatening to be more and more so as it advances; who say in their silent thoughts, "I shall live, perhaps, too long! I shall live, perhaps, till I am neglected, passed by, forgotten! I shall live, possibly, till I am a burden to others and to myself! Oh! what may my state be before I die!"

Yes, "the creature was made subject to misery;" and if you will find a rational being, not under that law, you must seek him, without the bounds of this world.

To this case then, to this great problem involved in human existence, let us give our thoughts this evening.

And in the first place, I would say, let not the vast amount of happiness in this world, be forgotten in the sense of its miseries.

They who say that this is a miserable world, or that this is a miserable life, say not well. It is misanthropy, or a diseased imagination only, that says this. Life is liable to misery, but misery is not its very being; it is not a miserable existence. Witness—I know not what things to say, or how many. The eye is opened to a world of beauty, and to a heaven, all sublimity and loveliness. The ear heareth tones and voices that touch the heart with joy, with rapture. The great, wide atmosphere, breathes upon us, bathes us with softness and fragrance. Then look deeper. How many conditions are happy! Childhood is happy; and youth is prevailingly happy: and prosperity hath its joy, and wealth its satisfaction; and the warm blood that flows in the ruddy cheek and sinewy arm of honest poverty, is a still better gift. No song is so hearty and cheering, none that steals forth from the windows of gay saloons, as the song of honest labour among the hills and mountains. Oh! to be a man— with the true energies and affections of a man; all men feel it to be good. To be a healthful, strong, true-hearted, and loving man; how much better is it, than to be the minion, or master of any condition— lord, landgrave, king, or Cæsar! How many affections too are happy; gratitude, generosity, pity, love, and the consciousness of being beloved! And to bow the heart, in lowliness and adoration, before the Infinite, all-blessing, ever-blessed One; to see in the all-surrounding brightness and glory, not beauty and majesty only, but the all-Beautiful, all-Majestic, all-Conscious *Mind* and *Spirit* of love; this is to be filled with more than created fulness; it is to be filled with all the fulness of God!

A world where such things are, a world above all, where such a presence is, seemeth to me, a goodly world. I look around upon it, I meditate upon it, I feel its blessings and beatitudes; and I say, surely it is a world of plenteousness and beauty and gladness, of loves and friendships, of blessed homes and holy altars, of sacred communions and lofty aspirations and immortal prospects; and I remember that He who made it, looked upon it, and saw that it was very good.

And strange it seemeth, indeed, to our earlier contemplation of it, that in such a world, and beneath the bright skies, there should be the dark stroke of calamity—a serpent winding through this Eden of our existence.

But it is here; and now let us draw nearer, and behold this wonder beneath the heavens—*misery!*

What is its nature? What account are we to take of it? What are we to think of it? On this point, I must pray your attention to something of detail and speculation; though I must be, necessarily, brief.

What then is the nature of misery? Is it an evil principle, or a good principle in the universe? Is it designed to do us harm, or to do us good? Doubtless the latter; and this can be shown without any very extended or laborious argument.

Misery then, evidently springs from two causes: from the perfection of our nature, and from the imperfection of our treatment of it; that is, from our ignorance, error, and sin.

I say, that misery springs, first, from the perfection or excellence of our nature. Thus remorse, a pained conscience, that greatest, and though half-benumbed, most wide-spread of all misery, never would afflict us, had we not a moral nature. Make us animals, and we should feel nothing of this. So of our intellectual nature; let poor, low instinct take its place, and we should never suffer from ignorance, error, or mistake. And our very bodies owe many of their sufferings and diseases to the delicacy of our nerves, fibres, and senses. Gird a man with the mail of leviathan; arm him with hoofs and claws; and he would have but few hurts, diseases, or pains. But now he is clothed with these vails of living tissues, with this vesture of sensitive feeling, spread all over his frame, that his whole body may be an exquisite instrument of communication with the whole surrounding universe; that earth, air, sky, waters, all their visions, all their melodies, may visit his soul through every pore, and every sense. In such a frame, suffering evidently is the incident, not the intent. And then, in fine, if you ask, whence comes this ever-craving desire of more, more; more happiness, more good, more of every thing that it grasps; what does this show primarily, but the extent of the grasp, the largeness of the capacity, the greatness of the nature? That universal sighing, of which I have spoken, which is forever saying, "who will show me any good?" comes not from the dens and keeps of animals, but from the dwellings of thoughtful, meditative, and immortal men.

But in the next place, I say, that our misery cometh from the imperfection of our treatment of this elevated and much-needing nature; from our ignorance, error, and sin. We do not satisfy this nature, and it suffers, from vague, ever-craving want. We cannot satisfy it, perhaps; which only the more shows its greatness; but we do not, what we *can*, to satisfy it. We wound it too by transgression, and it groans over the abuse. We err perhaps from want of reflection, and the consequences teach us wisdom. The child that puts his hand in the fire, will not put it there again. A cut finger is a brief lesson, a short copy writ in blood, to teach discretion. The *man* is taught to transfer that lesson to the whole scene of life. All elements, all the laws of things around us, minister to this end; and thus, through the paths of painful error and mistake, it is the design of providence to lead us to truth and happiness.

Is then, the principle of misery in *this* view, an evil principle? If erring but taught us to err; if mistakes confirmed us in imprudence; if the pains of imperfection only fastened its bonds upon us, and the miseries of sin had a natural tendency to make us its slaves, then were all this suffering, only evil. But the evident truth on the contrary is, that it all tends and is designed, to produce amendment, improvement. This so clearly results from the principles of reason, and is so uniformly sustained by the testimony of scripture, that I do not think it necessary to quote from the one, nor any farther to argue from the other.

Misery then is a beneficent principle in the universe. He who subjected the creature to misery, subjected him in hope. There is a brightness beyond that dark cloud. It is not an inexplicable, unutterable, implacable, dark doom, this ministration of misery; it is meant for good. It is meant to be a ministration to virtue and to happiness. I say, to virtue and happiness. These are the specifications of what I mean, when I say that suffering is a beneficent principle. It springs from the perfection or excellence of our nature, and thus far certainly, all is well with our argument. It springs from imperfection in our treatment of it; but it is designed to remove that imperfection; and still therefore the path of our argument, though it lead over desolations and ruins, is clear and bright. But still further I say, that it is not an abstract argument; a mere fair theory having no foundation in truth and fact.

I will reason from your own experience. The pained thought, the painful feeling in you; tell me what it is, and I will tell you, how it is made to work out good for you. Is it ennui, satiety, want? All this urges and compels you to seek for action, enlargement, supply. Is it that most sad and painful conviction, the conviction of deficiency or of sin? This directly teaches you to seek for virtue, improvement; for pardon, and the blessedness of pardon. Is it the sorrow of unrequited affection, or a sighing for friendship, in this cold and selfish world too seldom found? This is an occasion for the loftiest generosity, magnanimity and candour. Is it sickness or bereavement, the body's pain or the heart's desolation? Fortitude, faith, patience, trust in heaven, the hope of heaven; these are so much meant as the end, that, indeed, there are no other resources for pain and deprivation.

And these happy results, I say, have not failed to be produced in the experience of multitudes. It is no visionary dreaming of which I have spoken, but a matter of fact. Even as Christ was made perfect through sufferings, so are his followers. How many have said, in their thoughts, when at last the true light has broken upon them—" Ah! it *is* no contradiction; the dark path *does* lead to light; pain *is* a means of pleasure; misery of happiness; penitential grief, of virtue; loss, deprivation, sorrow, are the elements, or rather they are the means, of all that is best in my character; it is fortunate for me that I have suffered; it is good for me that I have been afflicted; it is better, how far better with me now, than if I had been always and only happy."

Nay, and even from that comparison, by which past suffering enhances all present and coming enjoyment, I could draw an argument almost sufficient for its vindication in the great scheme of providence. The pains of a sick and dying child, are often referred to, as the most mysterious things in providence; but that child, it should be remembered, may be, and probably will be, happier forever, for that dark cloud that brooded over the cradle of its infancy. And for myself I must say, that if I were now standing on the verge of a tried life with the prospects of everlasting happiness before me,

I should not regret that I had been a sufferer; I should count it all joy rather, and be sure that my eternal joy would be dearer for it.

But this is not, it is true, the chief consideration. Suffering is the discipline of virtue, that which nourishes, invigorates, perfects it. Suffering, I repeat, is the discipline of virtue; of that which is infinitely better than happiness, and yet which embraces all essential happiness in it. Virtue is the prize, of the severely contested race, of the hard-fought battle; and it is worth all the strifes and wounds of the conflict.

This is the view, which we ought, I think, manfully and courageously to take of our present condition. Partly from our natural weakness, partly from want of reflection, and partly from the discouraging aspects which infidel philosophy and ascetic superstition, have thrown over human life, we have acquired a timidity, a pusillanimity, a peevishness, a habit of complaining, which enhances all our sorrows. Dark enough they are, without needing to be darkened by gloomy theories. Enough do we tremble under them, without requiring the misgivings of cherished fear and weakness. Philosophy, religion, virtue should speak to man, not in a voice, all pity, not in a voice, all terror; but rather in that trumpet tone that arouses and cheers the warrior to battle.

With a brave and strong heart should man go forth to battle with calamity. He shall not let it be his master, but rather shall he master it; yea, he shall be as an artificer, who taketh in his hand an instrument to work out some beautiful work. When Sir Walter Raleigh took in his hand the axe, that was in a few moments to deprive him of life, and felt its keen edge, he said, smiling, "this is a sharp medicine, but it will cure all diseases." Indeed, the manner in which the brave English Noblemen and Clergy of the olden time went to death, even when it was to appease the jealousy or wrath of unjust monarchs, is illustrative of the spirit I would recommend. Fortitude, manliness, cheerfulness, with modesty and humility, dressed them, even on the scaffold, in robes of eternal honour. And surely he who takes an instrument in his hand, which is not to slay him, but with which he may work out the model and perfection of every virtue in him, should take it with resolution and courage; should say, " with this sore pain or bitter sorrow, is a good and noble work for me to do, and well and nobly will I strive to do it. I will not blench nor fly from what my Father above, has appointed me. I will not drown my senses and faculties with opiates to escape it. I will not forsake the post of trial and peril." Do you remember that noble boy who stood on the burning deck at the battle of the Nile? Many voices around said, " come down!—come away!" But the confiding child said, " father, shall I come?" Alas! that father's voice was hushed in death; and his child kept his post till he sunk in the whelming flame. Oh! noble child! thou teachest us firmly to stand in our lot, till the great word of providence shall bid us fly, or bid us sink!

But while I speak thus, think me not insensible to the severity of man's sufferings. I know what human nerves and sinews and feelings are. When the sharp sword enters the very bosom, the iron enters the very soul—I see what must follow. I see the uplifted hands, the writhen brow, the written agony in the eye. But God's mercy, which " tempers the blast to the shorn lamb," does not suffer these to be the ordinary and permanent forms of affliction. No, thou sittest down in thy still chamber; and sad memories come there; or it may be, strange trials gather under thy brooding thought. Thou art to die; or thy friend must die; or worse still, thy friend is faithless. Or thou sayest that coming life is dark and desolate. And now as thou sittest there, I will speak to thee; and I say—though sighs will burst from thy almost broken heart, yet when they come back in echoes from the silent walls, let them teach thee. Let them tell thee that God wills not thy destruction, thy suffering for its own sake; wills thee not, cannot will thee, any evil; how could that thought come from the bosom of infinite love! No, let thy sorrows tell thee, that God wills thy repentance, thy virtue, thy happiness, thy preparation for infinite happiness! Let that thought spread holy light through thy darkened chamber. That which is against thee, is not as that which is for thee. Calamity, a dark speck in thy sky, seemeth to be against thee; but God's goodness, the all-embracing light and power of the universe, forever lives, and shines around thee and for thee.

" Evil and good, before him stand
Their mission to perform."

The angel of gladness is there; but the angel of affliction is there too; and both alike for good. May the angel of gladness visit us as often as is good for us!—I pray for it. But that angel of affliction! what shall we say to it? Shall we not say, "come thou too, when our Father willeth; come thou, when need is; with saddened brow and pitying eye, come; and take us on thy wings, and bear us up to hope, to happiness, to heaven; to that presence where is fulness of joy, to that right hand, where are pleasures for evermore!"

There is one further thought which I must not fail to submit to you, on this subject, before I leave it. The greatness of our sufferings points to a correspondent greatness in the end to be gained. When I see what men are suffering around me, I cannot help feeling that it was meant, not only that they should be far better than they are, but far better than they often think of being. The end must rise higher and brighter before us, before we can look through this dark cloud of human calamity. The struggle, the wounds, the carnage and desolation of a battle, would overwhelm me with horror, if it were not fought for freedom, for the fireside; to protect infancy from ruthless butchery, and the purity of our homes from brutal wrong. So is the battle of this life, a bewildering maze of misery and despair, till we see the high prize that is set before it. You would not send your son to travel through a barren and desolate wilderness, or to make a long and tedious voyage to an unhealthy clime, but for some great object: say, to make a fortune thereby. And any way, it seems to your parental affection, a strange and almost cruel proceeding. Nor would the merciful Father of life, have sent his earthly children to struggle through all the sorrows, the pains and perils of this world, but to attain to the grandeur of a moral fortune, worth all the strife and endurance. No, all this is not ordained in vain, nor in reckless indifference to what we suffer; but for an end, for a high end, for an end higher than we think for. Troubles, disappointments, afflictions, sorrows, press us on every side, that we may rise upward, upward, ever upward. And believe me, in thus rising upward, you shall find the very names that you give to calamity, gradually changing. Misery, strictly speaking and in its full meaning, does not belong to a good mind. Misery shall pass into suffering, and suffering into discipline, and discipline into virtue, and virtue into heaven. So let it pass with you. Bend now patiently and meekly, in that lowly "worship of sorrow," till in God's time, it become the worship of joy, of proportionably higher joy; in that world where there shall be no more sorrow nor pain nor crying; where all tears shall be wiped from your eyes; where beamings of heaven in your countenance, shall grow brighter by comparison with all the darkness of earth.

And remember too, that your forerunner into that blessed life, passed through this same worship of sorrow. A *man* of sorrows was that Divine Master, and acquainted with grief. This is the great Sabbath of the year* that commemorates his triumph over sorrow and pain and death. And what were the instruments, the means, the ministers of that very victory, that last victory? The rage of men, and the fierceness of torture; the arraignment before enemies—mocking, smiting, scourging; the thorny crown, the bitter cross, the barred tomb! With these he fought, through these he conquered, and from these he rose to heaven. And believe me, in something must every disciple be like the master. Clothed in some vesture of pain, of sorrow or of affliction, must he fight the great battle and win the great victory. When I stand in the presence of that high example, I cannot listen to poor, unmanly, unchristian complainings. I would not have its disciples account too much of their griefs. Rather would I say, courage! ye that bear the great, the sublime lot of sorrow! It is not forever that ye suffer. It is not for naught, that ye suffer. It is not without end, that ye suffer. God wills it. He spared not his own Son from it. God wills it. It is the ordinance of his wisdom for us. Nay, it is the ordinance of Infinite love, to procure for us an infinite glory and beatitude.

* Easter Sunday.

XIV.

ON THE SCHOOL OF LIFE.

O GOD, THOU HAST TAUGHT ME FROM MY YOUTH.—Psalm lxxi. 17.

LIFE is a school. This world is a house of instruction. It is not a prison nor a penitentiary, nor a palace of ease, nor an amphitheatre for games and spectacles; it is a school. And this view of life is the only one that goes to the depths of the philosophy of life; the only one that answers the great question, solves the great problem of life. For what is life given? If for enjoyment alone, if for suffering merely, it is a chaos of contradictions. But if for moral and spiritual learning, then everything is full of significance, full of wisdom. And this view too, is of the utmost practical importance. It immediately presents to us and presses upon us the question: what are we learning? And is not this, truly, the great question? When your son comes home to you at the annual vacation, it is the first question in your thoughts concerning *him;* and you ask him, or you ask for the certificates and testimonials of his teachers, to give you some evidence of his learning. At every passing term in the great school of life, also, this is the all-important question. What has a man got, from the experience, discipline, opportunity of any past period? Not, what has he gathered together in the shape of any tangible good; but what has he got—in that other and eternal treasure-house, his mind! Not, what of outward accomodation the *literal* scholar has had, should we think it much worth our while to inquire; not whether his text books had been in splendid bindings; not whether his study-table had been of rich cabinet-work, and his chair softly cushioned; not whether the school-house in which he had studied, were of majestic size, or adorned with columns and porticoes; let him have got a good education, and it would be comparatively of little moment, how or where he got it. We should not ask what honours he had obtained, but as proofs of his progress. Let him have graduated at the most illustrious university, or have gained, through some mistake, its highest distinctions, and still be essentially deficient in mind or in accomplishment; and that fatal defect would sink into every parent's heart, as a heavy and unalleviated disappointment. And are such questions and considerations any less appropriate to the great school of life; whose entire course is an education for virtue, happiness, and heaven? "O God!" exclaims the Psalmist, "thou hast taught me from my youth."

Life, I repeat, is a school. The periods of life, are its terms; all human conditions are but its forms; all human employments, its lessons. Families are the primary departments of this moral education; the various circles of society, its advanced stages; kingdoms are its universities; the world is but the material structure, built for the administration of its teachings; and it is lifted up in the heavens and borne through its annual circuits, for no end but this.

Life, I say again, is a school: and all its periods, infancy, youth, manhood and age, have their appropriate tasks in this school.

With what an early care and wonderful apparatus,

does Providence begin the work of human education! An infant being is cast upon the lap of nature, not to be supported or nourished only, but to be instructed. The world is its school. All elements around, are its teachers. Long ere it is placed on the first form before the human master, it has been at school; insomuch that a distinguished statesman has said with equal truth and originality, that he had probably obtained more ideas by the age of five or six years, than he has acquired ever since. And what a wonderful ministration is it! What mighty masters are there for the training of infancy, in the powers of surrounding nature! With a finer influence than any human dictation, they penetrate the secret places of that embryo soul, and bring it into life and light. From the soft breathings of Spring to the rough blasts of Winter, each one pours a blessing upon its favourite child, expanding its frame for action, or fortifying it for endurance. You seek for celebrated schools and distinguished teachers for your children; and it is well. Or you cannot afford to give them these advantages, and you regret it. But consider what you have. Talk we of far-sought and expensive processes of education? That infant eye hath its master in the sun; that infant ear is attuned by the melodies and harmonies of the wide, the boundless creation. The goings on of the heavens and the earth, are the courses of childhood's lessons. The shows that are painted on the dome of the sky and on the uplifted mountains, and on the spreading plains and seas, are its pictured diagrams. Immensity, infinity, eternity, are its teachers. The great universe is the shrine, from which oracles, oracles by day and by night, are forever uttered. Well may it be said that "of such;" of beings so cared for, " is the kingdom of heaven." Well and fitly is it written of him, who comprehended the wondrous birth of humanity and the gracious and sublime providence of heaven over it, that " he took little children in his arms and blessed them."

So begins the education of man in the school of life. It were easy, did the time permit, to pursue it into its successive stages; into the period of youth, when the senses not yet vitiated, are to be refined into grace and beauty, and the soul is to be developed into reason and virtue; of manhood, when the strength of the ripened passions is to be held under the control of wisdom, and the matured energies of the higher nature, are to be directed to the accomplishment of worthy and noble ends; of age, which is to finish with dignity, the work begun with ardour; which is to learn patience in weakness, to gather up the fruits of experience into maxims of wisdom, to cause virtuous activity to subside into pious contemplation, and to gaze upon the visions of heaven, through the parting veils of earth.

But in the next place, life presents lessons in its various pursuits and conditions, in its ordinances and events. Riches and poverty, gayeties and sorrows, marriages and funerals, the ties of life bound or broken, fit and fortunate or untoward and painful, are all lessons. They are not only appointments, but they are lessons. They are not things which must be, but things which are meant. Events are not blindly and carelessly flung together, in a strange chance-medley: providence is not schooling one man, and another screening from the fiery trial of its lessons; it has no rich favourites nor poor victims; one event happeneth to all; one end, one design, concerneth, urgeth all men.

Hast thou been prosperous? Thou hast been at school; that is all; thou hast been at school. Thou thoughtest perhaps, that it was a great thing, and that thou wert some great one; but thou art only just a pupil. Thou thoughtest that thou wast master and hadst nothing to do but to direct and command; but I tell thee that there is a Master above thee; the Master of life; and that He looks not at thy splendid state nor thy many pretensions; not at the aids and appliances of thy learning; but simply at thy learning. As an earthly teacher puts the poor boy and the rich, upon the same form, and knows no difference between them but their progress; so it is with thee and thy poor neighbour. *What* then hast thou learnt from thy prosperity? This is the question that I am asking, that all men are asking, when any one has suddenly grown prosperous, or has been a long time so. And I have heard men say in a grave tone, "he cannot bear it! he has become passionate, proud, self-sufficient, and disagreeable." Ah! fallen, disgraced man! even in the world's account. But what, I say again, hast thou learnt from prosperity? Moderation, temperance, candour, modesty, gratitude to God, generosity to man? Well done, good and faithful! thou hast honour with heaven and with men. But what, again I say, hast thou learnt from thy prosperity? Selfishness, self-indulgence and sin; to forget or overlook thy less fortunate fellow; to forget thy God? Then wert thou an unworthy and dishonoured being, though thou hadst been nursed in the bosom of the proudest affluence, or hadst taken thy degrees from the lineage of an hundred noble descents; yes, as truly dishonoured, before the eye of heaven, though dwelling in splendour and luxury, as if thou wert lying, the victim of beggary and vice by the hedge or upon the dung-hill. It is the scholar, not the school, at which the most ordinary human equity looks; and let us not think that the equity of heaven will look beneath that lofty mark.

But art thou, to whom I speak, a poor man? Thou, too, art at school. Take care that thou learn, rather than complain. Keep thine integrity, thy candour and kindness of heart. Beware of envy; beware of bondage; keep thy self-respect. The body's toil is nothing. Beware of the mind's drudgery and degradation. I do not say, be always poor. Better thy condition if thou canst. But be more anxious to better thy soul. Be willing, while thou art poor, patiently to learn the lessons of poverty; fortitude, cheerfulness, contentment, trust in God. The tasks I know are hard; deprivation, toil, the care of children. Thou must wake early: thy children, perhaps, will wake thee; thou canst not put them away from thee to a distant nursery. Fret not thyself because of this; but cheerfully address thyself to thy task; learn patience, calmness, self-command, disinterestedness, love. With these the humblest dwelling may be hallowed, and so made dearer and nobler, than the proudest mansion of self-indulgent ease and luxury. But above all things, if thou art poor, beware that thou lose not thine independence. Cast not thyself, a creature poorer than poor, an indolent, helpless, despised beggar, on the kindness of others. Choose to have God for thy master, rather than man. Escape not from his school, either by dishonesty or alms-taking, lest thou fall into that state worse than disgrace, where thou shalt have no respect for thyself. Thou mayest come out of that school; yet beware that thou come not out as a truant, but as a noble scholar. The world itself doth not ask of the candidates for its honours, whether they studied in a palace or a cottage, but what they have acquired and what they are; and heaven, let us again be assured, will ask no inferior title to its glories and rewards.

Again, the entire social condition of humanity is a school. The ties of society affectingly teach us to love one another. A parent, a child, a husband or wife or associate *without love,* is nothing but a cold marble image; or rather a machine, an annoyance, a something in the way to vex and pain us. The social relations not only teach love, but demand it. Show me a society, no matter how intelligent, and accomplished and refined, but where love is not; where there is ambition, jealousy and distrust, not simplicity, confidence and kindness; and you show me an unhappy society. All will complain of it. Its punctilious decorum, its polished insincerity, its "threatening urbanity," gives no satisfaction to any of its members. What is the difficulty? What does it want? I answer, it wants love: and if it will not have that, it must suffer; and it ought to suffer.

But the social state, also powerfully teaches modesty and meekness. All cannot be great; and nobody may reasonably expect all the world to be engaged with lauding his merits. All cannot be great; and we have happily fallen upon times, when none can be distinguished as a few have been in the days of semi-barbarous ignorance. All cannot be great; for then nobody were. The mighty mass of human claims presses down all individual ambition. Were it not so, it were not easy to see where that ambition would stop. Well that it be schooled to reason; and society, without knowing it, is an efficient master for that end. Is any one vexed and sore under neglect? Does he walk through the street unmarked, and say, that he deserves to be saluted oftener and with more respect? Does the pang of envy shoot through his heart, when notice is bestowed on others, whom he thinks less worthy than he is? Perhaps, society *is* unjust to him? What then? What shall he do? What can he do, but learn humility and patience and quietness? Perhaps the lesson is roughly and unkindly given. Then must society, through its very imperfection, teach us to be superior to its opinion; and our care must be, not to be cynical and bitter, but gentle, candid and affectionate still.

Society is doubtless often right in its neglect or its condemnation; but certainly it is sometimes wrong. It seems to be the lot, the chance, the fortune, the accident of some to be known, admired, and celebrated. Adulation and praise are poured out at their feet while they live, and upon their tomb when they die. But thousands of others intrinsically just as interesting, with sentiments that mount as high on earth, and will flourish as fair in heaven, live unpraised and die unknown. Nay, and the very delicacy of some minds forbids their being generally known and appreciated. Tact, facility, readiness, conversation, personal recommendations, manners and connexions, help on some; and all these may be wanting to minds that have none the less worth and beauty. Who then would garner up his heart in the opinion of this world? Yet neither let us hate it; but let its imperfection minister to our perfection.

There are also broken ties; and sometimes the holiest ties wear themselves out; like imperfect things, alas! as they are. What, *then*, is to be learnt? I answer, a great lesson. What is to be done? A great duty. To be just; to be true; to cherish a divine candour; to make the best of that which seems not well; to pour not vinegar upon the galling chain, but the oil of gentleness and forbearance. So shall many a wound be healed; and the hearts shall be knit together in a better bond than that of hasty impulse; the bond of mutual improvement, strengthening mutual love.

But not to insist more at large upon the disciplinary character of all the conditions of life and society, let us consider, for a moment farther, some of its events and ordinances.

Amidst all the gayety and splendour of life there is a dark spot; over its brightest career, there comes a sudden and overshadowing cloud; in the midst of its loud and restless activity there is a deep pause and an awful silence; what a lesson is death!—death, that stops the warm current and the vital breath, and freezes mortal hearts in fear and wonder; death, that quells all human power, and quenches all human pride; death, "the dread teacher," the awful admonisher, that tells man of this life's frailty, and of a judgment to come. What a lesson is death! Stern, cold, inexorable, irresistible—the collected might of the world cannot stay it, nor ward it off; the breath that is parting from the lips of king, or beggar, the breath that scarcely stirs the hushed air—that little breath—the wealth of empires cannot buy it, nor bring it back for a moment. What a lesson is this to proclaim our own frailty, and a power beyond us! It is a fearful lesson; it is never familiar. That which lays its hands upon all, walks through the earth, as a dread mystery. Its mandate falls upon the ear in as fearful accents now, as when it said to the first man, "thou shalt die! dust thou art, and unto dust shalt thou return." It is a universal lesson. It is read everywhere. Its message comes every year, every day. The years past are filled with its sad and solemn mementos; and could a prophet now stand in the midst of us and announce the future; to more than one of us, would he say, "set thy house in order; for this year thou shalt die." Yes, death is a teacher. I have seen upon the wall of our school-rooms, the diagram, that sets forth some humble theorem; but what a hand-writing is traced by the finger of death upon the walls of every human habitation! And what does it teach? Duty; to act our part well; to fulfil the work assigned us. Other questions, questions of pride and ambition and pleasure, may press themselves upon a man's life; but when he is dying, when he is dead, there is but one question—but one question: *has he lived well?* I have seen an old man upon his bier; and I said, "hath he done the work of many years faithfully? hath he come to his end like a shock of corn fully ripe? Then all is well. There is no evil in death, but what life makes." I have seen one fall amidst life's cares, manly or matronly, and when the end came, not like a catastrophe, not as unlooked for; when it came as that which had been much thought upon and always prepared for; when I saw the head meekly bowed to the visitation or the eye raised in calm bright hope to heaven, or when the confidence of long intimate friendship knows that it would be raised there though the kind veil of delirium be spread over it; I said, "the work is done, the victory is gained; thanks be to God who giveth that victory through our Lord Jesus Christ." I have seen an infant form, sweetly reposing on its last couch, as if death had lost all its terrors, and had become as one of the cherubim of heaven; and I said, "ah! how many live so, that they will yet wish that they had died, with that innocent child!"

Among our Christian ordinances, Brethren, there is one that celebrates the victory over death; and there is one, that is appropriate to the beginning of life.

They are both teachers. Baptismal waters, the emblems of a purity received from God and to be watched over for God; the consecration unto obedience to the great truths of Christianity; to the doctrine of the Father, and the Son, and the Holy Ghost; these teach us, parents, of a charge to be solemnly kept, of duties to be faithfully rendered. The sacramental table; what is it but an altar, set up amidst the realm of death, to the hope of everlasting life? To keep us in mind of him who conquered death, and brought life and immortality to light; who gave his life a ransom for many; who became a curse for us that we might be redeemed from the curse of sin; who died that we might live forever; lo! these symbols that are set forth from time to time in the house of God, in the school of Christ! Touching memorials of pain and sorrow and patient endurance! Blessed omens, on God's altar, of peace and forgiveness and glorious victory!

Such, my friends, are some of the lessons of the school of life. Indulge me in one or two observations on the general character of this school, and I shall have completed my present design.

Life is a finely attempered, and at the same time a very trying school.

It is finely attempered; that is, it is carefully adjusted, in all its arrangements and tasks, to man's powers and passions. There is no extravagance in its teachings; nothing is done for the sake of present effect. It excites man, but it does not excite him too much. Indeed, so carefully adjusted are all things to this raging love of excitement, so admirably fitted to hold this passion in check, and to attemper all things to what man can bear, that I cannot help seeing in this feature of life, intrinsic and wonderful evidence of a wise and over-ruling Order. Men often complain that life is dull, tame and drudging. But how unwisely were it arranged, if it were all one gala-day of enjoyment or transport! And when men make their own schools of too much excitement, their parties, controversies, associations and enterprises; how soon do the heavy realities of life fasten upon the chariot-wheels of success when they are ready to take fire, and hold them back to a moderated movement!

Everything, I say, is tempered in the system of things to which we belong. The human passions, and the correspondent powers of impression which man possesses, are all kept within certain limits. I think sometimes of angel forms on earth; of a gracefulness and beauty more than mortal; of a flash or a glance of the eye in the eloquent man, that should rend and inflame a thousand hearts, as lightning does the gnarled oak; but do we not see that for the sensitive frame of man, enough excitement is already provided; that the moderated tone of things is all man's ear could bear; the softened and shaded hue, enough for his eye; the expressions of countenance and gesture, such as they are, enough for his heart! Nay, how often is the excitement of thought and feeling so great, that but for the interruptions of humble cares and trifles—the interpositions of a wise providence—the mind and frame would sink under them entirely! It would seem delightful, no doubt, in the pilgrimage of life, to walk through unending galleries of paintings and statues; but human life is not such; it is a school.

It is a trying school. It is a school, very trying to faith, to endurance and to endeavour. There are mysteries in it. As to the pupil in a human school, there are lessons of which he does not understand the full intent and bearing, as he is obliged to take some things on trust; so it is in the great school of providence. There are hard lessons to be got in this school. As the pupil is often obliged to bend all his faculties to the task before him, and tears sometimes fall on the page he is studying; so it is in the school of God's providence; there are hard lessons in it.

In short, the whole course of human life is a conflict with difficulties; and if rightly conducted, a progress in improvement. In both these respects, man holds a position peculiar, and distinct from that of the animal races. They are *not* at school. They *never* improve. With them too, all is facility; while with man comparatively, all is difficulty. Look at the ant-hill, or the hive of bees. See how the tenant of the one, is provided with feet, so constructed that he can run all over his house, outside and inside—no heavy and toilsome steps required to go upward or downward; and how the wings of the other, enable him to fly through the air, and achieve the journey of days in an hour. Man's steps compared with these, are the steps of toilsome endeavour.

Why is this so? Why is man clothed with this cumbrous mass of flesh? Because it is a more perfect instrument for the mind's culture, though that end is not to be wrought out without difficulty. Why are his steps slow and toilsome? Because they are the steps of improvement. Why is he at school? That he may learn. Why is the lesson hard? That he may rise high on the scale of advancement.

Nor is it ever too late for him to learn. This is a distinct consideration; but let me dwell a moment upon it in close. Nor, I say, is it ever too late for man to learn. If any man thinks that his time has gone by, let me take leave to contradict that dangerous assumption. Life is a school; the whole of life. There never comes a time, even amidst the decays of age, when it is fit to lay aside the eagerness of acquisition or the cheerfulness of endeavour. I protest utterly against the common idea of growing old. I hold that it is an unchristian, a heathen idea. It may befit those who expect to lay down and end their being in the grave, but not those who look upon the grave as the birth-place of immortality. I look for old age as, saving its infirmities, a cheerful and happy time. I think that the affections are often full as warm then, as they ever are. Well may the affections of piety be so! They are approaching near to the rest that remaineth; they almost grasp the prize that shall crown them; they are ready to say, with aged Simeon, "now let thy servant depart." The battle is almost fought; the victory is near at hand. "Why,"—does any one still ask—"why does the battle press hard to the very end? Why is it ordained for man that he shall walk, all through the course of life, in patience and strife, and sometimes in darkness?" Because from patience is to come perfection. Because, from strife, is to come triumph. Because, from the dark cloud, is to come the lightning-flash, that opens the way to eternity!

Christian! hast thou been faithful in the school of life? Art thou faithful to all its lessons? Or hast thou, negligent man! been placed in this great school, only to learn nothing, and hast not cared whether thou didst learn or not. Have the years passed over thee, only to witness thy sloth and indifference? Hast thou been zealous to acquire every thing but virtue, but the favour of thy God?

But *art* thou faithful, Christian? God help thee to be yet more so, in years to come. And remember for thine encouragement, what is written. "These things saith the first and the last, who was dead and is alive; I know thy works and tribulation and poverty, (but thou art rich;) fear none of those things which thou shalt suffer; be faithful unto death, and I will give thee a crown of life."

XV.

ON THE VALUE OF LIFE.

(Preached on New-Year's day.)

AND JOB SPARE AND SAID, LET THE DAY PERISH, WHEREIN I WAS BORN.—
Job iii. 2—3.

THERE is a worldly habit of viewing this life, and especially of depreciating its value, against which, in this discourse, I wish to contend. It is the view of life which many of the heathens entertained, and which better became them, than those who hold the faith of Christians. "When we reflect," says one of the Grecian sages, "on the destiny that awaits man on earth, we ought to bedew his cradle with our tears." Job's contempt of life, so energetically expressed in the chapter from which my text is taken, was of the same character. We may observe, however, that Job's contempt of life, consisted not with the views entertained by the children of the ancient dispensation, and was emphatically rebuked, in common with all his impious complaints, in the sequel of that affecting story. The birth of a child among the Hebrews was hailed with joy, and its birth-day was made a festival.

But there are times and seasons, events and influences in life, which awaken in many, sentiments similar to those of Job, and which require to be considered.

The sensibility of youth sometimes takes this direction. It is true, indeed, that, to the youthful mind, life for a while is filled with brightness and hope. It is the promised season of activity and enjoyment, of manly independence, of successful business, or of glorious ambition; the season of noble enterprises and lofty attainments. There is a time, when the youthful fancy is kindling with the anticipations of an ideal world; when it is thinking of friendship and honour of another sort than those which are commonly found in the world; when its promised mansion is the abode of perfect happiness, and its paths as they stretch into life, seem to it as the paths that shine brighter and brighter forever.

But over all these glowing expectations, there usually comes, sooner or later, a dark eclipse; and it is in the first shock of disappointed hope, before the season of youth is yet fully past, that we are probably exposed to take the most opposite and disconsolate views of life. It is here that we find real, in opposition to factitious sentimentalism. Before this great shock to early hope comes, the sentimental character is apt to be affectation, and afterwards it is liable to be misanthropy. But now it is a genuine and ingenuous sorrow, at finding life so different from what it expected. There is a painful and unwelcome effort to give up many cherished habits of thinking about it. The mind encounters the chilling selfishness of the world, and it feels the miserable insufficiency of the world to satisfy its longings after happiness; and life loses many of the bright hues, that had gilded its morning season. Indeed, when we take into account the unwonted and multiplied cares of this period, the want of that familiarity and habit which renders the ways and manners of life easy, the difficulties and embarrassments that beset the youthful adventurer, the anxiety about establishing a character and taking a place in the world, and above all, perhaps, the want of self-discipline; when we take all this into the account, to say nothing of the freshness of disappointment, we may well doubt whether the period of entrance into life, is the happiest, though it is commonly looked upon as such. It is not, perhaps, till men proceed farther in the way, that they are prepared, either rightly to estimate or fully to enjoy it. And it is worthy of notice in this connection, that those diseases which spring from mental anxiety, are accounted, by physicians, to be the most prevalent between the ages of twenty and forty.

Manhood arrives at a conclusion unfavourable to life, by a different process. It is not the limited view occasioned by disappointment, that brings it to think poorly of life; but it assumes to hold the larger view taken by experience and reflection. It professes to have proved this life, and found it little worth. It has deliberately made up its mind, that life is far more miserable than happy. Its employments, it finds, are tedious, and its schemes are baffled. Its friendships are broken, or its friends are dead. Its pleasures pall and its honours fade. Its paths are beaten and familiar and dull. It has grasped the good of life; and every thing grasped loses half of its charm; in the hand of possession everything is shrivelled and shrunk to insignificance.

Is *this manhood*, then, sad or sentimental? No; farthest possible from it. Sentiment, it holds to be ridiculous; sadness, absurd. It smiles, in recklessness. It is merry, in despite. It sports away a life, not worth a nobler thought, or else it wears away a life, not worth a nobler aim, than to get tolerably through it. This is a worldly manhood; and no wonder that its estimate of the value of existence is low and earthly.

Poetry has often ministered to a state of mind, loftier indeed, but of alike complexion. "Life," says the Grecian Pindar, "is the dream of a shadow."

"What," says the melancholy Kirk White—

> "What is this passing life?
> A peevish April day:
> A little sun, a little rain,
> And then night sweeps along the plain,
> And all things fade away."

The melancholy of Byron is of a darker complexion; one might anticipate, indeed, that his misanthropy, as well as gloom, would repel every reader; and yet a critic has observed that this is the very quality which has caught and held the ear of the sympathizing world. If the world does sympathize with it, it is time that the Christian preacher should raise his voice against it. One may justly feel, indeed, for the sufferings as well as perversions of that extraordinary mind; but its skepticism and scorn must not be suffered to fling their shadows across the world, without rebuke or remonstrance. Its sufferings, indeed, are a striking proof, which the Christian teacher might well adduce, of the tendency of earthly passion and unbelief to darken all the way of human life.

The pulpit, also, I must allow, has fallen, under the charge of leaning to the dark side of things. It may be said, perhaps, that if its instructions are to have any bias, it is expedient that it should lean to the dark side. But error or mistake is not to be vindicated by its expediency, or its power to affect the mind. And its expediency, in fact, if not its power, in this case, is to be doubted. Men of reflection and discernment are, and ought to be, dissatisfied with disproportionate and extravagant statements, made with a view to support the claims of an ascetic piety, or a cynical morality.

And one mistake, the preacher may find is to the hearer, an intrenchment strong, against a hundred of his arguments.

It is true, also, that religious men in general, have been accustomed to talk gloomily of the present state. I do not mean such religious men as the wise and holy saints of old. Let the rejoicing apostles, rejoicing in the midst of the greatest calamities; let the mild cheerfulness of their Master, stand as monuments against the perversions of later times. It has strangely come to be thought a mark of great piety towards God to disparage, if not to despise, the state which he has ordained for us; and the claims of this world have been absurdly set up, not in comparison only, but in competition, with the claims of another; as if both were not parts of one system; as if a man could not make the best of this world and of another at the same time; as if we should learn to think better of other works and dispensations of God, by thinking meanly of these. Jesus and his apostles did not teach us to contemn our present condition. They taught that every creature and every appointment of God is good, and to be received thankfully. They did not look upon life as so much time lost; they did not regard its employments as trifles unworthy of immortal beings; they did not tell their followers to fold their arms as if in disdain of their state and species; but it is evident that they looked soberly and cheerfully upon the world, as the theatre of worthy action, of exalted usefulness, and of rational and innocent enjoyment.

But I am considering the disparaging views of life; and against these views, whether sentimental, worldly, poetical or religious, I must contend. I firmly maintain, that with all its evils, life is a blessing. There is a presumptive argument for this, of the greatest strength. To deny that life is a blessing, is to destroy the very basis of all religion, natural and revealed; and the argument I am engaged upon therefore, well deserves attention. For the very foundation of all religion, is laid in the belief that God is good. But if life is an evil and a curse, there can be no such belief, rationally entertained. The Scriptures do not prove, nor pretend to prove, that God is good. They assume that truth as already certain. But what makes it certain? Where does, or can the proof come from? Obviously, from this world, and from nowhere else. Nowhere else can our knowledge extend, to gather proof. Nay more, I say, the proof must come from this *life*, and from nothing else. For it avails not, if life itself is doomed to be unhappy—it avails not to the argument to say that this world is fair and glorious. It avails not to say that this outward frame of things, this vast habitation of life, is beautiful. The architecture of an Infirmary may be beautiful, and the towers of a prison may be built on the grandest scale of architectural magnificence; but it would little avail the victims of sickness or bondage. And so if this life is a doomed life, doomed by its very conditions to sufferings far greater than its pleasures; if it is a curse and not a blessing; if sighs and groans must rise from it, more frequent and loud, than voices of joy and gladness, it will avail but little that heaven spreads its majestic dome over our misery; that the mountain walls, which echo our griefs, are clothed with grandeur and might; or that the earth, which bears the burthen of our woes, is paved with granite and marble, or covered with verdure and beauty.

Let him then, who says that this life is not a blessing; let him who levels his satire at humanity and human existence, as mean and contemptible; let him who with the philosophic pride of a Voltaire or a Gibbon looks upon this world as the habitation of a miserable race, fit only for mockery and scorn, or who with the religious melancholy of Thomas a Kempis or of Brainard, overshadows this world with the gloom of his imagination, till it seems a dungeon or a prison, which has no blessing to offer but escape from it; let all such consider that they are extinguishing the primal light of faith and hope and happiness. If life is not a blessing, if the world is not a goodly world, if residence in it is not a favoured condition, then religion has lost its basis, truth its foundation in the goodness of God; then it matters not what else is true or not true; speculation is vain and faith is vain; and all that pertains to man's highest being, is whelmed in the ruins of misanthropy, melancholy and despair.

The argument in this view is well deserving of attention. Considered as a merely speculative point, it is nevertheless one on which every thing hangs. And this indeed is the consideration which I have been stating; that the whole superstructure of religious truth is based upon this foundation truth—that life is a blessing.

And that this is not a mere assumption, I infer in the next place, from experience. And there are two points in this experience to be noticed. First, the love of life proves it is a blessing. If it is not, why are men so attached to it? Will it be said, that it is "the dread of something after death," that binds man to life? But make the case a fair one for the argument: say, for instance, that the souls of men sleep, after death, till the resurrection; and would not almost every man rather live on, during the intermediate space, than to sink to that temporary oblivion?

But to refer in the next place to a consideration still

plainer and less embarrassed; why are we so attached to our local situation in life, to our home, to the spot that gave us birth, or to any place, no matter how unsightly or barren,—though it were the rudest mountain or rock,—on which the history of years had been written? Will it be said, that it is habit which endears our residence? But what kind of habit? A habit of being miserable? The question needs no reply. Will you refer me to the pathetic story of the aged prisoner of the Bastile, who, on being released and coming forth into the world, desired to return to his prison; and argue from this, that a man may learn to love, even, the glooms of a dungeon, provided they become habitual? But why did that aged prisoner desire to return? It was not because he loved the cold shadow of his prison-walls: but it was, as the story informs us, because his friends were gone from the earth; it was because no living creature knew him, that the world was darker to him, than the gloomy dungeons of the Bastile. It shows how dear are the ties of kindred and society. It shows how strong and how sweet are those social affections, which we never appreciate, till we are cut off from their joys; which glide from heart to heart, as the sunbeams pass unobserved, in the daylight of prosperity; but if a ray of that social kindness visits the prison of our sickness and affliction, it comes to us like a beam of heaven. And though we had worn out a life in confinement, we go back again to meet that beam of heaven, the smile of society; and if we do not find it, we had rather return to the silent walls that know us, than to dwell in a world that knows us not.

"But after all, and as a matter of fact, how many miseries," it may be said, "are bound up with this life, too deeply interwoven with it, and too keenly felt, to allow it to be called a favoured and happy life! Besides evils of common occurrence and account, besides sickness and pain and poverty, besides disappointment and bereavement and sorrow, how many evils are there that are not embraced in the common estimate; evils that are secret and silent, that dwell deep in the recesses of life, that do not come forth to draw the public gaze or to awaken the public sympathy! How many are there who never tell their grief; how many who spread a fair and smiling exterior over an aching heart!"

Alas! it is but too easy to make out a strong statement: and yet the very strength of the statement, the strong feeling, at least, with which it is made, disproves the cynical argument. The truth is, and it is obvious, that misery makes a greater impression upon us, than happiness. Why? Because, misery is not the habit of our minds. It is a strange and unwonted guest, and we are more conscious of its presence. Happiness—not to speak now of any very high quality or entirely satisfying state of mind, but only of a general easiness, cheerfulness and comfort—happiness, I say, dwells with us, and we forget it; it does not excite us; it does not disturb the order and course of our thoughts. All our impressions about affliction, on the other hand, show that it is more rare, and at the same time, more regarded. It creates a sensation and stir in the world. When death enters among us, it spreads a groan through our dwellings; it clothes them with unwonted and sympathizing grief. Thus, afflictions are like epochs in life. We remember them as we do the storm and earthquake, because they are out of the common course of things. They stand like disastrous events in a table of chronology, recorded because they are extraordinary; and with whole periods of prosperity between. Thus do we mark out and signalize the times of calamity ; but how many happy days pass ; unnoted periods in the table of life's chronology ; unrecorded either in the book of memory or in the scanty annals of our thanksgiving ? How many happy months are swept beneath the silent wing of time, and leave no name nor record in our hearts ! How little are we *able*, much as we may be disposed, to call up from the dim remembrances of the year that is just ended, the peaceful moments, the easy sensations, the bright thoughts, the movements of kind and blessed affections, in which life has flowed on, bearing us almost unconsciously upon its bosom, because it has borne us calmly and gently ! Sweet moments of quietness and affection ! glad hours of joy and hope ! days, ye many days begun and ended in health and happiness ! times and seasons of heaven's gracious beneficence ! stand before us yet again, in the light of memory, and command us to be thankful and to prize as we ought, the gift of life.

But, my brethren, I must not content myself with a bare defence of life as against a skeptical or cynical spirit, or as against the errors and mistakes of religion. I must not content myself with a view of the palpable and acknowledged blessings of life. Life is more than what is palpable, or often acknowledged. I contend against the cynical and the superstitious disparagement of life, not alone as wrong and as fatal indeed to all religion ; but I contend against it as fatal to the highest improvement of life. I say, that life is not only good, but that it was made to be glorious. Ay, and it has been glorious in the experience of millions. The glory of all human virtue arrays it. The glory of sanctity and beneficence and heroism is upon it. The crown of a thousand martyrdoms is upon its brow.

Through this visible and sometimes darkened life, it was intended that the brightness of the soul should shine; and that it should shine through all its surrounding cares and labours. The humblest life which any one of us leads may be what has been expressively denominated "the life of God in the soul." It may hold a felt connection with its infinite source. It may derive an inexpressible sublimity from that connection. Yes, my Brethren, there may be something of God in our daily life; something of might in this frail inner man; something of immortality in this momentary and transient being.

This mind—I survey it with awe, with wonder—encompassed with flesh, fenced around with barriers of sense; yet it breaks every bound, and stretches away, on every side, into infinity. It is not upon the line only of its eternal duration, that it goes forth, forth from this day of its new annual period, through the periods of immortality; but its thoughts, like diverging rays, spread themselves abroad and far, far into the boundless, the immeasurable, the infinite. And these diverging rays may be like cords to lift up to heaven. What a glorious thing, then, is this life! To know its wonderful Author; to bring down wisdom from the eternal stars; to bear upward its homage, its gratitude, its love to the Ruler of all worlds; what glory in the created universe is there, surpassing this? "Thou crownest it, says the Psalmist, thou crownest it with glory and honour; thou hast made it a little lower than the angelic life."

Am I asked, then, what is life? I say, in answer, that it is good. God saw and pronounced that it was good, when he made it. Man feels that it is good when he preserves it. It is good in the unnumbered sources of happiness around it. It is good in the ten thousand buoyant and happy affections within it. It is good in its connection with infinite goodness, and in its hope of infinite glory beyond it. True, our life is frail in its earthly state, and it has often bowed down with earthly burthens; but still it endures and revives and flourishes; still it is redeemed from destruction, and crowned with loving kindness and tender mercy. Frail too, and yet strong is it, in its heavenly nature. The immortal is clothed with mortality; and the incorruptible with corruption. It is like an instrument formed for heavenly melody; whose materials were taken indeed, from the mouldering and unsightly forest; but lo! the hand of the artificer has been upon it; it is curiously wrought; it is fearfully and wonderfully made; it is fashioned for every tone of gladness and triumph. It may be relaxed, but it can be strung again. It may send forth a mournful strain; but it is formed also for the music of heavenly joy. Even its sadness is "pleasing and mournful to the soul." Even suffering is hallowed and dear. Life has that value, that even misery cannot destroy it. It neutralizes grief, and makes it a source of deep and sacred interest. Ah! holy hours of suffering and sorrow; hours of communion with the great and triumphant Sufferer; who that has passed through your silent moments of prayer and resignation and trust, would give you up, for all the brightness of prosperity?

Am I still asked what is life? I answer, that it is a great and sublime gift. Those felicitations with which this renewed season of it is welcomed, are but a fit tribute to its value, and to the gladness which belongs to it. "Happy," says the general voice, "happy New-Year!" to all who live to see it. Life is felt to be a great and gracious boon, by all who enjoy its light; and this is not too much felt. It is the wonderful creation of God; and it cannot be too much admired. It is light sprung from void darkness; it is power waked from inertness and impotence; it is being created from nothing; well may the contrast enkindle wonder and delight. It is a stream from the infinite and overflowing goodness; and from its first gushing forth to its mingling with the ocean of eternity, that goodness attends it. Yes: life, despite of all that cynics or sentimentalists say, is a great and glorious gift. There is gladness in its infant voices. There is joy in the buoyant step of its youth. There is deep satisfaction in its strong maturity. There is holy peace in its quiet age. There is good for the good; there is virtue for the faithful; there is victory for the valiant. There is spirituality for the spiritual; and, there is, even in this humble life, an infinity for the boundless in desire. There are blessings upon its birth; there is hope in its death; and there is—to consummate all—there is eternity in its prospect.

As I have discoursed upon this theme, it is possible that some may have thought that it has nothing to do with religion; that it is a subject merely for fine sentiments and for nothing more. Let me tell such a thinker that this subject has not only much to do with religion every way, but that it furnishes, in fact, a test of our religion. To the low-minded, debased and sensual, this life must, doubtless, be something very poor, indifferent and common-place; it must be a beaten path, a dull scene, shut in on every side, by the earthly, palpable, and gross. But break down the barriers of sense; open the windows of faith; fling wide the gates that darken the sensual world, and let the light of heaven pour in upon it; and then what is this life? How changed is it! how new! a new heavens, indeed, and a new earth. Yes, this earth which binds one man in chains, is to the other, the starting place, the goal of immortality. This earth which buries one man in the rubbish of dull cares and wearying vanities, is to the other, the lofty mount of meditation, where heaven and infinity and eternity are spread before him and around him. Yes, my friend, the life thou leadest, the life thou thinkest of, is the interpreter of thine inward being. Such as life is to thee, such thou art. If it is low and mean, and base, if it is a mere money-getting or pleasure-seeking or honour-craving life, so art thou. Be thou lofty-minded, pure and holy; and life shall be to thee the beginning of heaven, the threshold of immortality.

XVI.

LIFE'S CONSOLATIONS IN VIEW OF DEATH.

JESUS SAID UNTO HER, I AM THE RESURRECTION AND THE LIFE.—John xi. 25

These words, my brethren, so stupendous in their import, so majestic in their tone; when and where were they uttered? They were uttered in a world of the dying; in a world which is the tomb of all past generations; in a world from whose dreary caverns, from whose dark catacombs, and alike from whose proud mausoleums and towering pyramids, no word ever issued that spake of any thing but death. They were uttered in an hour, when bereavement, dimmed with tears and fainting with sorrow, was sighing for help more than human.

It was at Bethany. You remember the affecting story of Mary, and Martha her sister, and of Lazarus their brother. So simply and truly is it told, that it seems as if it were the relation of what had taken place in any village around us. "Now a certain man, named Lazarus of Bethany, was sick." How does such an event, when it becomes sufficiently marked with peril to attract attention, spread anxiety and apprehension through a whole neighbourhood. Life pauses, and is suspended on the result. "Lazarus was sick." What fears, watchings, and agonies of solicitude, hover around the sick man's couch; none but the inmates of his dwelling can know. It was in such an emergency that Mary and Martha, fearful and troubled, sent a message to their chief comforter and friend, saying, "behold, he whom thou lovest, is sick." Jesus, for reasons perhaps beyond our knowledge, does not immediately answer the call of distress. He remains two days in the same place. Then the dreaded event had taken place; all was over; and he calmly says to his disciples, "our friend Lazarus sleepeth." So does he contemplate death, not as a dread catastrophe, but as a quiet sleep; a sacred repose, succeeding the weary and troubled day of life. Beautifully says our great dramatist,

"After life's fitful fever, he sleeps well."

But so does it not appear to the bereaved and sorrowing sisters. They are plunged into the deepest distress. It is a time of mourning in that still and desolate house at Bethany. The dead is buried; but grief lives, and the hours pass in silent agony. The sympathizing neighbours from the village are still there; and many friends from Jerusalem are with the afflicted sisters to comfort them concerning their brother.

At length, the Master approaches. Martha, ever more alert and attentive to what is passing, first hearing of it, goes forth to meet him. Soon however she returns, and says to Mary, her sister, secretly, gives her a private intimation—how much passes in the dumb show, in whispers, where deep grief is!—she says, in a low tone, "the Master is come, and calleth for thee. And as soon as she heard that, she arose quickly and came unto him." The language of both when they met him is the same, turns upon the same point: "Lord, if thou hadst been here, our brother had not died." What natural and living truth is there, in this simple trait of feeling! How natural is it for the bereaved to think that if this or that had been done;

if this or that physician had been called; if some other course had been adopted, or some other plan or clime had favoured, the blow might have been averted. The thoughts all shrink from the awful certainty, revert to the possibility of its having been avoided; and catch at all possible suppositions to find relief. But the awful certainty nevertheless overwhelmed the mourning sisters; "the end had come; their brother was dead—was dead! no help now; no change to come over that still sleep;" so mourned they; and Jesus beholding their distress, groaned in spirit and was troubled. "Jesus wept." He was not one, who, with cold philosophy or misplaced rapture in his countenance, looked on bereavement and agony—looked on death. He was not one who forbade tears and sorrows. He was not one who approached the grave with an air of triumph, though he had gained a victory over it; but it is written, that "again groaning within himself, he came to the grave." No, humanity shudders, and trembles, and groans when it comes there; and may not, by any true religion, be denied these testimonies to its frailty.

But still there were words of soothing and comfort uttered by our Saviour on this occasion; and let us now turn to them and consider their import. "Martha said to Jesus, Lord, if thou hadst been here, my brother had not died. But I know that even now, whatsoever thou wilt ask of God, God will give it thee. Jesus saith unto her, thy brother shall rise again. Martha saith unto him, I know he shall rise again in the resurrection, at the last day." She had probably heard the doctrine of a future life from himself; but alas! that life seems far off; dim shadows spread themselves over the everlasting fields; they seem unreal to a person of Martha's turn of mind; she wants her brother again as he was but now by her side; she entertains some hope that Jesus will restore him; she says, "even now, I know that whatsoever thou wilt ask of God, God will give it thee." Jesus does not reply to this suggestion; he does not tell her whether her brother shall immediately come back to her; but utters himself in a more general and a grander truth. "I am the resurrection and the life; he that believeth in me, though he were dead, yet shall he live; and whosoever liveth and believeth in me shall never die; believest thou this?" As if he had said, be not too curious nor anxious in your thoughts, but confide, Martha, in me. You believe in a future resurrection, or renewal of life; you hope for the immediate resurrection of your brother; but be satisfied with this, "I am the Resurrection;" all that resurrection, renewal of life, heavenly happiness means, is embodied, consummated, fulfilled in me. Nay, it is not some future return to being of which I speak; he that liveth and believeth in me, shall never die. Already, he hath begun to live immortally. Death is for the body; but for that soul, no death. Its affections are in their very nature immortal; and have in them the very elements of undecaying happiness.

Let us attend a moment to the two parts of this instruction; what our Saviour uttered as already the belief of Martha; and what he added in the emphatic declaration, "I am the Resurrection and the Life."

"Thy brother shall live again"—thy brother! Not some undefined spirituality, not some new and strange being shall go forth beyond the mortal bourne; but life—life, in its character, its affections, its spiritual identity, such as it is here; thy *brother* shall rise again." He is not lost to thee; he shall not be so spiritually changed as to be forever lost to thee. On some other shore—as if he had only gone to another hemisphere, instead of another world; on some other shore, thou shalt find him again—find thy brother. Thus much must have been taught, or there had been no pertinency, no comfort in the teaching. To have only said that in the eternal revolutions and metamorphoses of being, life, existence should in some sense be continued, or that all souls should be re-absorbed into the Parent Soul, would have been nothing, to this mourning sister. Without conscious identity, indeed, without continued existence, a future life has no intelligible meaning.; and certainly without it, there could be no such thing as reward or retribution. And since the social element is an essential part of our nature, that element must be found in a nature which is the same: and that being so, to suppose that friends should meet and commune together, without recognition, is as absurd, as it would be unsatisfactory. Most clearly—to confine ourselves to the case before us—such a promise of future existence, that is, of a vague, indefinite, unremembering existence, would be no comfort to sorrowing friendship. To individual expectation it would be something, but to bereaved affection, nothing. It is to such sorrow, one of the bitterest in this world—that of a sister left alone in the world—that Jesus speaks; and he says, "thy brother shall live again.'

"Thy brother shall live again." What words are these to be uttered—amidst the wrecks of time, the memorials of buried nations, the earth-mounds swelling far and wide above the silent dust of all that has ever lived and breathed in the visible creation! Whence comes such stupendous, such amazing words as these? From beyond the regions of all visible life, they come. From the dark earth beneath us, no voice issues; from the shining walls of heaven, no angel forms beckon us. Silence, dust, death are here; no more: the earth entombs us, the heavens crush us, till those words come to us, heaven-sent, from the great realm of invisible life. O blessed revelation! Life there is for us, somewhere; I ask not where. I can wait God's time for that. Blessed fields there are somewhere in the great embosoming universe of God, that stretch onward and onward forever, and the happy walk there. There shall we find our lost ones, and be with them evermore. "Father," said our Saviour when he was about to depart, "I will that they whom thou hast given me, be with me, where I am." Shall that prayer be answered? Then shall there be a glorious fellowship of good men with Jesus and with one another. Are we not sometimes when we think of this, like Paul, "in a strait between two"—between the claims of friendship on earth and of friendship in heaven,—and ready to say, "for us it is better to depart and be with Christ?" Are we not ready to say, as the disciples did of Lazarus—when our beloved ones are gone from us—" let us go and die with them?"

And then in addition to this inexpressible comfort and hope, what is it that our Saviour so emphatically says to Martha? "I *am* the Resurrection and the Life." Something *in addition*, we may well suppose it must be. And I understand it to be this: He that believeth on me, that is, receiveth me—hath the spirit, the spiritual life that is in me, the same love of God, the same trust in God, is already living an immortal life. He shall never die. That in him which partakes of my inward life, shall never die. It is essentially immortal, and immortally blessed; and no dark eclipse shall come over it, between death and the resurrection, to bury it in the gloom of utter unconsciousness, or to cause it to wander like a shadow in the dim realms of an intermediate state. "I *am* the Resurrection. Thy brother who hath part in me, lives *now*, as truly as I live." As he says in another place, "I am the bread of life; he that eateth me, even he shall live through me;" so he says, "I am the Resurrection and the Life; and to him that is partner and partaker with me, belongeth not death, but only resurrection, continued life, life everlasting."

Let us now proceed to consider one or two further grounds for consolation that are suggested by this teaching of our Saviour.

That which he especially proposes to his bereaved friends at Bethany, is faith in him. It was a faith in him as the Saviour of the world, as one who was commissioned to bring life and immortality clearly to light, as one who through his own death and resurrection should open the way to heaven. But we should not do justice to this sentiment of faith, if we did not regard it as something more than any mere view of him as Saviour; if we did not regard it as the most intimate participation of the spiritual life that was in him. That participation embraces, doubtless, general purity of heart and life, a humble resignation to God's will, a thoughtful consideration of the wise purposes and necessary uses of affliction; but especially it embraces as the sum and source of all, the love of God. Faith in Christ, is nothing more emphatically than it is the love of God, his Father. Upon nothing does he more earnestly insist, and upon this he especially insists as the pledge and the test of fidelity to him.

To this, then, let me particularly direct your attention as the most essential part of that faith which is **to** comfort us.

It is the love of God only that can produce a just sense of his love to us. It is only a deep and true sense of his love to us, that can assuage the wounds of our affliction. This results from the very nature of things. It is not a technical dogma, but a living and practical truth. It is not a truth merely for certain persons called Christians, who are supposed to understand this language; but it is a truth for all men. We suffer under the government of God. It is his will that has appointed to us change, trial, bereavement, sorrow, death. The dispensation therefore will be coloured to us throughout—it will be darkened or brightened all over, by our views of its great Ordainer. Ah! it is a doubt *here ;* it is some distrust or difficulty, or want of vital faith on this point, that often adds the bitterest sting to human affliction. When all is well with us, we can say that God is good, and think that we have some love to him; but when the blow of calamity or death falls upon our dearest possessions, strikes down innocent childhood, or lovely youth, or the needed maturity of all human virtue or source of all earthly help and comfort—strikes from our side, that which we could least of all spare; oh! it seems to us a cruel, cruel blow!—and we say, perhaps, in our distracted thoughts, " *is* God good, to inflict it upon us. *He* could have saved, and he did not; he would not. Why would he not? Does he love us; and yet afflict us so?—yet crush us, break us down, and blight all our hopes? Is this a loving dispensation?"

My friends, there is but one remedy for all this; **the** love, the true, pure, childlike love of God: such love and trust as Jesus felt; even as **he,** the smitten, afflicted, cast down, betrayed, crucified; who was urged, in the extremity of his sorrow to say, "Father, if it be possible, remove this cup from me;" yet immediately added, "Father, not my will, but thine be done." This is our example. This is our only salvation. Nothing but this love of God, can yield us comfort. If there is no ground for this, then there is no place for consolation in the universe. There may be enduring, there may be forgetting; but there can be no consolation. If there is ground for this love and trust, who in the day of trouble will not pray God to breathe it into his broken heart?

I have said that doubt, distrust, want of faith, is our difficulty. And yet, how *can* we doubt? How *can* the Infinite Being be any thing but good? What motive, what reason, what possibility I had almost said, can there be to Infinite power, Infinite sufficiency, to be any thing but good? How *can* we—except it be in some momentary paroxysm of grief—how, I say, *can* we doubt? How doubt, beneath these shining heavens; amidst the riches, the plenitude, the brightness and beauty of the whole creation; with capacities of thought, of improvement, of happiness in ourselves that almost transcend expression; nay, and with sorrows too, that proclaim the loss of objects so inexpressibly dear! Whence but from love in God, could have come a love in us so intense, so transporting, so full of joy and blessedness; nay, and so full too of pain and anguish? No! such a love in me assures me that it had its *origin* in love. Could the Being who made me intelligent, have been himself without intelligence? Nor could the Being want love, who has made me so to love, so to sorrow for what I love. By my very sorrows, then, I know that God loves me; I say not whether with approbation, but with an infinite kindness, an infinite pity. What *I* need is, but to *feel* it, to pray for that feeling, to meditate upon all, that should bring that feeling into my heart; to take refuge amidst my sorrows, in the assurance that God loves me; that he does not willingly grieve or afflict me; that he chastens me for my profiting; that he could not show so much love for me, by leaving me unchastened, untried, undisciplined. "We have had fathers of our flesh who chastened us"—put us to tasks, trials, griefs; "and we gave them reverence"—felt, amidst all, that they were good. "Shall we not much rather be in subjection to the Father of our spirits and live?" Great is the faith that must save us. It is a faith in the Infinite; a faith in the Infinite love of God!

From this faith arises another ground of consolation. It is, not only that all is well; but that in the great order of things, *that* which particularly concerns *us*—enters into our peculiar suffering, is well. Our case, perhaps, is bereavement, heavy and sorrowful bereavement. Is it a messenger of wrath? Is any one of its circumstances, of its peculiarities—so poignant and piercing to us—an indication of divine anger? Awful thought! Immitigable calamity, if it were so! But no; it is appointed in love. Can God do any thing for anger's sake? To me, it were not God, of whom this could be said. Let it be, that a *bad* man has died. Has God made him die, because he hated him? I believe it not. If he has lost his being, I believe that it is well that he has lost it. If he has gone to retribution, I believe it is well that he has gone to that retribution; that nothing could be better for him, being what it is. If *I* were that unhappy being, I would say, "let me be in the hands of the infinitely good God, rather than any where else." But if it is a good being that has gone from me, an innocent child, or one clothed with every lovely virtue, one whom Jesus loved as he loved the dear brother in Bethany; to what joys unspeakable has that being gone! In the bosom of God, in the bosom of infinite love, all with him is well. Could that departed one speak to us, that lovely and loving one, invested with the radiance and surrounded with the bliss of some heavenly land; would not the language be—" mourn not for me, or mourn not as having no hope. Dishonour not the good and blessed One, my Father and your Father, by any distrust or doubt. Mourn for me, remember me, as I too remember you, long for you; but mourn with humble patience and calm sustaining faith."

How is it with us, my brethren, in *this* world? and what, in contemplation of *death*, would we say to those that we shall leave behind us? " Grieve not for me," would not one say?—or "grieve not too much, when I am gone. I cannot bear that you should suffer that awful agony, that desolating sorrow, that is often seen in the house of mourning. Remembered I would be; oh! let me have a memorial in some living, affectionate hearts! I would never be forgotten; I would never have it felt that the tie with me is broken: but let the memory of me be calm, patient, sacred, gently sorrowing if need be, but yet ever partaking of the blessedness of that love which death cannot quench. Let not my name gather about it an awfulness or a sacredness, such that it may not be uttered in the places where I have lived; or if in the sanctuary where it is kept, there is a delicacy that forbids the easy utterance of it, still let it not be invested with gloom and sadness. Think of me when I am gone, as one who thought much on death; who had thoughts of it, more and greater than he could in the ordinary goings on of life, find fit occasion to utter. **If** you could wish that I had said more to you, on this and many other themes, yet give the confidence, that you must ask, for that secret world within us all, that world of a thousand tender thoughts and feelings, for which language has no expression. Think of me as still possessing those thoughts and feelings, as still the same to you, as one that loves you still; for death shall not destroy in us, that image of Christ, a pure and holy love. If I retain my consciousness, I must still think of you; with more than all the love I ever felt; it cannot be otherwise. And if I am to sleep till the resurrection, though my hope is far different: believing in Jesus, my hope is that I am already of the Resurrection; yet if it be so, that God has ordained that pause in my existence, it is surely for a wise purpose; it is doubtless best for me; and to the ever good and blessed will of God, I calmly and humbly submit myself: to that ever gracious will, I pray you to be patiently and cheerfully resigned. How much better is it than your will or mine! What boundless good may we not expect, from an Infinite Will, prompted by an Infinite Love! Lift up your lowly thoughts to this: lift them up to the heavenly regions, to the boundless universe, to the all-embracing eternity; and in these contemplations lose the too keen sense of this breathing hour of time, of this world of dust and shadows—and of brightness and beauty, too: for all is good; all in earth and in heaven, in time and eternity, is good."

Thus, I conceive, might a wise and good man, about to depart from this life, speak to those whom he was to leave behind him. And thus might those who have died in infant innocence; thus might angel-children speak from some brighter sphere. And if it were wisdom thus to speak, then let that wisdom sink into our hearts, and bring there its consolation. Perfect relief from suffering it cannot bring; sorrow we may, we must; many and bitter pains must we bear in this mortal lot; Jesus wept over such pains, and we may weep over them; but let us be wise; let us be trustful; let the love of God fill our hearts; let the heavenly consolation help us, all that it can. It can help us much. It is not mere breath of words to say that God is good, that all is right, all is well; all that concerns us is the care of Infinite Love. It is not a mere religious common-place, to say that submission, trust, love can help us. More than eye ever saw or the ear ever heard, or the worldly heart ever conceived, can a deep, humble, child-like, loving piety bring help and comfort in the hours of mortal sorrow and bitterness. *Believest* thou this? This was our Saviour's question to Martha, in her distress. "He that believeth on me, though he were dead, yet shall he live. And he that lieveth and believeth on me, shall never die. Believest thou this?" This humble-believing, this heart-believing, my friends, is what we need—must have—must seek. The breathing of the life of Jesus in us, the bright cloud around us, in which he walked, this can comfort us beyond all that we know, all that we imagine. May we find that comfort! Forlorn, forsaken; or deprived, destitute; or bereaved, broken-hearted; whatever be our strait or sorrow; may we find that comfort!

My Brethren, I have been communing now, with affliction. It is a holy and delicate office; and I have been afraid, when speaking with all the earnestness I felt, lest I should not speak with all the delicacy I ought; lest I should only add to grief, by touching its wound. But I felt that I was coming to meet sorrow;

I know that I often come to meet it here; it has of late, occupied much of my mind; and I could not refrain from offering my humble aid for its relief.

I reflected too that I was coming this morning, to this sacred table,* this altar reared for the comfort of all believing souls; reared by dying hands, to the resurrection, to the hope of everlasting life. It was the same night in which he was betrayed: it was when *he* was about to die, that Jesus set forth in the form of a feast, this solemn and cheering memorial of himself; and uttered many soothing and consoling words to his disciples. He did not build a tomb, by which to be remembered; but he appointed a feast of remembrance. He did not tell his disciples to put on sackcloth; but to clothe themselves with the recollections of him, as with the robe of immortality. Death indeed, was a dread to him; and he shrunk from it. It was a grief to his disciples; and he recognised it as such, and so dealt with it. But he showed to them a trust in God, a loving submission to the Father, that could stay the soul. He spoke of a victory over death. He assured them that man's last enemy was conquered. Here then amidst these memorials of death, let us meditate upon the life everlasting. Let us carry our thoughts to that world where Christ is, and where he prayed that all who love him, might be with him; where, we believe, they are with him. Let our faith rise so high—God grant it!—that we can say: "Oh! grave, where is thy victory? Oh! death, where is thy sting? Thanks be to God who giveth us the victory, through Jesus Christ, our Lord!"

* Preached before the Communion.

XVII.

THE PROBLEM OF LIFE, RESOLVED IN THE LIFE OF CHRIST.

IN HIM WAS LIFE, AND THE LIFE WAS THE LIGHT OF MEN.—John i. 4.

The words, "life and light," are constantly used by the Apostle John, after a manner long familiar in the Hebrew writings, for spiritual happiness, and spiritual truth. The inmost and truest life of man, the life of his life, is spiritual life—is, in other words, purity, love, goodness; and this inward purity, love, goodness, is the very light of life; that which brightens, blesses, guides it.

I have little respect for the ingenuity that is always striving to work out from the simple language of Scripture, fanciful and far-fetched meanings; but it would seem, in the passage before us, as if John intended to state one of the deepest truths in the very frame of our being; and that is, *that goodness is the fountain of wisdom.*

Give me your patience a moment, and I will attempt to explain this proposition. "In it, was life;" that is, in this manifested and all-creating energy, this outflowing of the power of God, was a divine and infinite love and joy; and this life was the light of men. That is to say—love first, then light. Light does not create love; but love creates light. The good heart only can understand the good teaching. The doctrine of truth that guides a man, comes from the divinity of goodness that inspires him. But, it will be said, does not a man become holy or good, *in view* of truth? I answer, that he cannot *view* the truth, but through the medium of love. It is the loving view only, that is effective; that is any view at all. I must desire you to observe that I am speaking now of the primary convictions of a man, and not of the secondary influences that operate upon him. Light may *strengthen* love; a knowledge of the works and ways of God may have this effect, and it is properly presented for this purpose. But light cannot *originate* love. If love were not implanted in man's original and inmost being; if there were not placed there, the moral or spiritual feeling, that loves while it perceives goodness; all the speculative light in the universe, would leave man's nature, still and forever cold and dead as a stone. In short, loveliness is a quality which nothing but love can perceive. God cannot be known in his highest, that is, in his spiritual and holy nature, except by those who love him.

Now of this life and light, as we are immediately afterwards taught, Jesus Christ, not as a teacher merely, but as a being, is to us the great and appointed source. And therefore when Thomas says, "how can we know the way of which thou speakest," Jesus answers, "*I am* the way, and the truth and the life; no man cometh to the Father but by me." That is, no man can truly come to God, but in that spirit of filial love, of which I am the example.

In our humanity there is a problem. In Christ only is it perfectly solved. The speculative solution of that problem, is philosophy. The practical solution is a good life; and the only perfect solution is, the life of Christ. "In him was life, and the life was the light of men."

In him, I say, was solved the problem of life. What is that problem? What are the questions which it presents? They are these: Is there anything that can be achieved in life, in which our nature can find full satisfaction and sufficiency? And if there be any such thing, any such end of life; then is there any adaptation of things to that end? Are there any means or helps provided in life, for its attainment? Now the end must be the highest condition of our highest nature; and that end, we say, is virtue, sanctity, blessedness. And the helps or means are found in the whole discipline of life. But the end was perfectly accomplished in Christ, and it was accomplished through the very means which are appointed to us. "He was tempted in all points as we are, yet without sin;" and "he was made thus perfect through sufferings."

Our Saviour evidently regarded himself as sustaining this relation to human life; the enlightener of its darkness, the interpreter of its mystery, the solver of its problem. "I am the light of the world," he says; "he that followeth me, shall not walk in darkness, but shall have the light of life." And again: "I am come a light into the world, that whosoever believeth on me, should not abide in darkness." It was not for abstract teaching to men that he came, but for actual guidance in their daily abodes. It was not to deliver doctrines alone, nor to utter or echo back the intuitive convictions of our own minds, but to live a life and to die a death; and so to live and to die, as to cast light upon the dark paths in which we walk.

I need not say that there *is* darkness in the paths of men; that they stumble at difficulties, are ensnared by temptations, are perplexed by doubts; that they are anxious and troubled and fearful; that pain and affliction and sorrow often gather around the steps of their earthly pilgrimage. All this is written upon the very tablet of the human heart. And I *do* not say that all this is to be erased; but only that it is to be seen and read in a new light. I *do* not say that ills and trials and sufferings are to be removed from life; but only that over this scene of mortal trouble a new heaven is to be spread; and that the light of that heaven is Christ, the sun of righteousness.

To human pride, this may be a hard saying; to human philosophy, learning, and grandeur, it may be a hard saying; but still it is true, that the simple life of Christ, studied, understood and imitated, would shed a brighter light than all earthly wisdom can find, upon the dark trials and mysteries of our lot. It is true that whatever you most need or sigh for, whatever you most want, to still the troubles of your heart or compose the agitations of your mind, the simple life of Jesus can teach you.

To show this, I need only take the most ordinary admissions from the lips of any Christian, or I may say, of almost any unbeliever.

Suppose that the world were filled with beings like Jesus. Would not all the great ills of society be instantly relieved? Would you not immediately dismiss all your anxieties concerning it; perfectly sure that all was going on well? Would not all coercion, infliction, injury, injustice, and all the greatest suffering of life, disappear at once? If, at the stretching out of some wonder-working wand, that change could take place, would not the change be greater far, than if every house, hovel and prison on earth, were instantly turned into a palace of ease and abundance and splendour? Happy then would be these " human years;" and the eternal ages would roll on in brightness and beauty! The "still, sad music of humanity," that sounds through the world, now in the swellings of grief, and now in pensive melancholy, would be exchanged for anthems, lifted up to the march of time, and bursting out from the heart of the world!

But let us make another supposition, and bring it still nearer to ourselves. Were any one of us a perfect imitator of Christ; were any one of us clothed with the divinity of his virtue and faith; do you not perceive what the effect would be? Look around upon the circle of life's ills and trials, and observe the effect. Did sensual passions assail you? How weak would be their solicitation to the divine beatitude of your own heart! You would say, "I have meat to eat that ye know not of." Did want tempt you to do wrongly, or curiosity to do rashly? You would say to the one, "man shall not *live* by bread alone; there is a higher life which I must live;" and to the other, "thou shalt not tempt the Lord thy God." Did ambition spread its kingdoms and thrones before you, and ask you to swerve from your great allegiance? Your reply would be ready: "Get thee hence, Satan, for it is written, thou shalt worship the Lord thy God, and him only shalt thou serve." Did the storm of injury beat upon your head, or its silent shaft pierce your heart? In meekness you would bow that head, in prayer, that heart; saying, 'Father forgive them, for they know not what they do." What sorrow could reach you; what pain, what anguish, that would not be soothed by a faith and a love like that of Jesus? And what blessing could light on you, that would not be brightened by a filial piety and gratitude like his? The world around you would be new, and the heavens over you would be new; for they would be all, and all around their ample range, and all through their glorious splendours, the presence and the visitation of a Father. And you yourself, would be a new creature; and you would enjoy a happiness new, and now scarcely known on earth.

And I cannot help observing here, that if such be the spontaneous conviction of every mind at all acquainted with Christianity, what a powerful independent argument there is for receiving Christ as a guide and example! It were an anomaly, indeed, to the eye of reason, to reject the solemn and self-claimed mission of one, whom it would be happiness to follow, whom it would be perfection to imitate. Yet if the former, the special mission, *were* rejected; if it were, as it may be, by possibility, honestly rejected; what is a man to think of himself, who passes by, and discards the latter, the teaching of the life of Christ? Let it be the man, Rousseau, or the man, Hume, or any man in these days, who says that he believes nothing in churches or miracles or missions from heaven. But he admits, as they did and as every one must, that in Jesus Christ was the most perfect unfolding of all divine beauty and holiness that the world ever saw. What, I say, is he to do with this undeniable and undenied Gospel of the *life* of Jesus? Blessed is he, if he receives it; that is unquestionable. All who read of him, all the world, admits that. But what shall we say if he rejects it? If any one could be clothed with the eloquence of Cicero or the wisdom of Socrates, and would not, all the world would pronounce him a fool, would say that he had denied his humanity. And surely if any one could be invested with all the beauty and grandeur of the life of Jesus, and would not; he must be stricken with utter moral fatuity; he must be accounted to have denied his highest humanity. The interpretation of his case is as plain as words can make it; and it is this: "light has come into the world, and men have loved darkness rather than light, because their deeds are evil."

"In him was life," says our text, "and the life was the light of men."

I have attempted to bring home the conviction of this, simply by bringing before your minds the supposition that the world, and we ourselves, were like him. But as no conviction, I think, at the present stage of our Christian progress, is so important as this, let me attempt to impress it, by another course of reflections. I say of *our* Christian progress. We have cleared away many obstacles, as we think, and have come near to the simplicity of the Gospel. No complicated ecclesiastical organization nor scholastic creed, stands between us and the solemn verities of Christianity. I am not now pronouncing upon those accumulations of human devices; but I mean especially to say, that no mystical notions of their necessity or importance, mingle themselves with *our* ideas of acceptance. We have come to stand before the simple, naked shrine of the original Gospel. We have come, through many human teachings and human admonitions, to Christ himself. But little will it avail us to have come so far, if we take not one step farther. *Now*, what I think we need is, to enter more deeply into the study and understanding of what Christ was.

This, let us attempt. And I pray you and myself, Brethren, not to be content with the little that can now be said; but let us carefully read the Gospels for ourselves, and lay the law of the life of Christ, with rigorous precision to our own lives, and see where they fail and come short. It is true indeed, and I would urge nothing beyond the truth, that the life of Jesus is not, in every respect, an example for us. That is to say, the manner of his life was, in some respects, different from what ours can, or should be. He was a teacher; and the most of us are necessarily and lawfully engaged in the business of life. He was sent on a peculiar mission; and none of us have such a mission. But the spirit that was in him, may be in us. To some of the traits of this spirit, as the only sources of light and help to us, let me now briefly direct your attention.

And first, consider his self-renunciation. How entire that self-renunciation was; how completely his aims went beyond personal ease and selfish gratification; how all his thoughts and words and actions were employed upon the work for which he was sent into the world; how his whole life, as well as his death, was an offering to that cause; I need not tell you. Indeed, so entirely is this his accredited character; so completely is he set apart in our thoughts not only to a peculiar office, but set apart too and separated from all human interests and affections, that we are liable to do his character in this respect, no proper justice. We isolate him, till he almost ceases to be an example to us; till he almost ceases to be a *virtuous* being. He stands alone in Judea; and the words—society, country, kindred, friendship, home—seem to have, to him, only a fictitious application. But these ties bound him as they do others; the gentleness and tenderness of his nature made him peculiarly susceptible to them; no more touching allusions to kindred and country can be found in human language, than his; as when he said, "Oh! Jerusalem! Jerusalem!" in foresight of her coming woes; as when he said on the cross, "behold thy mother! behold thy son!" Doubtless he desired to be a benefactor to his country, an honour to his family; and when Peter, deprecating his dishonour and degradation, said, "be it far from thee, Lord! this shall not be unto thee," and he turned and said unto Peter, "get thee behind me, Satan, thou savourest not the things that be of God, but those that be of men," it has been beautifully suggested that the very energy of that repulse to his enthusiastic and admiring disciple, shows perhaps that he felt that there was something in his mind that was leaning that way; that the things of men were contending with the things of God in him; that he too much dreaded the coming humiliation and agony, to wish to have that feeling fostered in his heart.

But he rejected all this; he renounced himself, renounced all the dear affections and softer pleadings of his affectionate nature, that he might be true to higher interests than his own, or his country's, or his kindred's.

Now I say that the same self-renunciation would relieve us of more than half of the difficulties and of the diseased and painful affections of our lives. Simple obedience to rectitude, instead of self-interest, simple self-culture, instead of ever cultivating the good opinion of others; how many disturbing and irritating questions would these single-hearted aims, take away from our bosom meditations! Let us not mistake the character of this self-renunciation. We are required, not to renounce the nobler and better affections of our natures, not to renounce happiness, not to renounce our just dues of honour and love from men. It is remarkable that our Saviour, amidst all his meekness and all his sacrifices, always claimed that he deserved well of men, deserved to be honoured and beloved. It is not to vilify ourselves that is required of us; not to renounce our self-respect, the just and reasonable sense of our merits and deserts; not to renounce our own righteousness, our own virtue, if we have any; such falsehood towards ourselves gains no countenance from the example of Jesus; but it is to renounce our sins, our passions, our self-flattering delusions; and it is to forego all outward advantages which can be gained only through a sacrifice of our inward integrity, or through anxious and petty contrivances and compliances. What we have to do, is to choose and keep the better part; to secure that, and let the worst take care of itself; to keep a good conscience, and let opinion come and go as it will; to keep high, self-respect, and to let low self-indulgence go; to keep inward happiness, and let outward advantages hold a subordinate place. Self-renunciation, in fine, is, not to renounce ourselves in the highest character; not to renounce our moral selves, ourselves as the creatures and children of God; *herein* rather it is to cherish ourselves, to make the most of ourselves, to hold ourselves inexpressibly dear. What then is it precisely to renounce ourselves? It is to renounce our selfishness; to have done with this eternal self-considering which now disturbs and vexes our lives; to cease that ever asking "and what shall we have?"—to be content with the plenitude of God's abounding mercies; to feast upon that infinite love, that is shed all around us and within us; and so to be happy. I see many a person, in society, honoured, rich, beautiful, but wearing still an anxious and disturbed countenance; many a one upon whom this simple principle, this simple self-forgetting, would bring a change in their appearance, demeanour, and the whole manner of their living and being; a change that would make them tenfold more beautiful, rich and honoured. Yes; strange as it may seem to them; what they want, is, to commune deeply, in prayer and meditation, with the spirit of Jesus, to be clothed, not with outward adorning, but with the simple self-forgetting, single-hearted truth and beauty of his spirit. This is the change, this is the conversion that they want, to make them lovely and happy beyond all the aspirations of their ambition, and all their dreams of happiness.

Have you never observed how happy is the mere visionary schemer, quite absorbed in his plans, quite thoughtless of everything else? Have you never remarked how easy and felicitous, is the manner in society, the eloquence in the public assembly, the whole life's action, of one who has forgotten himself? For this reason in part it is, that the eager pursuit of fortune is often happier than the after enjoyment of it; for now the man begins to *look about* for happiness, and *to ask* for a respect and attention which he seldom satisfactorily receives; and many such are found, to the wonder and mortification of their families, looking back from their splendid dwellings, and often referring to the humble shop in which they worked; and wishing in their hearts, that they were there again.

It is our inordinate self-seeking, self-considering, that is ever a stumbling-block in our way. It is this which spreads questions, snares, difficulties around us. It is this that darkens the very ways of Providence to us, and makes the world a less happy world to us, than it might be. There is one thought that could take us out from all these difficulties; but we cannot think it. There is one clue from the labyrinth; there is one solution of this struggling philosophy of life within us; it is found in that Gospel, that life of Jesus, with which we have, alas! but little deep, heart-acquaintance. Every one must know, that if he could be elevated to that self-forgetting simplicity and disinterestedness, he would be relieved from more than half of the inmost trials of his bosom. What then can be done for us, but that we be directed, and that too with a concern as solemn as our deepest wisdom and welfare, to the Gospel of Christ? "In him was life; and the life was the light of men."

In him was the life of perfect love. This is the second all-enlightening, all-healing principle that the Gospel of Christ commends to us. It is indeed the main and positive virtue, of which self-renunciation is but the negative side.

Again, I need not insist upon the pre-eminence of this principle in the life of our Saviour. But I must again remind you that this principle is not to be looked upon as some sublime abstraction, as merely a love that drew him from the bliss of heaven, to achieve some stupendous and solitary work on earth. It was a vital and heartfelt love to all around him; it was affection to his kindred, tenderness to his friends, gentleness and forbearance towards his disciples, pity to the suffering, forgiveness to his enemies, prayer for his murderers; love flowing all round him as the garment of life, and investing pain and toil and torture and death, with a serene and holy beauty.

It is not enough to renounce ourselves, and there to stop. It is not enough to wrap ourselves in our close garment of reserve and pride, and to say, " the world cares nothing for us, and we will care nothing for the world; society does us no justice, and we will withdraw from it our thoughts, and see how patiently we can live within the confines of our own bosom, or in quiet communion, through books, with the mighty dead." No man ever found peace or light in this way. The misanthropic recluse is ever the most miserable of men, whether he lives in cave or castle. Every relation to mankind, of hate or scorn or neglect, is full of vexation and torment. There is nothing to do with men, but to love them; to contemplate their virtues with admiration, their faults with pity and forbearance, and their injuries with forgiveness. Task all the ingenuity of your mind to devise some other thing, but you never can find it. To all the haughtiness and wrath of men, I say—however they may disdain the suggestion—the spirit of Jesus is the only help for you. To hate your adversary will not help you; to kill him will not help you; nothing within the compass of the universe can help you, but to love him. Oh! how wonderfully is man shut up to wisdom—barred, as I may say, and imprisoned and shut up to wisdom; and yet he will not learn it.

But let that love flow out upon all around you, and what could harm you? It would clothe you with an impenetrable, heaven-tempered armour. Or suppose, to do it justice, that it leaves you, all defencelessness, as it did Jesus; all vulnerableness, through delicacy, through tenderness, through sympathy, through pity; suppose that you suffer, as all must suffer; suppose that you be wounded, as gentleness only can be wounded; yet how would that love flow, with precious healing, through every wound! How many difficulties too, both within and without a man, would it relieve! How many dull *minds* would it rouse; how many depressed minds would it lift up! How many troubles, in society, would it compose; how many enmities would it soften; how many questions, answer! How many a knot of mystery and misunderstanding would be untied by one word spoken in simple and confiding truth of heart! How many a rough path would be made smooth, and crooked way be made strait! How many a solitary place would be made glad, if love were there; and how many a dark dwelling would be filled with light! "In him was life, and the life was the light of men."

Once more: there was a sublime spirituality in the mind of Jesus, which must come into our life, to fill up the measure of its light. It is not enough in my view, to yield ourselves to the blessed bonds of love and self-renunciation, in the immediate circles of our lives. Our minds must go into the infinite and immortal regions, to find sufficiency and satisfaction for the present hour. There must be a breadth of contemplation in which this world shrinks, I will not say to a point, but to the narrow span that it is. There must be aims, which reign over the events of life, and make us feel that we can resign all the advantages of life, yea, and life itself; and yet be "conquerors and more than conquerors through him who has loved us."

There is many a crisis in life when we need a faith like the martyr's to support us. There are hours in life like martyrdom—as full of bitter anguish, as full of utter earthly desolation; in which more than our sinews, in which we feel as if our very heart-strings were stretched and lacerated on the rack of affliction; in which life itself loses its value, and we ask to die; in whose dread struggle and agony, life might drop from us, and not be minded. Oh! then must our cry, like that of Jesus, go up to the pitying heavens for help, and nothing but the infinite and the immortal can help us. Calculate, then, all the gains of earth, and they are trash; all its pleasures, and they are vanity; all its hopes, and they are illusions; and then, when the world is sinking beneath us, must we seek the everlasting arms to bear us up, to bear us up to heaven. Thus was it with our great Example, and so must it be with us. "In him was life;" the life of self-renunciation, the life of love, the life of spiritual and all-conquering faith; and that life is the light of men. Oh! blessed light! come to our darkness; for our soul is dark, our way is dark, for want of thee; come to our darkness, and turn it into day; and let it shine brighter and brighter, till it mingles with the light of the all-perfect and everlasting day!

XVIII.

ON RELIGION, AS THE GREAT SENTIMENT OF LIFE

IF IN THIS LIFE ONLY WE HAVE HOPE, WE ARE OF ALL MEN MOST MISERABLE.
I Cor. xv. 19.

THERE is a nation in modern times, of which it is constantly said that it has no religion; that in this life only has it hope. One is continually assured, not by foreigners alone, but in that very country—I need not say that I speak of France—that the people there have no religion, that the religious sentiment has become nearly extinct among them.*

Although there is, doubtless, some exaggeration in the statement, as would be very natural in a case so very extraordinary, and the rather as the representation of it comes from a people who are fond of appearing an extraordinary and wonderful people, and of striking the world with astonishment; yet there is still so much truth in the representation, and it is a thing so unheard of in the history of all nations, whether Heathen, Mahometan, or Christian, that one is naturally led to reflect upon the problem which the case presents for our consideration. *Can* a nation go on without religion? Can a people live devoid of every religious hope, without being of all people the most miserable? Can human nature bear such a state? This is the problem.

* Such is the language which I heard fourteen years ago in France: but I trust, it is becoming every day less applicable.

It is the more important to discuss this problem, because, the very spectacle of such a nation, has some tendency to unhinge the faith of the world. The thoughtless at least, the young perhaps, who are generally supposed to feel less than others, the necessity of this great principle, may be led to say with themselves, " is not religion after all, an error, a delusion, a superstition, with which mankind will yet be able to dispense?"* A part of my reply to this question I propose to draw especially from the experience of the young. For I think, indeed, that instead of this being an age, when men, and the young especially, can afford to dispense with the aid and guidance of religion, it is an age which is witnessing an extraordinary development of sensibility, and is urging the need of piety beyond, perhaps beyond all former ages. The circumstances, as I conceive, which have led to this development, are the diffusion of knowledge, and the new social relationships introduced by free principles. But my subject, at present, does not permit me to enlarge upon these points.

Can the world, then, go on without religion? I will not inquire now whether human governments can go on. But can the human heart go on without religion? Can all its resistless energies, its swelling passions, its overburthening affections, be borne without piety? Can it suffer changes, disappointments, bereavements, desolations; ay, or can it satisfactorily bear overwhelming joy, without religion? Can youth and manhood and age, can life and death, be passed through, without the great principle which reigns over all the periods of life, which triumphs over death, and is enthroned in the immortality of faith, of virtue, of truth, and of God?

* The very opinion of the French Auguste Comte.

I answer, with a confidence that the lapse of a hundred nations into Atheism, could not shake, that it is not possible: in the eye of reason and truth, that is to say, it is not possible for the world, for the human heart, for life, to go on without religion. Religion, naturally, fairly, rightly regarded, is the great sentiment of life: and this is the point which I shall now endeavour to illustrate.

What I mean by saying that religion is the great sentiment of life, is this: that all the great and leading states of mind which this life originates or occasions in every reflecting person, demand the sentiment of religion for their support and safety. Religion, I am aware, is considered by many, as something standing by itself, and which a man may take as the companion of his journey, or not take, as he pleases; and many persons, I know, calmly, some, it is possible, contemptuously, leave it to stand aside and by itself, as not worthy of their invitation, or not worthy, at any rate, of being earnestly sought by them. But when they thus leave it, I undertake to say, that they do not understand the great mental pilgrimage on which they are going. If all the teachings of nature were withdrawn, if Revelation were blotted out, if events did not teach; yet the very experience of life, the natural development of human feeling, the history of every mind which, as a mind, has any history, would urge it to embrace religion as an indispensable resort. There is thus, therefore, not only a kind of metaphysical necessity in the very nature of the mind, and a moral call in all its situations, for religion; but there is wrapped up within the very germs of all human experience, of all human feeling, joyous or sorrowful; there is, attending the very development of all the natural affections, a want, a need inexpressible, of the power of that divine principle.

Let us trace this want, this need, in some of the different stages, through which the character usually passes. Let us see whether this great necessity does not press down upon every period of life, and even upon its commencement; yes, whether upon the very heart of youth, there are not already deep records of experience, that point it to this great reliance. I have in a former discourse, spoken of the disappointments of youth; I now speak of its wants and dangers.

In youth then—that is to say, somewhere between the period of childhood and manhood—there is commonly, a striking development of sensibility and imagination. The passions, then, if not more powerful than at any other period, are at any rate more vivid, because their objects are new: and they are then most uncontrollable, because neither reason nor experience have attained to the maturity necessary to moderate and restrain them. The young have not lived long enough, to see how direful are the effects of unbridled inclination, how baseless are the fabrics of ambition, how liable to disappointment are all the hopes of this world. And therefore the sensibility of youth, is apt to possess a character of strong excitement and almost of intoxication. I never look upon one at such a period, whose quick and ardent feelings mantle in the cheek at every turn, and flash in the eye and thrill through the veins, and falter in the hurried speech, in every conversation; yes, and have deeper tokens, in the gathering paleness of the countenance, in speechless silence, and the tightening chords of almost suffocating emotion; I never look upon such an one, all fresh and alive, and yet unused, to the might and mystery of the power that is working within; a being full of imagination too, living a life but half of realities, and full half of airy dreams; a being, whom a thousand things, afterwards to be regarded with a graver eye, now move to laughter or to tears; I never look upon such an one—how is it possible to do so?—without feeling that one thing is needful; and that is, the serenity of religion, the sobriety and steadiness of deep-founded principle, the strong and lofty aim of sacred virtue.

But the sensibility of youth, is not always joyous nor enthusiastic. Long ere it loses its freshness or its fascination, it oftentimes meets with checks and difficulties; it has its early troubles and sorrows. Some disappointment in its unsuspecting friendships, some school-day jealousy or affliction, some jar upon the susceptible nerves or the unruly passions, from the treatment of kindred or friends or associates; or, at a later period, some galling chain of dependence or poverty or painful restraint; or else, the no less painful sense of mediocrity, the feeling in the young heart that the prizes of ambition are all out of its reach, that praise and admiration and love all fall to the lot of others; some or other of these causes, I say, brings a cold blight over the warm and expanding affections of youth, and turns the bright elysium of life, for a season, into darkness and desolation. All this is not to be described as if it were a mere picture; just enough, perhaps, but to be considered no otherwise than as a matter of youthful feeling, soon to pass away and to leave no results. This state of mind has results. And the most common and dangerous is a fatal recklessness. The undisciplined and too often selfish heart says, "I do not care; I do not care what others say or think of me; I do not care how they treat me.

Those who are loved and praised and fortunate, are no better than I am; the world is unjust; the world knows me not: and I care not if it never knows me. I will wrap myself in my own garment; let them call it the garment of pride or reserve, it matters not; I have feelings, and my own breast shall be their depository." Perhaps this recklessness goes farther, and the misguided youth says, "I will plunge into pleasure; I will find me companions, though they be bad ones; I will make my friends care for me in one way, if they will not in another;" or he says, perhaps, "nobody cares for me, and therefore it is no matter what I do."

My young friends, have you ever known any of these various trials of youth? And, if you have, do you think that you can safely pass through them, with no better guidance than your own hasty and headstrong passions? Oh! believe it not. Passion is never a safe impulse; but passion soured, irritated and undisciplined, is least of all to be trusted. If in this life only you have hope, if no influence from afar take hold of your minds, if no aims stretching out to boundless and everlasting improvement strengthen and sustain you, if no holy conscience, no heavenly principle sets up its authority among your wayward impulses, you are indeed of all beings most to be pitied. Unhappy for you is all this ardour, this kindling fervour of emotion, this throng of conflicting passions, this bright or brooding imagination, giving a false colouring and magnitude to every object; unhappy for you, and all the more unhappy, if you do not welcome the sure guidance, the strong control of principle, of piety, of prayer.

But let us advance to another stage of life and of feeling; to the maturity of life. And I shall venture to say that where the mind really unfolds with growing years; where it is not absorbed in worldly gains or pleasures, so as to be kept in a sort of perpetual childhood; where there is real susceptibility and reflection, there is apt to steal over us, without religion, a spirit of misanthropy and melancholy. I have often observed it, and without any wonder; for it seems to me, as if a thoughtful and feeling mind, without any trust in the great providence of God, without any communion of prayer with a Father in heaven, or any religious, any holy sympathy with its earthly brethren, or any cheering hope of their progress, must become reserved, distrustful, misanthropic, and often melancholy.

Youth, though often disappointed, is yet always looking forward; and it is looking forward with indefinite and unchecked anticipation. But in the progress of life, there comes a time when the mind looks backward as well as forward; when it learns to correct the anticipations of the future, by the experience of the past. It has run through the courses of acquisition, pleasure or ambition, and it knows what they are, and what they are worth. The attractions of hope have not, indeed, lost all their power, but they have lost a part of their charm.

Perhaps, even the disappointment of youth, though it has more of passion and grief in it, is not so bitter and sad, as that of maturer life, when it says, " well, and this is all. If I should add millions to my store; if I should reap new honours, or gain new pleasures, it will only be what I have experienced before; I know what it is; I know it all. There is no more in this life; I know it all." Ah! how cold and cheerless is that period of human experience; how does the heart of a man die within him, as he stands thus in the very midst of his acquisitions; how do his very honours and attainments teach him to mourn; and to mourn without hope, if there is no spiritual hope! If the great moral objects of this life, and the immortal regions of another life, are not spread before him, then is he most miserable. Yes, I repeat, his very success, his good fortune brings him to this. There are untoward circumstances, I know; there are afflictions that may lead a man to religion; but what I now say, is, that the natural progress of every reflecting mind, however prosperous its fortunes, that the inevitable development of the growing experience of life, unfolds, in the very structure of every human soul, that great necessity, the necessity of religion.

This world is dark and must be dark, without the light of religion; even as the material orb would be dark without the light of Heaven to shine upon it. As if

> "The bright Sun were extinguished, and the stars
> Did wander darkling in the eternal space,
> Rayless and pathless; and the icy earth
> Swung blind and blackening in the moonless air;"

so would the soul, conscious of its own nature, be, without the light of God's presence shining around it, without those truths that beam like the eternal stars from the depths of heaven; without those influences, invisible and far off, like the powers of gravitation, to hold it steadily in its orbit, and to carry it onward with unerring guidance, in its bright career. And no philosopher, no really intellectual being, ever broke from the bonds of all religious faith, without finding his course dreary, "blind and blackening" in the spiritual firmament. His soul becomes, in the expressive language of Scripture, "like a wandering star, or a cloud without water." No mean argument is this, indeed, for the great truths of religion. But whether it is so or not, it is a fact. I know indeed that many persons possessed of sense and talent in this world's affairs, do live without religion, and ordinarily without any painful consciousness of wanting it. But what do men of mere sense and talent in this world's affairs, know of the insatiable and illimitable desires of the mind? What—what by very definition, as the votaries of worldly good, are they pursuing? Why, it is some object about as far distant, in the bounded horizon of their vision, as that which the painted butterfly is pursuing; some flower, some bright thing a little before them; bright honour, or dazzling gold, or gilded pleasure. But let any mind awake to its real and sublime nature; let it feel the expanding, the indefinite reaching forth of those original and boundless thoughts which God has made it to feel; let it sound those depths, soar to those heights, compass those illimitable heavens of thought, through which it was made to range; and then let that mind tell me, if it can, that it wants no religion; that it wants no central principle of attraction, no infinite object of adoration and love and trust. Nay, if any mind, whatever its pretensions, should tell me this, I should not hesitate in my own judgment, to pronounce its acquisitions shallow, or at any rate partial, or at the best, technical and scholastic. For it is not true, my brethren, that intellectual weakness most stands in need of religion, or is most fitted to feel the need of it; but it is intellectual strength. I hold no truth to be more certain than this; that every mind, in proportion to its real development and expansion, is dark, is disproportioned, and unhappy, without religion. If in this life alone it has hope, it is of all minds most miserable.

I have spoken of youth and manhood as developing

the need of religion. Does age any less need it? Where can that want exist if not in the aged heart? It is not alone, that its pulses are faint and low; it is not alone, that so many of its once cherished objects have departed from it; it is not that the limbs are feeble, the eye dim and the ear dull of hearing; it is not that the aged frame is bent towards that earth into which it is soon to sink and find its last rest; but what is the position of an old man? Where does he stand? One life is passed through; one season of being is almost spent; youth has found, long since, the goal of its career; manhood, at length, is gone; and he stands —where, and upon what? What is it that spreads before him? Is it a region of clouds and shadows? Is all before him, dread darkness and vacuity, an eternal sleep, a boundless void? Thus would it be without religion, without faith! But how must he, who stands upon that shore of all visible being, from whence he can never turn back, how must he long for some sure word of promise, for some voice, that can tell him of eternal life, of eternal youth; of regions far away in the boundless universe of God, where he may wander on and onward forever! Age, with faith, is but the beginning of life, the youth of immortality; the times and seasons of its being are yet before it; its gathered experience is but an education to prepare it for higher scenes and services: but age, without faith, is a wreck upon the shore of life, a ruin upon the beetling cliffs of time; tottering to its fall, and about to be engulfed, and lost forever!

I have thus attempted to show that religion is the great sentiment of each period of life. Let me now extend the same observation to those epochs in life, which are occasioned by changes in that material creation which surrounds us.

There are sentiments appropriate to the dying, and to the reviving year. What are they? How striking is the answer which is given in all literature and poetry! Men are able, no doubt, to walk through the round of the seasons, without much reflection; but the moment any sentiment is awakened, it is the sentiment of religion; it is a thoughtfulness about God's wisdom and beneficence, about life and death and eternity. Thus it is that every poet of the seasons, every poet of nature, is devout; devout in his meditations when he writes, if not devout in his habits always.

And what man, in thoughtful mood, can walk forth in the still and quiet season of Autumn, and tread upon the seared grass that is almost painfully audible to the serious emotions of his heart, and listen to the fall of the leaf that seems, idle as it is, as if it were the footstep of some predestined event, and hear the far echo of the hills and the solemn wind dirge of the dying year; and not meditate in that hour; and not meditate upon things above the world and above all its grosser cares and interests! "The dead, the loved, the lost" will come to him then; the world will sink like a phantom-shadow; and eternity will be a presence; and heaven, through the serene depths of those opening skies, will be to him a vision.

But again, a change cometh! The seals of winter are broken; and lo! the green herb and the tender grass, and bird and blossom come forth; the clouds dissolve into softness, and open the azure depths beyond; and man goeth forth from imprisoning walls, and opens his bosom to the warmth and the breeze, and feels his frame expand with gladness and exultation. Then what is he, if from the kindling joy of his heart arises no incense of gratitude! It is the hour of nature's, and ought to be of man's thanksgiving. The very stones would cry out; the green fields and the rejoicing hills would cry out against him, if he were not grateful. The sentiment of the spring-time, is the sentiment of religious gratitude!

Let us look at other changes. There is a sentiment of the morning. The darkness is rolled away from the earth; the iron slumber of the world is broken; it is the daily resurrection-hour of rejoicing millions. God hath said again, "let there be light;" and over the mountain-tops and over the waves of ocean it comes, and streams in upon the waking creation. Each morning that signal-light, calling to action, is at thy window; duly it cometh, as with a message, saying, "awake, arise!" Thou wakest; from dreamy slumbers, from helpless inactivity; and what dost thou find? Hast thou lost any thing of thyself in that slumber of forgetfulness? Hath not all been kept for thee? Hath there not been a watch over thy sleep? Thou wakest; and each limb is filled with life; each sense holds its station in thy wonderful frame; each faculty, each thought is in its place; no dark insanity, no dreary eclipse hath spread itself over thy soul. What shall the thoughts of that hour be, but wondering and adoring thoughts? Well are a portion of our prayers called *matins*. Morning prayers—morning prayers; orisons in the first light of day, from the bended soul, if not from the bended knee; were not the morning desecrated and denied, if a part and portion of it were not prayer?

And there is a sentiment of the eventide; when the sun slowly sinks from our sight; when the shadows steal over the earth; when the shining hosts of the stars come forth; when other worlds and other regions of the universe, are unveiled in the infinitude of heaven. Then to meditate, how reasonable, I had almost said how inevitable is it! How meet were it then, that in every house there should be a vesper-hymn! I have read of such a scene in a village, in some country—I think it was in Italy—where the traveller heard, as the day went down, and amidst the gathering shadows of the still evening, first from one dwelling and then from another, the voices of song—accompanied with simple instruments, flute and flageolet; it was the vesper hymn. How beautiful were it, in village or city, for dwelling thus to call to dwelling, saying, " great and marvellous are thy works, Lord God Almighty; just and true are thy ways; God of the morning! God of the evening! we praise thee; goodness and mercy hast thou caused to follow us all our days."

Thus have I attempted to show that religion is the great sentiment of life. It is our life. Our life is bound up with it, and in it; and without it, life would be both miserable and ignoble.

I will only add, in fine, that religion alone affords to us the hope of a future life, and that without this our present being is shorn of all its grandeur and hope.

Whether we look at our own death or at the death of others, this consideration, this necessity of a faith that takes hold of eternity, presses upon us. I know very well what the common and worldly consolation is. I know very well, the hackneyed proverb, that " time is the curer of grief;" but I know very well too, that no time can suppress the sigh that is given to the loved and lost. Time, indeed, lightens the constant pressure of grief rather than blunts its edge; and still more than either, perhaps, does it smooth over the outward aspect of that suffering: but often when all is outwardly calm and even bright, does the conscious heart say, " I hear a voice you cannot hear; I see a sign you cannot see;" and it pays the sad and dear tribute of bereaved love. No, the memory of the beloved ones parts not from us, as its shadow passes from our countenance. And who is there, around whose path such memories linger, that will not say, "I thank God, through our Lord Jesus Christ," through him who is the revealed "resurrection and life;" through him who said, "he that liveth and believeth in me, shall never die?" For now, blessed be God, we mourn not as those who have no hope. But surely, dying creatures as we are, and living in a dying world, if in this life only we had hope, we should of all beings be most miserable.

In fine, my view of life is such, that if it were not for my faith and hope, I should very little care what became of it. Let it be longer or shorter, it would but little matter, if all was to end when life ended; if all my hopes and aspirations, and cherished joys, were to be buried with me forever, in the tomb. Oh! that life of insect cares and pursuits, and of insect brevity! the mind that God has given me could only cast a sad and despairing look upon it, and then dismiss it, as not worth a farther thought. But no such sad and shocking incongruity, is there, thanks be to God, in the well ordered course of our being. The harmonies that are all around us, in all animal, in all vegetable life, in light and shade, in mountain and valley, in ocean and stream, in the linked train of the seasons, in the moving and dread array of all the heavenly hosts of worlds; the harmonies of universal nature, but above all, the teachings of the Gospel, assure us that no such shocking incongruity and disorder are bound up in the frame of our nature.

No; it is true; that which we so much need to support us, is true; *God doth look down upon our humble path with the eye of paternal wisdom and love; this universe is full of spiritual influences to help us in the great conflict of life; there is a world beyond in which we may assuredly trust.* The heart, full of weighty interests and cares, of swelling hopes and aspirations, of thoughts too big for utterance, is not given us merely that we may bear it to the grave, and bury it there. From that sleeping dust shall rise the free spirit, to endless life. Thanks—let us again say and forever say—thanks be to God, who giveth us this victory of an assured hope, through our Lord Jesus Christ.

XIX.

ON THE RELIGION OF LIFE.

HE HATH MADE EVERY THING BEAUTIFUL IN ITS TIME.—Ecclesiastes iii. 11.

In my last discourse on human Life, I spoke of religion as the great, appropriate and pervading sentiment, of life. *The religion of life,* by which I mean a different thing; the religion, the sanctity, the real, spiritual consecration naturally and properly belonging to all the appointed occupations, cultivated arts, lawful amusements and social bonds of life; this is the subject of my present discourse.

By most religious systems, this life, the life, that is, which the world is leading, and has been leading through ages, is laid under a dark and fearful ban. "*No religion*"—is the summary phrase which is written upon almost its entire history. Though it is held by these very systems, that the world was made for religion, made, that is to say, for the culture of religion in the hearts of its inhabitants; yet it is contended that this purpose has been almost entirely frustrated.

First, the heathen nations, by this theory, are cut off from all connection with real religion. Next, upon the mass of Christian nations, as being unregenerate and utterly depraved, the same sentence is passed. I am not disposed, on this subject, to exact the full measure of inference from any mere theory. Men's actual views are often in advance of their creeds. But is it not very evident, as a third consideration, that the prevailing views of the world's life, very well agree with the prevailing creeds? Is it not the common feeling, that mankind in the mass, in the proportion of thousands to one, have failed to attain to anything of true religion; to any, the least of that which fulfils the real and great design of the Creator? Is it not commonly felt that the mass of men's pursuits, of their occupations, of their pleasures, is completely severed from this great purpose? In labour, in merchandise, in the practice of law and of medicine, in literature, in sculpture, painting, poetry, music, is it not the constant doctrine or implication of the pulpit, that there is no religion, no spiritual virtue, nothing accordant with the Gospel of Christ? Men, amidst their pursuits, may *attain* to a divine life; but are not the pursuits themselves regarded, as having nothing, strictly speaking, to do with such a life, as having in them no elements of spiritual good, as having in them no tendency to advance religion and goodness in the world?

This certainly, upon the face of it, is a very extraordinary assumption. The pursuits in question, are —some of them necessary; others, useful; and all, natural; that is to say, they are developments, and inevitable and predestined developments of the nature which God has given us. And yet it is maintained and believed, that they have no tendency to promote his great design in making the world; that they have nothing in them allied to his purpose; that, at the most, they are only compatible with it, and that the actual office which they discharge in the world, is to lead men away from it. The whole, heaven-ordained ac**tivity**, occupation, care, ingenuity of human life, is at **war** with its great purpose. And if any one would **seek the** welfare of his soul, he is advised to leave all;

the farmer, his plow; the merchant, his ships; the lawyer, his briefs; and the painter his easel; and to go to a revival-meeting, or a confessional, or to retire to his closet. I need not say that I am not here objecting to meditation, to distinct, thoughtful and solemn meditation, as one of the means of piety and virtue; but I do protest against this ban and exclusion, which are thus virtually laid upon the beneficent and religious instrumentalities of a wise and gracious Providence.

On the contrary, I maintain that every thing is beautiful in its time, in its place, in its appointed office; that every thing which man is put to do, naturally helps to work out his salvation; in other words, that if he obey the genuine principles of his calling, he will be a good man; and that it is only through disobedience to the heaven-appointed tasks, either by wandering into idle dissipation, or by violating their beneficent and lofty spirit, that he becomes a bad man. Yes, if man would yield himself to the great training of Providence in the appointed action of life, we should not need churches nor ordinances; though they might still be proper for the *expression* of religious homage and gratitude.

Let us then look at this action of life, and attempt to see what is involved in it, and whether it is all alien, as is commonly supposed, to the spirit of sacred truth and virtue.

I. And the first sphere of visible activity which presents itself, is labour; the business of life, as opposed to what is commonly called study. I have before spoken of the moral ministration of labour; but let us, in connexion with this subject, advert to it again.

My subject in this discourse is the religion of life; and I now say that there is a religion of toil. It is not all drudgery, a mere stretching of the limbs and straining of the sinews to tasks. It has a meaning. It has an intent. A living heart pours life-blood into the toiling arm. Warm affections mingle with weary tasks.

I say not how pure those affections are, or how much of imperfection may mix with them; but I say that they are of a class, held by all men to be venerable and dear; that they partake of a kind of natural sanctity. They are, in other words, the home affections. The labour that spreads itself over tilled acres, all points, for its centre, to the country farm-house. The labour that plies its task in busy cities, has the same central point, and thither it brings daily supplies. And when I see the weary hand bearing that nightly offering; when I see the toiling days-man, carrying to his home the means of support and comfort; that offering is sacred to my thought, as a sacrifice at a golden shrine. Alas! many faults there are, amidst the toils of life; many hasty and harsh words are spoken; but why do those toils go on at all? Why are they not given up entirely; weary and hard and exasperating as they often are? Because in that home, is sickness, or age, or protected though helping woman, to be provided for. Because that there, is helpless infancy or gentle childhood, that must not want.

Such are the labours of life; and though it is true that mere selfishness, mere solitary need would prompt to irregular and occasional exertion, or would push some ambitious persons, of covetous desires, to continued and persevering effort; yet I am persuaded, that the selfish impulses would never create that scene of labour, which we behold around us.

Let us next look at the studious professions.

And I must confess that I have often been struck with surprise that a physician could be an undevout man. His study, the human frame, is the most wonderful display of divine wisdom in the world; the most astonishing proof of contrivance, of providence. Fearfully and wonderfully is it made; and if he who contemplates it, is not a reverent and heaven-adoring man, he is false to the very study that he calls his own. He reads a page, folded from the eyes of most men, a page of wondrous hieroglyphics; that handwriting of nerves and sinews and arteries; darkly he reads it, with a feeling enforced upon him that there is a wisdom above and beyond him; and if he is not a religiously inquiring and humble man, it seems to me that he knows not what he reads. Then again it is his office to visit scenes, where he is most especially taught the frailty of life, the impotence of man, and the need of a divine helper; where the strong man is bowed down by an invisible blow to debility, to delirium, to utter helplessness; where the dying stretch out their hands to heaven for aid, and to immortality for a reliance; where affliction, smitten to the dust and stript of all earthly supports, plainly declares that no sufficient resource is left for it, but Almighty Goodness. I do not say, that there is any thing in the physician's calling which necessarily makes him a religious and good man; but I do say, that if he obeys the true spirit of his calling, he must be led to the formation of such a character, as the inevitable result.

Turn next to the vocation of the lawyer; and what is it? It is to contribute his aid to the establishment and vindication of justice in the world. But what is justice? It is rectitude, righteousness. It is the right between man and man; and as an absolute quality, it is the high attribute of God. The lawyer may fall below this aim and view of his vocation; but that is not the fault of his vocation. His vocation is most moral, most religious; it connects him, most emphatically, with God; he is the minister of Almighty justice. In the strictest construction of things, the clergyman is not more truly God's minister, than he is. I know that the prevailing view is a different one. I know that the world looks upon this profession, as altogether irreligious, or altogether un-religious at the best. To say that the lawyer, however legitimately employed, is most religiously employed, sounds in most ears like mockery, I suppose. But let us look at his function, and let us put it in the most doubtful light. He goes up to the court of justice to plead the cause of his client. All the day long, he is engaged with examining witnesses, sifting evidence, and wrangling, if you please, for points of evidence and construction and law. He may commit mistakes, no doubt. He may err, in temper or in judgment. But suppose that his leading aim, his wish, is to obtain justice. And it is a very supposable thing, even though he be on the wrong side. He goes into the case, and he goes up to the court, not knowing what the right is, what the evidence is. He strenuously handles and sifts the evidence, to help on towards the right conclusion. Or if you say, it is to help his view of the case; still his function ministers to the same thing. For the conclusion is not committed to him; it lies with the judge and the jury; his office is ministerial; and he is to put forward every fair point on his side, as his opponent will, on the other side, because these are the very means, nay, the indispensable means, for coming to a righteous decision. And I say, that if he does this fairly and honestly, with a feeling of true self-respect, honour and conscience; with a feeling that God's justice reigns in that high tribunal; then he is acting a religious part; he is leading, that day, a religious life.

If righteousness, if justice is any part of religion, he is doing so. No matter whether during all that day, he has once appealed, in form or in terms, to his conscience or not; no matter whether he has once spoken of religion and of God, or not; if there has been the inward appeal, the inward purpose, the conscious intent and desire that justice, sacred justice should triumph, he has that day, led a good and religious life: and certainly, he has been making a most essential contribution to that religion of life and of society, the cause of equity between man and man, of truth and righteousness in the world.

There are certain other pursuits of an intellectual character, which require to be noticed in this connection; those, I mean, of literature and the arts. And the question here, let it be borne in mind, is not whether these pursuits are always conducted upon the highest principles; but whether they are in their proper nature and in their justest and highest character, religious and good; whether between these functions and religion there is any natural affinity; whether or not in their legitimate tendency, they are helping to work out the world's salvation from vice and sin, and spiritual misery. And certainly, to him who is looking with any anxiety to the great moral end of Providence, this is a very serious question. For in these forms, of literature and art, the highest genius of the world is usually revealed. The cost of time and money to which they put the world, is not a small consideration. The laboured works of art and the means lavished to obtain them; the writing, printing, selling and reading of books; all this presents one of the grandest features of our modern civilization. But the cost of mental labour is more than this; it is of the very life-blood of the world. This great power *of communication with men*, is not only working, and putting in requisition, much of the labour and time of the world; but it is often working painfully, and is wasting the noblest strength, in its strenuous toils. In silent and solitary places, genius is often found, consuming away in the fires which it has kindled. And now the question is: on what altars, are these priceless offerings laid?

Let it be considered then, in answer to this question, how few statues, paintings or books, have any bad design. Point me to one in an hundred, to one in a thousand or ten thousand that recommends vice. What then do they inculcate? Surely it is virtue, sanctity, the grandeur of the spiritual part of man. What do we see in these works? It is in sculpture, the fearful beauty of the god of Light, or the severe majesty of the Hebrew law-giver, or the solemn dignity of the Christ. It is in painting, some form of moral loveliness, some saint in the rapture of devotion, or a Christian, constant, serene, forgiving, victorious in the agonies of martyrdom. It is, in writing, in fiction, in poetry, in the drama, some actor or sufferer, nobly sustaining himself amidst temptations, difficulties, conflicts and sorrows, holding on his bright career through clouds and storms, to the goal of virtue and of heaven! Of course, I do not say that there are no moral defects in these representations; but most certain it is, nevertheless, that the highest literature and art of every age, embody its highest spiritual ideal of excellence. And even when we descend from their higher manifestations and find them simply amusing, there is nothing in this that is *hostile* to religion. Men must have recreation; and literature and art furnish that which is most pure, innocent and refining. They are already drawing away multitudes from coarser indulgences, and from places of low and vile resort. And the theatre, were it purged from certain offensive appendages, might be one of the most admirable ministrations conceivable, to the recreation and entertainment of the people. Nay, a great actor, as well as a great dramatist, in the legitimate walk of his art, may be a most effective and tremendous preacher of virtue to the people.

But, to go again to the main point; I must strenuously maintain, that books, to be of religious tendency, to be ministers to the general piety and virtue, need not be books of sermons, nor books of pious exercises, nor books of prayers. These all have their great and good office to discharge; but *whatever* inculcates pure sentiment, whatever touches the heart with the beauty of virtue and the blessedness of piety, is in accordance with religion; and this is the Gospel of literature and art. Yes, and it is preached from many a wall, it is preached from many a book, ay, from many a poem and fiction and Review, and Newspaper; and it would be a painful error, and a miserable narrowness, not to recognise these wide-spread agencies of heaven's providing, not to see and welcome these many-handed coadjutors, to the great and good cause. Christianity has, in fact, poured a measure of its own spirit into these forms; and not to recognise it there, is to deny its own specific character and claim. There are religious books indeed, which may be compared to the solid gold of Christianity; but many of its fairest gems have their setting in literature and art; and if it is a pitiable blindness, not to see its beautiful spirit even when it is surrounded by ignorance and poverty, what must it be not to recognise it, when it is set in the richest frame-work that human genius, imagination and art can devise for it?

There is one of the arts of expression, which I have

not mentioned; which sometimes seems to me a finer breathing-out of the soul than any other, and which certainly breathes a more immediate and inspiring tone into the heart of the world than any other; I mean music. Eloquent writing is great; eloquent speaking is greater; but an impromptu burst of song, or strain of music, like one of old Beethoven's voluntaries, I am inclined to say, is something greater. And now when this wonderful power, spreads around its spell, almost like inspiration; when, celebrating heroism, magnanimity, pity or pure love, it touches the heart with rapture and fills the eye with tears; is it to be accounted among things profane or irreligious? Must it be heard in church, to be made a holy thing? Must the words of its soul-thrilling utterance, be the technical words of religion, grace, godliness, righteousness, in order to mean anything divine? No, the vocation of the really great singer, breathing inspirations of truth and tenderness into the mind, is as holy as the vocation of the great preacher. In our dwellings, and in concert-rooms, ay, and in opera-houses—so the theme be pure and great—there is *preaching*, as truly as in church walls.

My brethren, give me your patience, if I must suppose that what I am saying, needs it. Do but consider what the great arts of mental and moral communication, express. Are they not oftentimes, the very same qualities that you revere in religion? Are goodness, pity, magnanimous self-sacrifice and heroic virtue, less divine, because they are expressed in literature, in painting or in song? And when you are moved to admiration, to tears, at some great example of heroism or self-sacrifice—be it by music or dramatic representation,—and when the same thing moves you in preaching; are you entirely to distinguish between the cases;

and to say that the one feeling is profane and the other holy?

Observe that I do not ask you to revere religion less, but to see and to welcome new, and perhaps before unthought of, instruments and agencies in the great field. You fear, perhaps, that they are not altogether pure. Then, I say, cut off and cast away the bad part; I plead not for that; but none the less accept the good. Nay, and I might ask, is religious teaching itself, all pure, all right? Indeed, I think that religion and religious teaching, have been as much perverted and abused as labour, literature or art.

It is every way most injurious and unjust to brand every thing as irreligious that is not specifically devoted to religion; to deny and as it were to forbid, to work any good work, those who "follow not after us." Our Saviour rebuked his disciples in such a case; saying, forbid them not; "he that is not against me, is for me." It is a bigotry totally unworthy of the generous and glorious Gospel, to hold in utter distrust and desecration all the beneficent activities of the world, all its kindly affections, all the high purposes and sentiments that live both in its physical and mental toils, because they do not come within the narrow pale of a technical religion; because they are not embraced in the mystic secret of what is called *religious experience*. All men are experiencing, more or less, what the Christian is experiencing. If his experience is higher and more perfect, is that a reason why he shall disdain and reject every thing that is like it in others? As well might the sage, the philosopher repudiate and scorn all the common sense and knowledge of the world. If he does so, we call him a bigoted and a scholastic philosopher. And if the Christian does so, we must call him a bigoted and mystic Christian. And, let me add, that if he were a generous and lofty-minded Christian, I cannot conceive what could be more distressing and mournful to him, than to hold all human existence, with the exception of his little peculiarity, to be a dark and desolate waste; to see all beside, as a gloomy mass of ignorance, error, sin and sorrow. It is the reproduction, on Christian ground, of the old Jewish exclusion and bigotry.

II. Let us now extend our view to another department of human life, recreation: and let us see whether we cannot embrace this within the great bond of religion; whether we cannot reclaim another lost territory to the highest service of man.

The isles of refreshment; the gardens and bowers of recreation; the play-grounds for sport; somewhere must they lie embosomed in this great world of labour; for man *cannot* always toil. Place for mirth and gayety, and wit and laughter; somewhere must it be found; for God hath made our nature to develop these very things. Is not this sufficient to vindicate the claim of recreation to be part of a good and religious life?

But let us look at the matter in another light. Suppose the world of men were created, and created in full maturity, but yesterday: and suppose it to be a world of beings, religious, devout, and devoutly grateful and good. The first employment that engages it, as a matter of necessity and of evident appointment too, is labour. But after some days or weeks of toil, it becomes acquainted with a new fact. It finds that incessant toil is impracticable; that it is breaking down both mind and body; in fact, that neither body nor mind was made for it. In short, the necessity of recreation becomes manifest. What then, under this view of the case, would men do? Social, and socially inclined, especially in their lighter engagements, would they not very naturally say, "let us devise games and sports, let us have music and dancing; let us listen to amusing recitations or dramatic stories of life's gayety or grandeur; and let us obey these tendencies and wants of our nature, in ever-kept, grateful veneration and love of Him who has made us." And if all this were followed out, in primeval innocence, with a religious devoutness and gratitude, I suppose that every objection to it would be removed from the minds of the most scrupulous.

The objection, then, lies against the abuse of these things. But what is the proper moral business of such an objection? Is it to extirpate the things in question? It cannot. Games, gayeties, sports, spectacles, there will be; as long as man have limbs or eyes or ears. It is no factitious choice which the world has made of its amusements. It chose them because it wanted them. The development here, is as natural as it is in the arts. You might as well talk of extirpating music and painting, as of driving the common amusements out of the world. Shall the religious objection then, since it cannot destroy, proceed to vilify these amusements? What! vilify an ordinance of nature, a necessity of man, a thing that cannot be helped? Is this the wisdom of religion; to degrade what it cannot destroy; to make of that which it cannot prevent, the worst that can be made; to banish alike from its protection and remedy, that which it cannot banish from the world? There lies the garden of recreation, close by the field of labour! and they cannot be severed; and men must and will pass from one to the other; and is it the office of religion to curse that garden, to pronounce it unholy ground, and so to give it up to utter levity or license? Nay, can any thing be plainer than that it is the business of religion to *reform* the amusements of the day? Reform, I believe, is the only measure that can be taken with the theatre; for that which has its root in the natural tastes, customs and literature of all civilized ages, is not likely to be eradicated. But how is any thing to be reformed? By invective, by opprobrium, by heaping contempt upon it? By casting it out from the pale of good influences, by withdrawing good men from all contact with it, by consigning it over to the irreligion, frivolity and self-indulgence of the world? Surely not. And therefore I am anxious to show that recreation must come within the plan of good life, and hence to show that it is not to be snatched as a forbidden pleasure; not to be distorted by the hand of reckless license; but to be welcomed, ay, and consecrated, by calm, conscientious, rational enjoyment

The objection I am considering, is, that the common and chosen recreations of the world, are abused. If they were pure and innocent, it would have nothing to say. But what is *not* abused? Is not business, is not religion itself abused? Are they therefore to be denounced and driven away from the sight of man? The objection carried out, would reduce the whole world to dead silence and inaction. But this cannot be tolerated. We must work; and we must do business; and we must relax into gayety and sportiveness, when our work is done. Improvements may be introduced into each sphere of action, and have been all along, through ages; but the sphere must remain; and it must remain essentially the same. You can no more get men to amuse themselves in some entirely new manner, than you can get them to do business, or to draw deeds, or to labour upon the arts, in some entirely new manner. I tell the ascetic religionist that there *will* be gayety and laughter; there *will* be assemblies and music and dancing; ay, and, as I think, cards and theatres, as long as the world stands. Whether *he* like it or not; whether *I* like it or not; it cannot be helped.

Now there are abuses of these things. What are we to say of the abuses? "Let them crush down and destroy the things themselves," do we say? But they cannot. Then let them be cut off. There is really nothing else to be done. Elevate, refine, purify the public amusements. Let religion recognise and restrain them. Let it not, as is too common, drive them to license and extravagance; but let it throw around them its gentle and holy bonds, to make them pure, cheerful, healthful; healthful to the great ends of life. What a blessed thing for the world, were it, if its amusements could thus be rescued, redeemed, and brought into the service of its virtue and piety! What a blessed thing for the weary world, for the youthful world, for the joyous world, if the steps of its recreation, trodden in cheerful innocence and devout gratitude, could be ever leading it to heaven!

I have now considered two great departments of life; labour, physical and mental, and recreation. My design has been, to rescue them from the common imputation of being necessarily or altogether worldly or irreligious; to resist the prevailing notion, that all true religion, all true spiritual goodness, is gathered up in certain and (so-called) sacred professions, peculiarities and places; to show that in all the heaven-ordained pursuits and conditions of life, there are elements of good; that the Spirit is breathing its gracious influence through the world; that there is a religion of life, unrecognised in our ordinary religious systems, but real and true, and either worthy of our welcome and admiration, or when defective or wrong, worthy of our endeavour to correct and improve it.

III. But, once more, there is a religion of society.

This topic, let me observe, is essentially distinct from those which I have already discussed. It is true that our labour and recreation are mostly social; but in the social bond, there is something more than the business or the amusement which takes advantage of it. It has a holiness, a grandeur, a sweetness of its own. The world, indeed, is encircled by that bond. And what is it? In business, there is something more than barter, exchange, price, payment; there is a sacred faith of man in man. When you know one in whose integrity you repose perfect confidence; when you feel that he will not swerve from conscience for any temptation; *that* integrity, that conscience is the image of God to you; and when you believe in it, it is as generous and great an act, as if you believe in the rectitude of heaven. In gay assemblies for amusement again; not instruments of music, not rich apparel, not sumptuous entertainments, are the chief things; but the gushing and mingling affections of life. I know what is said, and may be truly said, of selfishness and pride and envy in these scenes; but I know too, that good affections go up to these gathering places, or they would be as desolate as the spoil-clad caves and dens of thieves and robbers. Look at two kind-hearted acquaintances meeting in those places, or meeting in the market or on the exchange; and see the warm pressure of the hand, the kindling of the eye, the suffusion of the whole countenance with heartfelt gladness; and tell me if there is not a *religion* between those hearts; and true love and worshipping, in each other, of the true and good. It is not policy that spreads such a charm around that meeting, but the halo of bright and beautiful affection. It hangs, like the soft enfolding sky, over all the world, over all places where men meet, and toil or walk together; not over lovers' bowers and marriage altars alone, not over the homes of purity and tenderness alone—yet these are in the world—but over all tilled fields, and busy workshops, and dusty highways, and paved streets. There is not a trodden stone upon these side-walks, but it has been an altar of such offerings of mutual kindness. There is not a wooden pillar nor an iron railing, against which throbbing hearts have not leaned. True, there are other elements in the stream of life, that is flowing through these channels. But will any one dare to deny that *this* element is here and every where; honest, heart-felt, disinterested, inexpressible affection? If he dare, let him do so, and then confess that he is a brute or a fiend, and not a man. But if this element is here, is every where, what is it?

To answer this question, let us ask, what is God? And the Apostle answers, "God is love." And is not this, of which we have been speaking, love; true, pure love? Deny it, and bear upon your head, the indignation of all mankind. But admit it; and what do you admit? That God's love is poured into human hearts. Yes, into human hearts! Oh! sad, sad—frail, erring, broken, are they often; yet God's spirit is breathing through them; else were they despoiled, desolate, crushed, beyond recovery, beyond hope. It is that same spirit of love that enshrines the earth and enrobes the heavens with beauty; and if there were not an eye of love to see it, a heart of love to feel it, all nature would be the desolate abode of creatures as desolate.

I know full well, alas! that there are other things in life besides love. I know that in city streets, not far removed from us, are depths beneath depths of sorrow and sin ; that in cellars beneath cellars, and in stories above stories, are crowded together poverty and wretchedness and filth and vileness. Oh! desolate and dreary abodes; where, through the long bright day, only want and toil and sorrow knock at all your gates, only blows of passion and shrieks of children, and cursings of drunkenness and oaths of the profane, measure out the heavy hours!—are there no hearts to bleed for you? Are there no energies of love to interpose for you? Shall the stream of glad and prosperous life flow so near you, and *never* come to cleanse out your impurities and heal your miseries? Nay, in that stream of glad and joyous life, I know that there are ingredients of evil; the very ingredients indeed that prevent a consummation so blessed. I know that amidst gay equipages, selfishness is borne; and that amidst luxurious entertainments pride is nursed and sensuality gorged; and that through fair and fair-seeming assemblies, envy steals, and hatred and revenge spread their wiles; and that many a bad passion casts its shade over the brightest atmosphere of social life. All this I know. I do not refuse to see the evil that is in life. But tell me not that all is evil. I still see God in the world. I see good amidst the evil. I see the hand of mercy often guiding the chariot of wealth to the abodes of poverty and sorrow. I see truth and simplicity amidst many wiles and sophistries. There is a habit of berating fashionable life, which is often founded more in ignorance than ill-will. Those who know better, know that there is good every where. I see good hearts beneath gay robes; ay, and beneath tattered robes, too. I see love clasping the hand of love, amidst all the envyings and distortions of showy competition; and I see fidelity, piety, sympathy, holding the long night-watch, by the bed-side of a suffering neighbour, amidst all surrounding poverty and misery. God bless the kindly office, the pitying thought, the loving heart, wherever it is!—and it is every where!

Why, my Brethren, do I insist upon this? Why do I endeavour to spread life before you in a new light; in a light not recognised by most of our religious systems? I will endeavour, in few words, to tell you.

I am made to be affected, in many respects, by the consciousness of what is passing around me, but especially in my happiness and my improvement. I am more than an inhabitant of the world; I am a sympathizing member of the great human community. Its condition comes as a blessing, or weighs as a burthen, upon my single thought. It is a discouragement or an excitement, to all that is good and happy within me. If I dwell in this world as in a prison; if the higher faith, the religion of my being, compels me to regard it in this light; if all its employments are prison employments, mere penal tasks or drudgeries to keep its tenants out of mischief; if all its ingenious handicrafts are but prison arts and contrivances to while away the time; if all its relations are prison relations, relations of dislike or selfishness, or of compact and cunning in evil; if the world is such a place, it must be a gloomy and unholy place, a dark abode, a wilderness world: yes, though its walls were built of massive gold and its dome were spread with sapphire and studded with diamond-stars, I must look upon it with sadness; I must look upon its inhabitants with coldness, distrust and disdain. It is a picture which I have drawn; but it is mainly a picture of the world as viewed by the prevailing religion of our time. Nay, more; from this prison, it deems that thousands are daily carried to execution—plunged into a lake of fire

—there to burn forever. And if the belief of its votaries actually came up to its creed, gayety and joyousness in such a world, would be more misplaced and shocking a thousand times, than they would be in the gloomiest penitentiary that ever was builded. Is this fair and bright world—is God's world, such a place? If it is, I am sure that it was not made for any rational and reflective happiness; but mountain to mountain, and continent to continent, and age to age, should echo nothing but sighs and groans.

But if this world, instead of being a prison, is a school; if all its appointed tasks are teachings; if all its ordained employments are fit means for improvement, and all its proper amusements are the good recreations of virtuous toil and endeavour; if, however perverse and sinful men are, there is an element of good in all their lawful pursuits, and a diviner breathing in all their lawful affections; if the ground whereon they tread is holy ground; if there is a natural religion of life, answering, with however many a broken tone, to the religion of nature; if there is a beauty and glory of humanity, answering, with however many a mingled shade, to the loveliness of soft landscapes and embosoming hills and the overhanging glory of the deep, blue heavens; then all is changed. And it is changed not more for happiness than it is for virtue.

For then do men find that they may be virtuous, improving, religious, *in* their employments; that this is precisely what their employments were made for. Then will they find that all their social relations—friendship, love, family ties—were made to be holy. Then will they find that they may be religious, not by a kind of protest and resistance against their several vocations, but by conformity to their true spirit; that their vocations do not exclude religion, but demand it for their own perfection; that they may be religious labourers, whether in field or factory; religious physicians and lawyers; religious sculptors, painters and musicians; that they may be religious in all the toils and amusements of life; that their life may be a religion; the broad earth, its altar; its incense, the very breath of life; and its fires kindled, ever kindled by the brightness of heaven.

XX.

THE VOICES OF THE DEAD.

AND BY IT, HE BEING DEAD, YET SPEAKETH.—Hebrews xi. 4.

THIS is a record of virtue that existed six thousand years ago; but which yet liveth in its memory, and speaketh in its example. "Abel, it is written, offered unto God a more excellent sacrifice than Cain, by which he obtained witness, that he was righteous, God testifying of his gifts; and by it, he being dead, yet speaketh." How enduring is the memorial of goodness! It is but a sentence, which is read in a moment; it is but a leaf from the scroll of time; and yet, it is borne on the breath of ages; it takes the attributes of universality and eternity; it becomes a heritage, from family to family, among all the dwellings of the world.

But it is not Abel alone, the accepted worshipper and martyred brother, that thus speaks to us. The world is filled with the voices of the dead. They speak not from the public records of the great world only, but from the private history of our own experience. They speak to us in a thousand remembrances, in a thousand incidents, events, associations. They speak to us, not only from their silent graves, but from the throng of life. Though they are invisible, yet life is filled with their presence. They are with us, by the silent fireside and in the secluded chamber: they are with us in the paths of society, and in the crowded assemblies of men. They speak to us from the lonely way-side; and they speak to us, from the venerable walls that echo to the steps of a multitude, and to the voice of prayer. Go where we will, the dead are with us. We live, we converse with those, who once lived and conversed with us. Their well-remembered tone mingles with the whispering breezes, with the sound of the falling leaf, with the jubilee shout of the spring-time. The earth is filled with their shadowy train.

But there are more substantial expressions of the presence of the dead with the living. The earth is filled with the labours, the works, of the dead. Almost all the literature in the world, the discoveries of science, the glories of art, the ever-enduring temples, the dwelling-places of generations, the comforts and improvements of life, the languages, the maxims, the opinions of the living, the very frame-work of society, the institutions of nations, the fabrics of empire—all are the works of the dead: by these, they who are dead yet speak. Life; busy, eager, craving, importunate, absorbing life; yet what is its sphere, compared with the empire of death! What, in other words, is the sphere of visible, compared with the vast empire of invisible, life! A moment in time; a speck in immensity; a shadow amidst enduring and unchangeable realities; a breath of existence amidst the ages and regions of undying life! They live—they live indeed, whom we call dead. They live in our thoughts; they live in our blessings; they live in our life: "death hath no power over them."

Let us then meditate upon those, the mighty company of our departed brethren, who occupy such a space in the universe of being. Let us meditate upon their relation, their message, their ministry, to us. Let us look upon ourselves in this relation, and see what we owe to the dead. Let us look upon the earth, and see if death hath not left behind its desolating career, some softer traces, some holier imprint, than of destruction.

I. What memories, then, have the dead left among us, to stimulate us to virtue, to win us to goodness?

The approach to death often prepares the way for this impression. The effect of a last sickness to develop and perfect the virtues of our friends, is often so striking and beautiful, as to seem more than a compensation for all the sufferings of disease. It is the practice of the Catholic Church to bestow upon its eminent saints, a title to the perpetual homage of the faithful, in the act of canonization. But what is a formal decree, compared with the effect of a last sickness, to canonize the virtue that we love, for eternal remembrance and admiration? How often does that touching decay, that gradual unclothing of the mortal body, seem to be a putting on of the garments of immortal beauty and life! That pale cheek, that placid brow, that sweet serenity spread over the whole countenance; that spiritual, almost supernatural brightness of the eye, as if light from another world already shone through it; that noble and touching disinterestedness of the parting spirit, which utters no complaint, which breathes no sigh, which speaks no word of fear nor apprehension to wound its friend, which is calm, and cheerful, and natural, and self-sustained, amidst daily declining strength and the sure approach to death; and then, at length, when concealment is no longer possible, that last firm, triumphant, consoling discourse, and that last look of all mortal tenderness and immortal trust; what hallowed memories are these to soothe, to purify, to enrapture surviving love!

Death, too, sets a seal upon the excellence, that

sickness unfolds and consecrates. There is no living virtue, concerning which, such is our frailty, we must not fear that it may fall; or at least, that it may somewhat fail from its steadfastness. It is a painful, it is a just fear, in the bosoms of the best and purest beings on earth, that some dreadful lapse *may* come over them, or over those whom they hold in the highest reverence. But death, fearful, mighty as its power, is yet a power, that is subject to virtue. It gives victory to virtue. It brings relief to the heart, from its profoundest fear. It enables us to say, " now all is safe! The battle is fought; the victory is won. The course is finished; the race is run; the faith is kept: henceforth, it is no more doubt nor danger, no more temptation nor strife; henceforth is the reward of the just, the crown which the Lord, the righteous Judge, will give!' Yes, death, dark power of earth though it seem, does yet ensphere virtue, as it were, in heaven. It sets it up on high, for eternal admiration. It fixes its places never more to be changed; as a star to shine onward, and onward, through the depths of the everlasting ages!

In life there are many things which interfere with a just estimate of the virtues of others. There are, in some cases, jealousies and misconstructions, and there are false appearances; there are veils upon the heart that hide its most secret workings and its sweetest affections from us; there are earthly clouds that come between us and the excellence that we love. So that it is not, perhaps, till a friend is taken from us, that we entirely feel his value, and appreciate his worth. The vision is loveliest at its vanishing away; and we perceive not, perhaps, till we see the parting wing, that an angel has been with us!

Yet if we are *not*, from any cause, or in any degree,

blind to the excellence we possess, if we do feel all the value of the treasure which our affections hold dear; yet, I say, how does that earthly excellence take not only a permanent, but a saintly character, as it passes beyond the bounds of mortal frailty and imperfection! How does death enshrine it, for a homage, more reverential and holy, than is ever given to living worth! So that the virtues of the dead gain, perhaps, in the power of sanctity, what they lose in the power of visible presence; and thus—it may not be too much to say—thus the virtues of the dead benefit us sometimes, as much as the examples of living goodness.

How beautiful is the ministration, by which those who are dead, thus speak to us, thus help us, comfort us, guide, gladden, bless us! How grateful must it be to their thoughts of us, to know that we thus remember them; that we remember them, not with mere admiration, but in a manner that ministers to all our virtues! What a glorious vision of the future is it, to the good and pure who are yet living on earth, that the virtues which they are cherishing and manifesting, the good character which they are building up here, the charm of their benevolence and piety, shall live, when they have laid down the burthen and toil of life, shall be an inspiring breath to the fainting hearts that are broken from them, a wafted odour of sanctity to hundreds and thousands that shall come after them. Is it not so? Are there not those, the simplest story, the frailest record of whose goodness, is still and ever, doing good? But, frail records, we know full well, frail records they are *not*, which are in our hearts. And can we have known those, whom it is a joy as well as a sorrow to think of, and not be better for it? Are there those, once, our friends, now bright angels in some blessed sphere; and do we not sometimes say, "perhaps, that pure eye of affection is on me now; and I will do nothing to wound it?" No, surely, it cannot be, that the dead will speak to us in vain. Their memories are all around us : their footsteps are in our paths; the memorials of them meet our eye at every turn; their presence is in our dwellings; their voices are in our ears; they speak to us—in the sad reverie of contemplation, in the sharp pang of feeling, in the cold shadow of memory, in the bright light of hope—and it cannot be, that they will speak in vain.

II. Nay, the very world we live in; is it not consecrated to us by the memory of the dead? Are not the very scenes of life made more interesting to us, by being connected with thoughts that run backward far beyond the range of present life? This is another view of the advantage and effect with which those who are "dead, yet speak to us."

If we were beings to whom, present, immediate, instant enjoyment were every thing; if we were animals, in other words, with all our thoughts prone to the earth on which we tread, the case would be different; the conclusion would be different. But we are beings of a deeper nature, of wider relations, of higher aspirations, of a loftier destiny. And being such, I cannot hesitate to say for myself, that I would not have every thing which I behold on earth, the work of the present, living generation. The world would be, comparatively, an ordinary, indifferent place, if it contained nothing but the workmanship, the handicraft, the devices of living men. No, I would see dwellings, which speak to me of other things, than earthly convenience, or fleeting pleasure; which speak to me the holy recollections of lives which were passed in them, and have passed away from them. I would see temples in which successive generations of men have prayed. I would see ruins, on whose mighty walls is inscribed the touching story of joy and sorrow, love, heroism, patience, which lived there, there breathed its first hope, its last sigh, ages ago. I would behold scenes, which offer more than fair landscape and living stream to my eye; which tell me of inspired genius, glorious fortitude, martyred faith, that studied there, suffered there, died there. I would behold the earth, in fine, when it is spread before me, as more than soil and scenery, rich and fair though they be; I would behold the earth as written over with histories; as a sublime page, on which are recorded the lives of men, and empires.

The world, even of nature, is not one laughing, gay scene. It is not so in fact; it appears not so in the light of our sober, solemn, Christian teachings. The dark cloud sometimes overshadows it: the storm sweeps through its pleasant valleys; the thunder smites its everlasting hills; and the holy record hath said, "thorns and thistles shall it bring forth to thee." It has been said that all the tones in nature are, to use the musical phrase, on the minor key. That is to say, they are plaintive tones. And although the fact is probably somewhat exaggerated, when stated so strongly and unqualifiedly, yet to a certain extent it is true. It is true, that that tone always mingles with the music of nature. In the winds that stir the mountain pine, as well as in the wailing storm; in the soft-falling shower, and in the rustling of the autumn leaves; in the roar of ocean, as it breaks upon the lonely sea-beach; in the thundering cataract, that lifts up its eternal anthem amidst the voices of nature; and so likewise, in those inarticulate interpretations of nature, the bleating of flocks, the lowing of herds, and even in the song of birds, there is usually something plaintive; something that touches the sad and brooding spirit of thought. And the contemplation of nature in all its forms, as well of beauty as of sublimity, is apt to be tinged with melancholy. And all the higher musings, the nobler aspirations of the mind, possess something of this character. I doubt if there were ever a manifestation of genius in the world, that did not bear something of this trait.

It can scarcely be the part of wisdom, then, to refuse to sympathize with this spirit of nature and humanity. And it can be no argument against a contemplation of this world as having its abodes sanctified by the memory of the departed, as having its brightness softly veiled over by the shadow of death; it can be no argument against such contemplation, that it is somewhat sober and sad. I feel then, that the dead have conferred a blessing upon me, in helping me to think of the world thus rightly; in thus giving a hue of sadness to the scenes of this world, while, at the same time, they have clothed it with every glorious and powerful charm of association. This mingled spirit of energy and humility, of triumph and tenderness, of glorying and sorrowing, is the very spirit of Christianity. It was the spirit of Jesus, the conqueror and the sufferer. Death was before him; and yet his thoughts were of triumph. Victory was in his view; and yet, what a victory! No laurel crown was upon his head; no flush of pride was upon his brow; no exultation flashed from his eye; for his was a victory to be gained over death, and through death. No laurel crown sat upon his head—but a crown of thorns, no flush of pride was on his brow—but meekness was enthroned there; no exultation flashed from his eye— but tears flowed from it: "Jesus wept."

Come then, to us, that spirit at once of courage and

meekness; of fortitude and gentleness; of a life hopeful and happy, but thoughtful of death; of a world bright and beautiful, but passing away! So let us live, and act; and think, and feel; and let us thank the good providence, the good ordination of heaven, that has made the dead our teachers.

III. But they teach us more. They not only leave their own enshrined and canonized virtues for us to love and imitate; they not only gather about us the glorious and touching associations of the past, to hallow and dignify this world to us, and to throw the soft veil of memory over all its scenes; but they open a future world to our vision, and invite us to its blessed abodes.

They open that world to us, by giving, in their own deaths, a strong proof of its existence.

The future, indeed, to mere earthly views, is often "a land of darkness as darkness itself, and of the shadow of death without any order, and where the light is as darkness." Truly, death is "without any order." There is in it, such a total disregard to circumstances, as shows that it cannot be an ultimate event. That must be connected with something else; that cannot be final, which, considered as final, puts all the calculations of wisdom so utterly at defiance. The tribes of animals, the classes and species of the vegetable creation, come to their perfection, and then die. But is there any such order for human beings? Do the generations of mankind go down to the grave, in ranks and processions? Are the human, like the vegetable races, suffered to stand till they have made provision for their successors, before they depart? No; without order, without discrimination, without provision for the future, or remedy for the past, the children of men depart. They die—the old, the young; the most useless, and those most needed; the worst and the best, alike die; and if there be no scenes beyond this life, if there be no circumstances nor allotments to explain the mystery, then all around us is, as it was to the doubting spirit of Job, "a land of darkness as darkness itself." The blow falls, like the thunder-bolt beneath the dark cloud; but it has not even the intention, the explanation that belongs to that dread minister. The stroke of death must be more reckless than even the lightning's flash; yes, that solemn visitation that cometh with so many dread signs—the body's dissolution, the spirit's extremity, the winding up of the great scene of life, has not even the meaning that belongs to the blindest agents in nature, if there be no reaction, no revelation hereafter! Can this be? Doth God take care for things animate and inanimate, and will he not care for us?

Let us look at it for a moment. I have seen one die—the delight of his friends, the pride of his kindred, the hope of his country: but he died! How beautiful was that offering upon the altar of death! The fire of genius kindled in his eye; the generous affections of youth mantled in his cheek; his foot was upon the threshold of life; his studies, his preparations for honoured and useful life, were completed; his breast was filled with a thousand glowing, and noble, and never yet expressed aspirations: but he died! He died; while another, of a nature dull, coarse and unrefined, of habits low, base and brutish, of a promise that had nothing in it but shame and misery—such an one, I say, was suffered to encumber the earth. Could this be, if there were no other sphere for the gifted, the aspiring and the approved, to act in? Can we believe that the energy just trained for action, the embryo thought just bursting into expression, the deep and earnest passion of a noble nature, just swelling into the expansion of every beautiful virtue, should never manifest its power, should never speak, should never unfold itself? Can we believe that all this should die; while meanness, corruption, sensuality, and every deformed and dishonoured power, should live? No, ye goodly and glorious ones! ye godlike in youthful virtue! ye die not in vain: ye teach, ye assure us, that ye are gone to some world of nobler life and action.

I have seen one die; she was beautiful; and beautiful were the ministries of life that were given her to fulfil. Angelic loveliness enrobed her; and a grace as if it were caught from heaven, breathed in every tone, hallowed every affection, shone in every action—invested as a halo, her whole existence, and made it a light and blessing, a charm and a vision of gladness, to all around her: but she died! Friendship, and love, and parental fondness, and infant weakness, stretched out their hand to save her; but they could not save her: and she died! What! did all that loveliness die? Is there no land of the blessed and the lovely ones, for such to live in? Forbid it reason, religion!—bereaved affection, and undying love! forbid the thought! It cannot be that such die in God's counsel, who live even in frail human memory forever!

I have seen one die—in the maturity of every power, in the earthly perfection of every faculty; when many temptations had been overcome, and many hard lessons had been learned; when many experiments had made virtue easy, and had given a facility to action, and a success to endeavour; when wisdom had been learnt from many mistakes, and a skill had been laboriously acquired in the use of many powers; and the being, I looked upon, had just compassed that most useful, most practical of all knowledge, how to live, and to act well and wisely: yet I have seen such an one die! Was all this treasure gained, only to be lost? Were all these faculties trained, only to be thrown into utter disuse? Was this instrument, the intelligent soul, the noblest in the universe; was it so laboriously fashioned, and by the most varied and expensive apparatus, that on the very moment of being finished, it should be cast away forever? No, the dead, as we call them, do not *so* die. They carry our thoughts to another and a nobler existence. They teach us, and especially by all the strange and seemingly untoward circumstances of their departure from this life, that they, and we, shall live forever. They open the future world, then, to our faith.

They open it also, and in fine, to our affections. No person of reflection and piety can have lived long, without beginning to find, in regard to the earthly objects which most interest him, his friends, that the balance is gradually inclining in favour of another world. How many, after the middle period of life, and especially in declining years, must feel, if the experience of life has had any just effect upon them, that the objects of their strongest attachment are not here. One by one, the ties of earthly affection are cut asunder; one by one, friends, companions, children, parents, are taken from us; for a time, perhaps, we are "in a strait betwixt two," as was the apostle, not deciding altogether whether it is better to depart; but shall we not, at length, say with the disciples, when some dearer friend is taken, "let us go and die with him?"

The dead have not ceased their communication with us, though the visible chain is broken. If they are still the same, they must still think of us. As two friends on earth, may know that they love each other, without any expression, without even the sight of each other; as they may know though dwelling in different and distant countries, without any visible chain of communication, that their thoughts meet and mingle together, so may it be with two friends of whom the one is on earth, and the other is in heaven. Especially where there is such an union of pure minds that it is scarcely possible to conceive of separation, that union seems to be a part of their very being: we may believe that their friendship, their mutual sympathy, is beyond the power of the grave to break up. "But ah! we say, if there were only some manifestations; if there were only a glimpse of that blessed land; if there were, indeed, some messenger bird, such as is supposed in some countries to come from the spirit land, how eagerly should we question it!" In the words of the poet, we should say,

> " But tell us, thou bird of the solemn strain,
> Can those who have loved, forget?
> We call—but *they* answer not again—
> *Do* they love, do they love us yet?
> We call them far, through the silent night,
> And they speak not from cave nor hill;
> We know, we know, that their land is bright,
> But say, do they love there still?"

The poetic doubt, we may answer with plain reasoning, and plainer scripture. We may say, in the language of reason, if they *live* there, they love there. We may answer in the language of Jesus Christ, " he that liveth and believeth in me, shall never die." And again: " have ye not read," saith our Saviour, " that which was spoken unto you by God, saying, I am the God of Abraham, and the God of Isaac, and the God of Jacob? God is not the God of the dead, but of the living." Then it is true, that they live there; and they yet speak to us. From that bright sphere, from that calm region, from the bowers of life immortal, they speak to us. They say to us, " sigh not in despair over the broken and defeated expectations of earth. Sorrow not as those who have no hope. Bear calmly and cheerfully thy lot. Brighten the chain of love, of sympathy; of communion with all pure minds, on earth and in heaven. Think, Oh! think of the mighty and glorious company that fill the immortal regions. Light, life, beauty, beatitude, are here. Come, children of earth! come to the bright and blessed land!" I see no lovely features, revealing themselves through the dim and shadowy veils of heaven. I see no angel forms enrobed with the bright clouds of eventide. But "I hear a voice, saying, write, blessed are the dead who die in the Lord, for they rest—for they rest, from their labours, and their works, works of piety and love recorded in our hearts and kept in eternal remembrance—their works do follow them." Our hearts, their workmanship, do follow them. We will go and die with them. We will go and live with them forever l

Can I leave these meditations, my brethren, without paying homage to that religion which has brought life and immortality to light; without calling to mind that simple and touching acknowledgment of the great apostle, "I thank God through our Lord Jesus Christ." Ah! how desolate must be the affections of a people, that spurn this truth and trust! I have wandered among the tombs of such a people; I have wandered through that far-famed cemetery, that overlooks from its mournful brow, the gay and crowded metropolis of France; but among the many inscriptions upon those tombs, I read scarcely one; I read,—to state so striking a fact with numerical exactness—I read not more than four or five inscriptions in the whole Pere La Chaise, which made any consoling reference to a future life. I read, on those cold marble tombs, the lamentations of bereavement, in every affecting variety of phrase. On the tomb of youth, it was written that "its broken-hearted parents, who spent their days in tears and their nights in anguish, had laid down here their treasure and their hope." On the proud mausoleum where friendship, companionship, love, had deposited their holy relics, it was constantly written, "Her husband inconsolable;" "His disconsolate wife;" "A brother left alone and unhappy" has raised this monument; but seldom, so seldom that scarcely ever, did the mournful record close with a word of hope; scarcely at all was it to be read amidst the marble silence of that world of the dead, that there is a life beyond; and that surviving friends hope for a blessed meeting again, where death comes no more!

Oh! death! dark hour to hopeless unbelief! hour to which, in that creed of despair, no hour shall succeed! being's last hour! to whose appalling darkness, even the shadows of an avenging retribution were brightness and relief; death! what art thou to the Christian's assurance? Great hour of answer to life's prayer; great hour that shall break asunder the bond of life's mystery; hour of release from life's burden; hour of reunion with the loved and lost; what mighty hopes, hasten to their fulfilment in thee! What longings, what aspirations,—breathed in the still night beneath the silent stars; what dread emotions of curiosity; what deep meditations of joy; what hallowed imaginings of never experienced purity and bliss; what possibilities, shadowing forth unspeakable realities to the soul, all verge to their consummation in thee!

Oh! death! the Christian's death! what art thou, but the gate of life, the portal of heaven, the threshold of eternity!

Thanks be to God; let us say it, Christians! in the comforting words of holy scripture: "thanks be to God who giveth us the victory, through our Lord Jesus Christ!" What hope can be so precious as the hope in him? What emblems can speak to bereaved affection, or to dying frailty, like those emblems at once of suffering and triumph, which proclaim a crucified and risen Lord; which proclaim that Jesus the Forerunner, has passed through death, to immortal life? Well, that the great truth should be signalized and sealed upon our heart by a holy rite! Well, that amidst mortal changes, and hasting to the tomb, we should, from time to time, set up an altar, and say, " by this heaven-ordained token, do we know that we shall live forever!" God grant the fulfilment of this great hope—what matter all things beside?—God grant the fulfilment of this great hope, through Jesus Christ!

ON THE NATURE OF RELIGION.

XXI.

THE IDENTITY OF RELIGION WITH GOODNESS, AND WITH A GOOD LIFE.

IF A MAN SAY, I LOVE GOD, AND HATETH HIS BROTHER, HE IS A LIAR; FOR HE THAT LOVETH NOT HIS BROTHER WHOM HE HATH SEEN, HOW CAN HE LOVE GOD WHOM HE HATH NOT SEEN?—1 John iv. 24.

IF there is any mission for the true teacher to accomplish in this age, it is to identify religion with goodness; to show that they are the same thing, manifestations, that is to say, of the same principle; to show, in other words and according to the Apostle, that no man is to be accounted a lover of God, who is not a lover of his brother. It is, I say again, to identify religion with morals, religion with virtue; with justice, truth, integrity, honesty, generosity, disinterestedness; religion with the highest beauty and loveliness of character. This, I repeat, is the great mission, and message of the true teacher to-day. What it may be some other day, what transcendental thing may be waiting to be taught, I do not know; but this, I conceive, is the practical business of religious instruction now. Let me not be misunderstood, as if I were supposed to say that this or any other mere doctrine, were the *ultimate end* of preaching. *That* is, to make men holy. But how shall any preaching avail to make men holy, unless it do rightly and clearly teach them what it *is* to be holy? If they mistake here, all their labour to be religious, all their hearing of the word, Sabbath keeping, praying, and striving, will be in vain. And therefore, I hold that to teach this, and especially to show that religion is not something else than a good heart, but is that very thing; this, I say, is the burden of the present time.

I use now an old prophetic phrase, and I may remark here, that every time has its burden. In the times of the Old Testament, the burden of teaching was, to assert the supremacy and spirituality of God, in opposition to Idolatry. In the Christian time, it was to set forth that universal and impartial, and that most real and true love which God has for his earthly creatures, in opposition to Jewish peculiarity and Pagan indifference and all human distrust; a love, declared by one who came from the bosom of the Father, sealed in his blood, and thus bringing nigh to God, a guilty, estranged, and unbelieving world. The burden of the Reformation time, was to assert the freedom of religion; to bring it out from the bondage of human authority into the sanctuary of private judgment and sacred conscience. But now, religion having escaped from Pagan idolatry and Jewish exclusion and papal bondage, and survived many a controversy since, has encountered a deeper question concerning its own nature. What especially is religion itself? This, I say, is the great question of the present day. It underlies all our controversies. It is that which gives the main interest to every controversy. For whether the controversy be about forms or creeds, the vital question is, whether this or that ritual or doctrine ministers essentially to true religion; so that if a man embraces some other system, he is fatally deficient of the vital means of salvation. And this brings us to the question, what is true religion itself?

This question, as I have intimated, presses mainly upon a single point, which I will now state and argue as a contested point: viz. whether religion, in its essence, consists in a principle of rectitude, of goodness, in a simple and true love of the true and divine, or whether it consists in something else; or in other words—whether it consists in certain intelligible affections, or in something, to the mass of men, unknown and unintelligible.

This question craves some explanation, both that you may understand what it is, and may perceive that it is a question; and I must bespeak your patience.

In entering upon these points, let us consider, in the first place, what is the ground on which the general assertion in our text proceeds.

There is, then, but one true principle in the mind, and that is the love of the true, the right, the holy. There is but one character of the soul, to which God has given his approbation, and with which he has connected the certainty of happiness here and hereafter. There is something in the soul which is made the condition of its salvation; and that something is one thing, though it has many forms. It is sometimes called grace in the heart; sometimes, holiness, righteousness, conformity to the character of God; but the term for it most familiar in popular use, is *religion*. The constant question is, when a man's spiritual safety or well-being is the point for consideration, when he is going to die, and men would know whether he is to be happy hereafter; has he got religion? or has he been a religious man? I must confess that I do not like this use of the term. I am accustomed to consider religion as reverence and love towards God; and to consider it therefore, as only one part of rectitude or excellence. But you know that it commonly stands for the whole of that character which God requires of us. Now what I am saying is, that this character is, in principle, *one thing*. It is, being right; and being right is but one thing. It has many forms; but only one essence. It may be the love of God, and then it is piety. It may be the love of men, and then it is philanthropy. But the love of God, and the love of man as bearing his image, are in essence the same thing. Or to discriminate with regard to this second table of the law: it may be a love of men's happiness, and then it is the very image of God's benevolence; or it may be the love of holiness in men, of their goodness, justice, truth, virtue, and then it is a love of the same things that form, when infinitely exalted, the character of God. All these forms of excellence, if they cannot be resolved into one principle, are certainly parts of one great consciousness, the consciousness of right; they at any rate have the strictest alliance; they are inseparably bound together as parts of one whole; the very nature of true excellence in one form, is a pledge for its existence in every other form. He who has the right principle in him, is a lover of God, and a lover of good men, and a lover of all goodness and purity, and a labourer for the happiness of all around him. The tree is one, though the branches and the leaves and the blossoms, be many and various; all spring from one vital germ; so that the Apostle, in our text, will not allow it to be said, that a man is a lover of God, who does not love his brethren of the human family.

Now it may surprise you at first, to hear it asserted that this apparently reasonable account of the matter, does not accord with the popular judgment. To this point of explanation, therefore, I must invite your attention, lest I seem to fight as one that beateth the air.

It is true then, that it is admitted in general, that the Christian, the object of God's favour here and hereafter, must be a good man; a just, honest, pure, benevolent man. These admissions are general and vague. We must penetrate into this matter, with some more discriminating inquiry. What is it, specifically, that makes a man spiritually a Christian, and entitles him to hope for future happiness? The common answer is; it is religion, it is piety, it is grace in the heart, it is being converted, it is being in Christ, and being a new creature. These phrases I might comment upon, if I had time, and I might show that they have a very true and just meaning. But what is the meaning that they actually convey to most hearers? What is this inmost and saving principle of religion, this grace or godliness, this spirit of the regenerated man? Is it not something peculiar to the regenerate—not something *more* of goodness in them than in other men, but something different in them from goodness in others? Is it not something possessed by them alone, unshared with the rest of the world, unknown, completely unknown, and in fact inconceivable to the great body of mankind? Are not the saints, God's people as they are called, supposed to have some secret of experience wrapped up in them, with which the stranger intermeddleth not; of which the world knoweth nothing? I do not wish to have this so understood if it is not true. But if it is true, it is too serious a point to be tampered with or treated with any fastidious delicacy. I say then plainly and earnestly, is it not true? If you ask most men around you what is that gracious state of the heart, which is produced by the act of regeneration, will they not say that they do not *know*? And all that they can say about it, provided they have any serious thoughts, will it not be this: that they hope they *shall* know sometime or other? But they know what truth, kindness, honesty, self-denial, disinterestedness are. They know, or suppose that they know, what penitence, sorrow for doing wrong, is. Gratitude to God, also, the love of God, they deem, is no enigma to them. They certainly have some idea of these qualities. I do not say *how much by experience*, they know of all these things; but I say they have some idea of what these things mean. If then they are told, and if they believe, that all this does not reach to the true idea of religion, it follows that religion must be, in their account, some enigma or mystery; it is some inconceivable effect of divine grace, or moving of gracious affections in the heart; it must be something different from all that men are wont to call goodness, excellence, loveliness.

But to make this still plainer, if need be; what, let it be asked, are most men looking for and desiring, when they seek religion? In a Revival of religion, as it is termed, what is the anxious man seeking? Is it not something as completely strange and foreign to his ordinary experience, as would be the effect of the mystery called Animal Magnetism? A man is declining into the vale of years, or he is lying upon the bed of death, and he wants religion, wants that something which will prepare him for a happy hereafter. He has got beyond the idea that the priest can save him, or that extreme unction can save him, or that any outward rite can save him. He knows that it must be something in his own soul. And now, what shall it be? What does he set himself to do, or to seek? What is the point about which his anxious desires are hovering? "Oh! that that *thing* could be wrought in me, on which all depends! I know not what it is; but I want it; I pray for it." And this something that is to be done in him, is something that can be done in a moment! Can anything be plainer then, than this which I am saying; that he is not looking to the increase and strengthening and perfection of truth, kindness, disinterestedness, humility, gratitude to God, to save him; not for the increase and strengthening of anything that is already in him; but for the *lodgment* in him, of *something new* that will save him. He does not set himself, in seeking religion, about the cultivation of known affections, but about the attainment of unknown affections.

Look again for further proof, at the language of the popular religion, whether heard from the pulpit, or coming from the press. What is more common than to hear morality decried, and the most lovely virtue disparaged, in comparison with something called grace in the heart? Morality is allowed to be a very good thing for this world, but no preparation for the next; or it is insisted on as a consequence of grace, but is considered as no part of grace itself; or if it is admitted that by an infusion of grace, morality may become a holy thing, still, by this supposition, the grace maintains its position as the distinct, peculiar and primal essence of virtue. Observe, that I do not say that any body preaches against kindness, honesty and truth-telling, absolutely. Nay, they are insisted on. But in what character? Why, as evidences of that other thing, called religion or grace. They are not that thing, nor any part of it; but only evidences of it. And observe too, that if it were only said, that much that is called morality and kindness, is not real morality or kindness; that the ordinary standard of virtue is too low and needs to be raised; to that discrimination, I should have nothing to object. But the point maintained is, that nothing that is called simple kindness or morality, ever comes, or ever can, by any increase come, up to the character of saving virtue.

There is one further and decisive consideration which I am reluctant to mention, but which I will suggest, because it is, first of all, necessary that I should clearly make out the case upon which my discourse proceeds. The Church has ever been accustomed to hold that the virtues of heretics are nothing worth. Now suppose a case. Here is a body of men, called heretics; Protestants they were once—Church of England men, Puritans, Presbyterians. No age has wanted the instance. Here is a body of men, I say, called heretics. To all human view, they are as amiable, affectionate and true hearted; as honest, diligent and temperate, as any other people. They profess to reverence religion too; they build churches, meet together for worship; and their worship seems as hearty and earnest as any other. By any standard of judging save that of theology, they appear to be as good and devout men as any other. Now what does the popular theology, what does the pulpit say, of them? Why this, briefly and summarily,—*that they have no religion.* They may be very good men, very amiable, kind, honest and true, and after their manner, devout; but they have no religion. Is not the case clear? Must not religion be a secret in the bosom of these confident judges? *They* must know what it is: but others do not know and cannot find out. We must sit down in silence and despair; for we can know nothing about it. Or if we say anything, there is nothing for us but to say with Job, " no doubt, ye are the men, and wisdom shall die with you!" But this, at least, is clear:

whatever this religion is, of which they speak; whether it consist in a certain belief, or in some secretly imparted grace, it must be something different from all that men generally understand, by goodness and devotion.

In short, the prevailing idea of religion is, unquestionably, that it is some heavenly visitant to the soul; some divine guest that takes up its abode there; some essence or effluence, not merely proceeding from God as its cause, which it does, but partaking of unknown attributes; something that comes into the soul from without, and is sustained there by a foreign influence; something that is, at a certain time, created in the heart, and is totally unlike anything that was there before; something that is ingrafted upon our nature, and does not, in any sense, grow out of it; something, in fine, that is put into us, and does not, in any sense, spring out of us; is not *originally* the result of any culture or care of ours, is not wrought out of any materials found in us, not reducible to any ordinary laws of cause and effect; but is the result of a special and supernatural working of divine power, brought to bear upon us. This doctrine, as I have latterly stated it, is undoubtedly modified by some of the New Schools of Theology that are rising around us; and this whole idea of religion is, doubtless, rejected by some orthodox persons; as it was completely rejected in the old English theology of Paley and Bishop Butler; but it is nevertheless very generally taught in this country, and it is the faith, or rather the fear and trouble, of the multitude.

Nor do I know of any recent modification of the prevailing Theology, that materially affects the point now before us. When I say that, according to that theology, religion is not wrought out of any materials found in us, it may be thought that I do injustice to the views of some of its adherents. They hold perhaps that the necessary *powers are* within us; and simply maintain that they have never been rightly exercised, and that without a special impulse from above, they never will be. On this supposition, the moral faculties of our nature stand like machinery, waiting for the stream of influence that is to move them. In the unregenerate nature, they have never been moved, or have never been *rightly* moved; and they never will be, by any power among them or inherent in them. That motion or that right motion when it comes, will be religion. But on *this* supposition, is not religion a thing, still and equally unknown? Can the unregenerate man foresee, can he conjecture, what that *motion* will be? Can any body understand what it is; saving and excepting the converted man himself?

I suppose that this conclusion is incontrovertible; and I presume that almost every convert to the popular forms of religion, would be found to say: "I cannot tell you what it is that I have got; I cannot tell you what religion is; but I know by experience what it is; and that is enough for me."

This view of religion, I propose to make the subject of some free discussion. It demands the most serious consideration; and I do not remember that it has received at any hand, the attention that it deserves.

I shall first state the opposite, and as I conceive, the true view of religion, and briefly show why it is true: and I shall then proceed to consider more at large, the consequences that must result and do result, from the prevailing, and as I conceive, the false view.

And here let me distinctly observe, that I am not about to consider these consequences as matters foreign and indifferent to ourselves. They belong to us, indeed, as they concern the general state of religion in the world. But they concern us yet more nearly, as they enter more or less into the state of our own minds. No age can escape the influence of the past. The moral history of the world, is a stream, that is not to be cut off at a single point. In *us*, doubtless, are to be found the relics of all past creeds, of all past errors.

But before I proceed to these consequences, I am briefly to state and defend what I conceive to be the true view of religion, as a principle in the mind.

For statement then I say, in the first place, that all men know what God requires of them, what affections, what virtues, what graces, what emotions of penitence and piety; in the second place, that all men have a capacity for these affections and some exercise of them, however slight and transient; and in the third place, that what God requires, what constitutes the salvation of the soul, is the culture, strengthening, enlargement, predominance of these very affections; that he who makes that conscience and rectitude and self-denial, and penitence and sacred love of God which he already perceives and feels, or has felt in himself, however imperfectly; he who makes these affections the fixed, abiding, and victorious habits of his soul, is accepted with God, and must be happy in time and in eternity.

This is the statement; and for defence of this view of religion, I submit its own reasonableness; nay, and I contend for its absolute certainty as a matter of Scriptural interpretation.

First, its reasonableness. For if men, if all men do not know what religion is, they do not know what is required of them. To say that God demands that to be done in us and by us, of which we have no conception or no just conception, is to make a statement which carries with it its own refutation. To make a *mystery* of a *commandment*, is a solecism amounting to absolute self-contradiction. Again, we could not know what are the affections that are required of us, unless it were by some experience of them. It is philosophically impossible; it is, in the nature of things, impossible that we should. No words, no symbols could teach us what moral or spiritual emotion is, unless we had in ourselves some feeling of what it is; any more than they could teach a blind man what it is to see, or a deaf man what it is to hear. Excellence, holiness, justice, disinterestedness, love, are words which never could have any meaning to us, if the originals, the germs of those qualities were not within us. Let any person ask himself what he understands by love, the love of man or of God, and how he obtained the idea of that affection; and he will find that he understands it, because he feels it, or has, sometime or other, felt it. Once more; I have said that these feelings of benevolence and piety, cultivated into the predominant habit of the soul, are the very virtues and graces that are required of us. And is not this obviously true? We all know by something of experience, what it is to love those around us; to wish them well; to be kindly affected and mercifully disposed towards them. And we all have had some transient emotions at least of gratitude and love to the Infinite Father. Now if all these affections were to fill our hearts, and shine in our lives always, what would this be, but that character in which all true religion and happiness are bound up?

Thus reasonable is the ground which we are defending. But I have said also, that it is certain, from the principles that must govern us in the interpretation of Scripture. The Bible addresses itself to the world, and demands a certain character. In describing that character it adopts terms in common use. It tells us that we must be lovers of God, and lovers of men; that we must be gentle, forbearing and forgiving; true, pure, and faithful. Now if it does not mean by these words as to their radical sense, what we all mean by them; if it uses them in an altogether extraordinary and unintelligible manner, then, in the first place, it teaches nothing; and next, it leads us into fatal error. The conclusion is inevitable. What the Bible presupposes to be a right knowledge of religion, *is* a right knowledge.

I am not denying that we are to grow in this knowledge, through experience; and that, from our want of this enlightening experience, much is said to us in the Scriptures of our own blindness: much of the new light that will break in upon us, with the *full* experience of the power of the Gospel. But to a world totally blind, wrapped in total darkness, and having no conception of what light is, the Bible would not have spoken of light. The word stands for an idea. If the idea, and the just idea did not exist, the word would not be used.

There is then a light in the human soul, amidst all its darkness; an inward light; a divine light, which, if it were increased instead of being dimmed, would shine brighter and brighter, even to the perfect day. Let any man have taken the best feeling that ever was in him—some feeling, however transient, of kindness to his fellow, or some emotion of reverence and gratitude to his Creator; let him have taken that feeling and all that class of feelings, and cultivated and carried it up to an abiding habit of mind, and he would have become a good and pious man. This change, from transient to habitual emotions of goodness and piety, is the very regeneration that is required of us. The being, so changed, would be " born again,' would be " a new creature ;" " old things with him would have passed away, and all things would have become new."

Now, according to the common doctrine, instead of this slow, thorough, intelligible and practical change, we are to look for a new and unknown element to be introduced among our affections. A man feels that he must become a Christian, that he must obtain that character on which all happiness, here and hereafter, depends. And now what does he do? Finding in himself an emotion of good-will, of affection for his neighbour, does he fasten upon that, and say, " this must I cherish and cultivate into a genuine philanthropy and a disinterested love?" Feeling the duty of being honest, does he say, " this practical conscience must I erect into a law?" Sensible, in some gracious hour, of the goodness of God or the worth of a Saviour, does he say, " let me keep and bear upon my heart, the reverent and sacred impression?" No, all this, the popular theology repudiates, and represents as a going about to establish our own righteousness. " No, it says, you must feel that you can do nothing yourself; you must cast yourself, a helpless, despairing sinner, upon the mercy of God; you must not look to the powers of a totally depraved nature to help you at all; you must cast yourself wholly upon Christ; you must look to the renewing power of the Holy Ghost, and to the creation in you of something totally different from any thing that is in you now."

The question between these two views of religion is certainly one of a very serious character; one on which momentous consequences depend. And it is a question too, which concerns not one or another form of sectarian faith alone, but the entire condition of Christianity in the world. The idea of religion on which I have dwelt so much in this discourse with a view to controvert it, has penetrated the whole mass of religious opinion. No body of Christians has entirely escaped it; not even our own; though our characteristic position, as I conceive, at the present moment, is one of protest against it. I say at the present moment. We have gone through with a speculative controversy. It may be renewed, no doubt; but there will be hardly anything new to be said upon it. We have gone through, then, with the argument about the Trinity, the Atonement, Election, and such speculative matters; and we have come now to the greater question, what is religion itself? And what we say, is, that religion is a principle, deep-imbedded in the conscience and consciousness of all mankind; and that from these germs of it, which are to be found in human nature, it is to be cultivated and carried up to perfection. What is maintained on the contrary is, that religion, the true and saving religion, is a principle of which human nature is completely ignorant; that to make a man a Christian, is to implant in him a principle, entirely new, and before unknown. Whether it be called a principle, or a new mode of spiritual action, for some may prefer the latter description, it is the same thing in this respect. The man unregenerate, according to this teaching, can no more tell what he is to feel when made regenerate, than a man can anticipate what a shock of electricity will be, or what will be the effect upon his system of a new poison; or what would be the experience of a sixth sense.

The establishment of this point is so material in this whole discussion, that I shall occupy the few moments that remain to me, with the attempt to relieve the views I have offered, from all misapprehension.

Let it then be distinctly observed, in the first place, that the question is not at all about the nature or necessity or degree of divine influence. Not, what power from above, is exerted to produce religion in the soul, but what the religion is, however produced; not what divine aid is given to human endeavour, but what is the nature and result of that endeavour; not what grace from God, but what grace in man, is; this is the question. Of course, we believe in general, that all true religion, in common with every thing else good, proceeds from God. And for myself, I firmly believe, that it pleases the Almighty to give special assistance to the humble and prayerful efforts of his weak and tempted creatures; and this, not only when those efforts are resolutely commenced, but in every successive step of the religious course; not merely nor peculiarly in the hour of conversion, but equally in the whole process of the soul's sanctification. I know of no Scripture warrant for supposing that this divine influence is limited to any particular season, or is concentrated upon any particular exigency of the soul's experience.

In the next place, I do not say that the notion of religion as a mystery or an enigma, embraces or usurps the whole of the popular idea of religion. When I shall come to speak of the injurious consequences of this idea, I shall maintain that an enigma cannot be the object of any moral admiration, or love, or culture, or sensibility; and I may then be asked if I mean to say that there is no religious goodness or earnestness among those who embrace this idea. And to this, I answer beforehand and decidedly, "no, I do not mean to say this." If the idea were not modified nor qualified in any way, if no other ideas mixed themselves up with that of a mystic religion, this would be the result. It is seldom that error practically stands alone. Still it is proper to single it out, and to consider it by itself. And I do maintain too, that this error predominates sufficiently to exert the most disastrous influence upon the religion of the whole Christian world.

The whole of Christianity as it is commonly received, is, in my view, greatly perverted, corrupted and enfeebled by this error. Christianity is not regarded as a clearer and more impressive exhibition of the long established, well known, eternal laws of man's spiritual welfare, but as the bringing in of an entirely new scheme of salvation. The common interpretation of it, instead of recognising the liberal Apostolic doctrine, that the "way of salvation is known to all men, that those not having the written law are a law to themselves, and that in every nation he that worships God and works righteousness," is accepted of him, holds in utter derogation and sovereign scorn, all heathen light and virtue. The prevailing idea is, that the Gospel is a certain device or contrivance of divine wisdom, to save men; not helping them in the way which they already perceive in their own consciousness, but superseding all such ways and laying them aside entirely; not opening and unfolding new lights and encouragements to that way, by revelations of God's paternal mercy and pledges of his forgiving love, but revealing a way altogether new.

Thus the Gospel itself is made a kind of mystic secret. I cannot allow a few of the more intelligent expounders of it to reply, as if that were sufficient, that *they* do not regard it in this light. I ask them to consider what is the *general* impression conveyed by most preachers of Christianity. They may be offended when we say that vital religion is commonly represented as a mystery, an enigma, to the mass of their hearers. But let us not dispute about words. They *do* represent it as something created in their heart, which was not there before; of which no element was there before; of which no man's previous experience ever gives him any information, any conception. If this is not a mystery to mankind, it would be difficult to tell what there is that deserves the name. Suppose the same thing to be applied to men's general *knowledge*. Men *know* many things; but suppose it were asserted that in all their knowing there is not one particle of true knowledge, and that only here and there one, who has been specially and divinely enlightened, possesses any such knowledge. Would not such knowledge then, be a secret shared by a few, and kept from the rest of the world? Would it not be a profound mystery to the mass of mankind? Yes; and a mystery all the darker for the seeming light that surrounded it!

How much is there that passes in the bosom of society, unquestioned and almost unknown! It is this which prevents us from seeing the momentous fact and the character of the fact, which I have now been attempting to strip bare and to lay before you. It would seem that we least know that which is nearest to us, which is most familiar and most certain, which is mixed up most intimately with all present thought and usage, and with the life that we daily live. A thing must become history, it would seem, before we can fairly read it. This is commonly allowed to be true of political affairs; but it is just as true of all human experience. Thus, if there had been a sect, among the old philosophers, which pretended to hold the exclusive possession of all science; if certain persons had stood up in the ancient time, and said, "that which other men call science, is all an illusion; we alone truly know any thing; all other men are but fools and idiots in this matter; they suppose themselves to know, but they know nothing; they use words, and make distinctions, and write books, as if they knew, but they know nothing; they do not even know, what knowing is;" such a pretension we should not hesitate to characterize as a strange mixture of mysticism and arrogance. But the same assumption in regard to religion, is now put forth among ourselves; it is announced every week from the pulpit; it is constantly written in books; it enters into every argument about total depravity and regeneration and divine grace; and men seem totally insensible to its enormity; it is regarded as a mark of peculiar wisdom and sanctity; the men who take this ground, are the accredited Christian teachers of multitudes; they speak as if the secret of the matter were in them, and as if they were perfectly entitled, in virtue of a certain divine illumination which they have received, to pronounce all other religious claims to be groundless and false; to say of all other men but the body of the elect, "they think they know what religion is; they talk about it; they make disquisitions and distinctions as if they knew, but they know nothing about it; they do not even know what true religious knowing is." And all the people say, amen. There is no rebuke; there is no questioning; the light of coming ages has not yet shone upon this pretension; and the people say, it is all very right, very true.

I pray you, in fine, not to regard what I have now been saying as a sectarian remonstrance. Nay, and if it were so, it would not be likely to be half strong enough. There is a heavy indifference on this subject of religion that weighs down remonstrance, and will not let it rise as it ought. If certain ship-masters or merchants should say that they only understood navigation; if certain mechanicians or manufacturers should assert that they only understood their art or their business; if certain lawyers or physicians should lay exclusive claim to the knowledge of law or medicine, there would be an outburst of indignation and scorn on every hand. "What presumption! what folly! these people are deranged!"—would be the exclamation. But men may make this claim in religion; a few persons comparatively in Christendom, may say, "we only have religion; we alone truly know what religion is;" and the indifference of society replies, "no matter; let them claim it: let them have it;" as if the thing were not worth disputing about. And if some one arouses himself to examine and to resist this claim, indifference still says, "this is but a paltry, sectarian dispute."

No, sirs, I answer, this is not a sectarian dispute. It is not a sectarian remonstrance that is demanded here; but the remonstrance of all human experience. Religion is the science of man's intrinsic and immortal welfare. What is a true knowledge, what is a true experience here, is a question of nothing less than infinite moment. All that a man is to enjoy or suffer for ever, depends upon the right, practical solution of this very question. Every where else, in business, in science, in his profession, may a man mistake with comparative impunity. But if he mistakes here, if he does not know, and know by experience, what it is to be good and pure, what it is to love God and to be conformed to his image, he is, in spite of all that men or angels can do for him, a ruined creature.

Settle it then with yourselves, my Brethren, what

true religion, true goodness, is. I will attempt, in some further discourses, to lead you to the inferences that follow from this discussion. But it is so fruitful in obvious inferences, that I am willing for the present to leave it with you, for your reflections. But this I say now. Settle it with yourselves what true religion is. If it is a mystery, then leave no means untried to become acquainted with that mystery. If it is but the cultivation, the increase in you, of what you already know and feel to be right, then address yourselves to that work of self-culture, as men who know that more than fortunes and honours depend upon it; who know that the soul, that heaven, that eternity, depend upon it.

XXII.

ON THE IDENTITY OF RELIGION WITH GOODNESS, AND WITH A GOOD LIFE.

IF A MAN SAY, I LOVE GOD, AND HATETH HIS BROTHER, HE IS A LIAR; FOR HE THAT LOVETH NOT HIS BROTHER WHOM HE HATH SEEN, HOW CAN HE LOVE GOD WHOM HE HATH NOT SEEN?—1 John iv. 20.

I HAVE presented, in my last discourse, two views of religion, or of the supreme human excellence; and I have offered some brief, but as I conceive, decisive considerations to show which is the right view. The one regards religion or the saving virtue, as a new creation in the soul; the other as the culture of what is already in the soul. The one contemplates conversion as the introduction of an entirely new element, or of an entirely new mode of action, into our nature; the other, as a strengthening, elevating and confirming of the conscience, the reverence and the love that are already a part of our nature. A simple comparison drawn from vegetable nature will show the difference. Here is a garden of plants. The rational gardener looks upon them all as having in them, the elements of growth and perfection. His business is to cultivate them. To make the comparison more exact—he sees that these plants have lost their proper beauty and shapeliness, that they are distorted and dwarfed and choked with weeds. But still the germs of improvement are in them, and his business is to cultivate them. But now what does the theological gardener say?

"No, in not one of these plants, is to be found the germ of the right production. To obtain this, it is necessary to graft upon each one, a new principle of life."

Now I have said, that, upon the theory in question, this new creation, this new element, this graft upon the stock of humanity, is, and must be to the mass of mankind, a mystery, an enigma, a profound secret. And is not this obviously true? Man, in a state of nature, it is constantly taught, has not one particle of the true saving excellence. How then should he know what it is? "Very true," says the popular theorist; "I accept the conclusion; is it not *written*, the natural man receiveth not the things of God, neither can he know them, because they are spiritually discerned?" That is to say, the popular theorist understands by the natural man, in this much quoted and much misunderstood passage, *human nature*. If he construed it to mean, the *sensual* man, I conceive that he would arrive at a just exposition. But that is not the point in question now. He does construe it to mean human nature; this is constantly done. Human nature being nothing but one mass of unmingled depravity, having never had one right motion or one right feeling, can, of course, have no knowledge of any such motion or feeling.

And to show that this is not a matter of doctrine only, but of experience too, let me spread before you a single supposition of what often, doubtless, takes place in fact. A man of generally fair and unexceptionable life, is lying upon his bed of death, and is visited and questioned, with a view to his spiritual condition. Suppose now he were to say, "I have had for some time past, though I never confessed it before, a certain, unusual, indescribable feeling in my heart on the subject of religion. It came upon me, for I remember it well, in such a month of such a year; it was a new feeling; I had never felt any thing like it before. Ever since, I have had a hope that I then experienced religion. Not that I trust myself, or any thing in myself; I cast all my burthen upon Christ; nothing but Christ—nothing but Christ, is the language upon my lips with which I would part from this world;" and would not this declaration, I ask, though conveying not one intelligible or definite idea to the most of those around him, be held to be a very satisfactory account of his preparation for futurity? But now suppose that he should express himself in a different manner, and should utter the thoughts of his heart thus: "I know that I am far from perfect, that I have, in many things, been very unfaithful; I see much to repent of, for which I hope and implore God's forgiveness. But I do trust, that for a number of years, I have been growing in goodness; that I have had a stronger and stronger control over my passions. Alas! I remember sad and mournful years, in which they had dominion over me; but I do trust that I did at length gain the victory; and that latterly, I have become, every year, more and more pure, kind, gentle, patient, disinterested, spiritual and devout. I feel that God's presence, in which I am ever happiest, has been more abidingly with me; and in short, I hope that the foundations of true happiness have been laid deep in my soul; and that through God's mercy, of which I acknowledge the most adorable manifestation and the most blessed pledge in the Gospel, I shall be happy forever." And now I ask you, do you not think that this account, with many persons, would have lost just as much in satisfactoriness as it has gained in clearness? Would not some of the wise, the guides in Israel, go away, shaking their heads, and saying, they feared it would never do? "Too much talk about his own virtues!" they would say; "too little about Christ!" with an air itself mysterious in that solemn reference. And doubtless if this man had talked more mystically about Christ and grace and the Holy Spirit, it would have been far more satisfactory. And yet he has stated, and clearly stated, the essential grounds of all human welfare and hope.

How often in life, to take another instance, does a highly moral and excellent man say, "I hope I am not a bad man; I mean to do right; I trust I am not devoid of all kind and generous affections towards my fellow-men, or of all grateful feelings towards my Maker; but then I do not profess to have religion. I do not pretend that I am a Christian in any degree." Let not my construction of this case, be mistaken. Doubtless in many such persons there are great defects; nay, and defects proceeding partly from the very error which I am combatting. For if I were to say to such persons, "yes, you have some good and pious affections in you, which God approves, and your only business is, to give the supremacy to these very affections which are already in you;" I should be thought to have lulled his conscience, fostered his pride, and ruined his soul. I should be regarded as a worldly moralizer, a preacher of smooth things, a follower of the long-doomed heresy of Pelagius. "No," it would be said, "there is no saving virtue in that man; there is nothing in him that can be strengthened, or refined or elevated or confirmed into holiness; there is no spark to be fanned into a flame, no germ to be reared into saving life and beauty; all these things are to be flung aside to make way for the reception of something altogether new; as new as light to the blind or as life to the dead. That something, when it comes, will be what he never knew before, never felt before, never before truly saw or conceived of; and it is, undoubtedly, though that is an unusual way of describing it—it is, to depraved human nature, a mystery."

This unquestionable assumption of the popular religion, I shall now proceed freely to discuss in several points of view; in its bearing on the estimate and treatment of religion, on its culture, and on its essential vitality and power.

In the present discourse I shall consider its bearing on the estimate, and on the treatment of religion.

First, the general estimate of the nature, reasonableness and beauty of religion; what can it be, if religion is a mystery, an enigma, a thing unknown? We may feel *curiosity* about a mystery; and I have seen more than one person, seeking religion from this impulse; because they would know what it can be. This is uncommon, doubtless; but taken in any view, can men be in love with a mystery? Can they feel any moral admiration for an enigma? Can their affections be strongly drawn to what is completely unknown? Can they feel even the rectitude of that, of which they have no appreciation, no idea? Certainly not; and in accordance with this view is the old Calvinistic doctrine concerning the means of grace; which utterly denied the force of moral suasion, and held that there is no natural tendency in preaching to change the heart; that the connection between preaching and regeneration was as purely arbitrary as that between the voice of Ezekiel over the valley of dry bones and their resurrection to life.

But suppose this view of preaching be modified, and that a man *designs* to impress his hearers with the reasonableness and beauty of religion, and so to draw their hearts to it. What, let us ask him, can you do, upon the principle that religion is utterly foreign to human nature, an absolute secret to humanity? You have denied and rejected the only means of *rational* impression—some knowledge and experience in the hearers, of that about which you are speaking to them. You have disannulled the very laws and grounds of penitence; for how can men feel to blame for not possessing the knowledge of a secret? In fine, you may be a magician to men, upon this principle; but I do not perceive how you can be a rational preacher. You may say, "this, of which I speak to you, is something wonderful; try it; you have no idea what it will be to you; you will find—" you cannot say, you see—but, "you will find that it is something delightful and beautiful beyond all things." And have we never witnessed a preaching which seemed to work upon the hearers, as it were, by a kind of art magic: solemn and affecting tones, a preternatural air, a talking as of some secret in heaven ready to come right down into the hearts of the hearers, if they will: an awful expostulation with them for their refusal; a mysterious influence drawn around the place; dark depths of wo here; a bright haze of splendour there; heaven above, hell beneath; and the sinner suspended between them by a parting cord! And how, oh! how, was he now to escape? Mark the answer; for if there ever was a mystery, here is one. By some stupendous change then and there to take place; not by rationally cultivating any good affections; not by solemnly resolving to do so; not at all by that kind of change; but by a change instant, immense, mysterious, incomprehensible; a change that would wrap up in that moment the destinies of eternity, that should gather up all the welfare or wo of the infinite ages of being, into the mysterious bosom of that awful moment!

Can such teaching as this, go to the silent depths of real and rational conviction? Did Jesus Christ teach in this manner? Think how natural, how moral, how simple, his teachings were. Think how he taught men their duty in every form, which the instant occasion suggested. Think of his deep sobriety, of his solemn appeals to conscience rather than to imagination, to what was *in* man rather than what was out of him; and then answer me. Did the great Bible preachers, teach so? Behold the beauty of holiness, they say, behold the glory of the Lord; "know and see that it is an evil thing and bitter to depart" from them. "Come, ye children, and I will teach you the fear of the Lord. What man is he that desireth life and loveth many days that he may see good? Keep thy tongue from evil, and thy lips from speaking guile. Depart from evil and do good; seek peace and pursue it. The eyes of the Lord are upon such righteous ones, and his ears are open to their cry." All simple; all intelligible; all plain and level to the humblest apprehension; no talking of a mysterious secret here; no mysterious talking any way!

It is very difficult to speak the exact and undisputed truth upon any point, amidst the endless shapings and shadowings of language and opinion. I myself, who protest against making a secret of religion, may be found speaking of most men as very ignorant of religion; of the depths of the Gospel as yet to be sounded by them; of the preciousness of the great resource as yet to be felt, yet to be found out by them. But I am well understood, by those who are accustomed to hear me, not to mean any thing, which is radically a secret of humanity, but simply the increase and consummation in the soul, of that which it already knows and experiences. The change from transient and unstable, to habitual and abiding emotions of goodness and piety, is the most immense, the most important, the most glorious on earth; and it is one, of which those who are ignorant of it, cannot clearly foresee all the blessed fruits.

Again, it is very difficult to describe what is deemed a great error, without seeming to do it harshly. I would gladly avoid this imputation. God forbid that I should speak lightly of the preaching of good and earnest men. I must speak plainly of it. I must remonstrate against what I deem to be its errors. But I do not forget that with all error there is a mixture of truth. No doubt, there are, in all pulpits, many appeals, however inconsistent with the prevailing theology, to what men naturally know and feel of the rectitude and beauty of religion. But from this mass of teaching, I single out one element which, I say, is not accordant with truth; which, I must say, is not only false, but fatal to all just appreciation of religion.

And does not the actual state of things show this to be the fact? With what eyes are men, in fact, looking upon a religion which holds itself to be a mystic secret in the bosom of a few? Do you not know that the entire literature and philosophy of the age, are in a state of revolt against it? Our literature has its ideals of character, its images of virtue and worth; it portrays the moral beauty that it admires; but is there one trace of this mystic religion in its delineations? Our philosophy, our moral philosophy especially, whose very business it is to decide what is right, calmly treads this religion under foot, does not consider its claims at all. And the cultivators of literature, of science and of art, with a multitude of thoughtful and intelligent men besides them—is it not a well-ascertained fact that they are remarkably indifferent to this kind of religion? Here and there one has fallen in with it; but the instance is rare. But if religion were presented to them as a broad and rational principle, we might expect the reverse to be the fact. Thoughtful men, cultivators of literature and art, are the very men whose minds are most conversant with images of moral beauty. Show them that all true moral beauty, is a part of religion; tell them that a Christian, in the true sense, is a man of principle, of truth and integrity, of kindness and modesty, of reverence and devotion to the Supreme Glory; and they must feel that all this is interesting. But if religion is some mysterious property ingrafted into the soul, differing altogether from all that men are wont to call rectitude and beauty, must not all intellect and taste and all moral enthusiasm and all social generosity and love, shrink from it? In truth, I wonder that they are so patient as they are; and nothing but indifference about the whole matter, can account for this patience. When the preacher rises in his pulpit and tells the congregation, that, excepting that grace which is found in a few, all their integrity and virtue, all their social love and gentleness, all their alms and prayers, have not in the sight of God, one particle of true goodness or worth; nothing, I say, but profound apathy and unbelief can account for their listening to the sermon with any patience, with an instant's toleration of the crushing burthen of that doctrine. Or suppose this doctrine embodied into a character, and then how does it appear? Suppose one person in a family, possessing this mystic grace; in no other respect, that any body can see, better than the rest; no more amiable nor gentle nor disinterested, no more just nor forbearing nor loving: and suppose this person to take the position of being the only one in that family that is approved of God, to hold all the rest as reprobate, and doomed to destruction; is it possible, I ask, to feel for that person in that character, any respect, or admiration, or love? Nay, I have known persons of the greatest defects of character and even of gross vices, to take this ground of superiority, in virtue of a certain inward grace, which they conceive has been applied to them. And I say not this for the sake of opprobrium; but because this ground is, in fact, a legitimate consequence of the doctrine that saving grace in the heart, is an entirely distinct and different thing from what men ordinarily call virtue and goodness.

But further; what is the state of feeling towards religion among those who *accept* this doctrine? In those strong holds of theology or of Church institution, where this doctrine is entrenched, where it is preserved as a treasure sacred from all profane invasion, or held as a bulwark against what are called the inroads of insidious error; in these places, I say, what is the feeling? If religion is not any known or felt sentiment or affection of human nature to be cultivated, but is a spell that comes upon the heart of one and another, and nobody can tell how or when it will come, I can conceive that there may be much fear and anxiety about it; but how there should be much true freedom or genuine and generous love, I cannot conceive. I do not profess to have any very intimate acquaintance with the mind of such a congregation; but if religion does not press as an incubus upon the minds of many there; if it is not a bugbear to the young, and a mystery to the thoughtful, and a dull, dead weight upon the hearts of the uninitiated; if, in its *votaries*, it is not ever swaying between the extremes of death-like coldness and visionary rapture; if it is not a little pent-up hope of salvation, rather than a generous and quickening principle of culture; if the fire in the secret shrine, does not wither the gentle and lofty virtues; I must confess that I understand nothing of the tendencies of human nature. There may be much religiousness in such a state of things; but much of this has existed in many a state, Heathen, Mahometan, Catholic and Protestant too, without much of true religion. I do not say, that the churches consist generally of bad people; many influences unite to form the character; but I say that in so far as any churches hold their religion, to be some special grace implanted in them, and different from all that other men feel of goodness and piety, so far their assumption tends directly to make them neglect the cultivation of all true worth and nobleness of character. And I am not shaken in this position by the admission which I am willing to make, that there are probably more good men, in proportion, *in* the churches than *out* of them; for profession itself, the eye of the world upon them, and the use of certain ordinances, are powerful influences. They are powerful, and yet they are not the loftiest influences. They restrain, more than they impel. And the very morality of an exclusive religion, is apt to wear features hard, stern, ungenial and unlovely.

I have said in the opening of my last discourse, that the great mission of the true teacher in this age is to establish the identity of religion and goodness. And the reason is, that by no other means can religion be really esteemed and loved. Feared it may be; desired it may be; but by no other means, I repeat, can it be truly and heartily esteemed and loved.

Now consider that religion stands before the world, with precisely this claim, the claim to be, above all other things, reverenced and loved. Nay, it demands this love on pain of perdition for failure. Does the world respond to this claim? Does public sentiment any where yield to it? There *are* things that unite the moral suffrages of mankind—honesty, integrity, disinterestedness, pity for the sorrowful, true love, true sanctity, self-sacrifice, martyrdom, and among them and above them all, the character of Jesus Christ. Among these, does Calvinistic piety hold any place? This is a fair and unexceptionable question in the sense in which I mean it. I am not speaking at all, of persons, I am speaking of an idea. Is the Calvinistic idea of piety, among the beautiful and venerable ideals and objects of the world's conscience, of the world's moral feeling? Surely not. But it will not do to say that this is because the world is so bad. For the character of our Saviour *is* among those objects! Bad as the world is, yet all sects and classes and communities, all Infidels and Mahometans and Heathen, have agreed, without one single solitary whisper of contradiction, that this character is a perfect example of true, divine excellence! Does the Calvinistic idea of religion draw to it, any such testimony? Then what clearer evidence can there be, that it is wrong?

And if it be wrong, if it is an error; what terrible and awful mischiefs must follow in its train! Mankind required, as the supreme duty, to love that which all their natural sentiments oblige them to dislike, and none of their natural powers, in fact, enable them to understand! What peril must there be of their salvation in such a case! What a calamitous state of things must it be for their highest hopes! What confusion, what embroilment and distraction to all their moral convictions! Nothing else can account for that blind wandering of many souls after the true good, which we see; for that wild fanaticism, which has taken the place of sober and intelligent seeking; for that distracted running up and down, of men who know not what they are to get, nor how to get it, nor what, in any way, to do; and yet more, for that profound and dreadful apathy of many, who have concluded that they can do nothing, who have given up all thoughts of life as the voyage of the soul, and have resigned themselves to wait for some chance wave of excitement to bear them to the wished-for haven.

Believe me, my friends, this is no abstract matter. It touches the vital ideas of human welfare. It concerns what is most practical, most momentous. In all congregations, in all townships and villages through the land, an image is held up of religion, an idea of what is the supreme excellence. It is regarded with doubt and fear and misgiving; not with love, or enthusiasm, or admiration. It is not fair loveliness or beauty; but a dark enigma. It is not the supreme excellence, but the supreme necessity. It is not intelligently sought, but blindly wished for. Alas! it is hard enough to get men to pursue the true excellence when they are plainly told what it is. But here is a dread barrier on the very threshold, and they cannot proceed a single step. They can do nothing till they are converted; they know not what it is to be converted; and they wait for the initiative to come from heaven; not knowing, alas! that to be converted is, with heaven's help, to begin; to take the first determined step and the second, and thus to go onward; to begin upon the ground of what they actually know, and thus to go on to perfection. Religion, the beauty of the world; that which mingles as their pervading spirit with the glory of the heavens and the loveliness of nature; that which breathes in the affections of parents and children and in all the good affections of society; that which ascends in humble penitence and prayer to the throne of God: this is no mystic secret. It is to be good and kind, penitent and pure, temperate and self-denying, patient and prayerful; modest and generous and loving, as thou knowest how to be; loving, in reverent thoughts of the good God, and in kind thoughts of all his children. It is plain, *not easy*, not in that sense natural; but natural in its accordance with all the loftiest sentiments of thy nature, easy in this, that nothing ever sat with such perfect peace and calm upon thy soul as that will. It is so plain, that he who runs, may read. It is the way in which fools need not err. "For what doth the Lord require of thee," saith the prophet, indignant at the complaint of ignorance, "what doth the Lord require of thee, but to do justice, and to love mercy, and to walk humbly with thy God?"

Let me now proceed in the next place, from the estimate to the treatment of religion. The topics indeed are closely connected; for the treatment of the subject will, of course, depend on the estimate formed of its character and merits. This consideration, it is evident, might carry us through the whole subject; but I shall not, at present, touch upon the ground of religious culture and religious earnestness, which I have reserved for separate discussion. In the remainder of this discourse, I shall confine myself to the *treatment* of religion; as a matter of investigation, and of institution, and as a matter to be approached in practical seeking. The space that remains to me will oblige me to do this very briefly; and indeed to touch upon one or two topics under these several heads, is all that I shall attempt.

Under the head of investigation, the subject of religious controversy presents itself.

Every one must be aware that religious controversy is distinguished by certain remarkable traits, from all other controversy. There has generally been a severity, a bigotry, an exclusion and an obstinacy in it, not found in any other disputes. What has invested, with these strange and unseemly attributes, a subject of such tender, sublime and eternal interest? I conceive, that it is this: the idea that within the inmost bosom of religion, lies a secret, a something peculiar, distinct from all other qualities in the human character, and refusing to be judged of as other things are judged of, a secret wrapped about with the divine favour, and revealed only to a few. There is an unknown element in the case, and it is difficult to obtain a solution. The question is perplexed by it, as a question in chemistry would be, by the presence of some undetected substance. Or if the element is known to some, it is held to be unknown to others, and this assumption lays the amplest ground for bigotry and exclusion. If I know what religion is, and another man does not know, I am perfectly entitled, if I think proper, to reject his claim to it, to say that some defect of faith, or of ritual in him, forbids the possibility of his having it. Nothing is easier than, on this basis, to form an exclusive sect; it is, in fact, the legitimate and the only legitimate basis of such a sect. I say the only legitimate basis; because, if every thing in this matter be fairly submitted to inquiry and decision, the vitality of religion as well as its creed and ritual; if all men can, by care and study, know what it is; if all men must know what it is, by the very law written on their hearts; then it is absurd for one party to lay claim to the sole knowledge and possession of it. Wrap it up in secrecy, and then, and then only, may you consistently wrap it up in exclusion.

Only think of an exclusive party in science or art. Think of such a sect, saying to all others, "we only have the true love of science or art; we only have the true spirit of science or art;" and why would not their claim stand, for a moment? Because all other men of learning and skill would say, "we are as competent to judge of this matter as you are. There is no secret in knowledge. There is no exclusive key to wisdom. There is no hidden way to art. Prove that there is, and then it may be that the mystery is in your possession. But until you establish this point, your claim is absurd and insufferable, and not worth examination."

Now the whole evil as well as the whole peculiarity of religious controversy, lies in this spirit of exclusion, in the assumption that opponents cannot be good men. Otherwise, controversy is a good thing. That is to say, honest and friendly discussion is good. The whole evil, I say, lies in the assumption of an exclusive knowledge of religion. Persecution proceeds upon no other ground. Men have been imprisoned, tortured, put to death, not merely because they erred, not simply because they differed from their brethren, but because that error, that difference, was supposed to involve the very salvation of the soul. Men have been punished, not as errorists simply, but as men irreligious and bad, and as making others so. I speak now of honest persecution. Its object has been the salvation of souls. Its doctrine has been: "painful as torture is, it is better than perdition; better fires on earth, than fires in hell." But the persecuted brethren say, "we are not irreligious and bad men. We wish the truest good to ourselves and others; and though you oppose us, as you must, you ought not to hate, or torture or vilify us; we no more deserve it than you do." And what is the reply? "You know nothing about the matter. You suppose yourselves to be good and true, and to have favour with God and a good hope of heaven; but we know better; we *know* what true religion is, and we say that you are totally devoid of it." And this judgment, I repeat, can fairly proceed upon nothing but the notion that religion is a secret in the possession of the persecutors.

Let it be otherwise, as surely it ought to be, if any thing ought; let religion, the great sentiment, the great interest of humanity, be common ground, open and common to all; let men take their stand upon it, and say, as they say in other differences of opinion, "we all wish the same thing; we would all be happy, we would get to heaven; what else can we wish?" and do you not see how instantly religious disputes would take on a new character; how gentle and charitable and patient and tolerant they would become? But now, alas! the toleration of science, of art, nay, and of politics too, goes beyond the toleration of religion! Men do not say to their literary or political opposers, "ye are haters of science or art; ye hate the common country;" but in religion, they say: "ye are haters of God, and of good men, and of all that is truly good." Yes, the occasion for this tremendous exclusion, is found in religion; in that which was ordained to be the bond of love, the bosom of confidence, the garner of souls into heaven; the theme of all grandeur and of all tenderness; the comforter of affliction, the loving nurse of all human virtues, the range of infinity, the reach to eternity, the example of the One meek and lowly; the authority, at once, and the pity of the heavenly Father!

The next subject for the application of the point I am considering, is religious institutions. Under this head, I must content myself with briefly pointing out a single example. The example is the ordinance of the Lord's Supper. The question I have to ask, is: why do so many sober, conscientious and truly religious persons, refrain from a participation in this rite? And the anwer with many, is doubtless to be found in the notion, that religion involves some secret, or the experience of some secret grace, something different from moral uprightness, and religious gratitude, with which they are not acquainted. I do not say that this account embraces every case of neglect, but I say that it embraces many. I will suppose a person, conscious of a sincere intent to be in all things, a true and good man, conscious too of religious affections, and desirous of cultivating them; one, believing in Christ, believing that his life and his death are the most powerful known ministration to human sanctity and blessedness; one, also, truly disposed to impress the spirit of Christ upon his own heart, and persuaded that the meditations of the Communion season, would be a help and comfort to him; and why now, I ask, shall he not avail himself of that appointed means? He is desirous of sacred culture. This is a means, and he wishes to embrace it. Why does he not? I am sure that I may answer for him, that he would do so, if he felt that he were qualified. But this is the difficulty; he is afraid that there is some qualification, *unknown* to *him;* and that he shall commit a sin of rashness and presumption if he comes to the sacred ordinance.

My friends, it is all a mistake. You *do* know, in a greater or less measure, what Christian virtue, what Christian piety, is. You *can* know, whether you desire to cultivate this character. If you do, that very desire is the qualification. Means are for those who need them, not for those who need them not; for the imperfect, not for the perfect. The felt need of means, the sincere desire of means, is the qualification for them. If, being believers in Christianity, you also believe that our Communion meditations would help you, you should as much come to them, as you come to the prayers of the Sanctuary. And you should as freely come. The Lord's Supper is a service no more sacred than the service of prayer. Nothing can be more solemn than solemn prayer.

There is one more subject to be noticed under this head of treatment of religion, by far the most important of all, and that is religious seeking; the seeking, in other words, to establish in one's self that character, on which God's approbation and all true good, all true happiness, depend, and will forever depend. Momentous pursuit! that for which man was made, and life, with all its ordinances, was given; and the Gospel, with all its means of grace and manifestations of mercy, was published to the world; that in which every man should be more vitally and practically interested than in every other pursuit on earth. Every thing else may a man seek and gain; the whole world may he gain, and after all lose this supreme interest. And yet to how many, alas! will this very statement which I am making, appear technical, dry and uninteresting!—to how many more, irrelevant to *them*, foreign to their concerns, appropriate to other persons, but a matter with which they have nothing to do! A kind of demure assent they may yield to the importance of religion, but no vital faith; nothing of that which carries them with such vigour and decision, to the pursuit of property, pleasure and fame.

Now is there any difficulty in accounting for this deplorable condition of the general mind? Make religion a mystic secret, divest it of every attractive and holy charm, sever it from every thing that men already know and feel of goodness and love, tell them that they are totally depraved, totally destitute, totally ignorant; and they may "wonder and perish;" but can they rationally seek any thing? Men may be very depraved, they may be extremely deficient of the right affections, as they doubtless are; but if they saw the subject in the right light, they could not be indifferent. There could not be this heavy and benumbing cloud of apathy, spreading itself over the whole world. I have seen the most vicious men, intensely conscious, conscious with mingled anger and despair, that the course of virtue is the only happy course. And do you preach to the most selfish and corrupt of men, in this wise, saying, "nothing but purity, gentleness, love, disinterestedness, can make you happy, happy in yourself, in your family, or in society; and nothing but the love of God can make you happy amidst the strifes and griefs of this life and the solemn approaches to death;" and they know that what you say is true; they know that you are dealing with realities; and they cannot be indifferent. They may be angry; but anger is not indifference. But now, do you speak to them in a different tone and manner, and say, "you must get religion; you must experience the grace of God, in order to be happy," and immediately their interest will subside to that state of artificial acquiescence and real apathy, which now characterizes the mass of our Christian communities.

Nor is this, save for its extent, the most affecting view of the common mistake. There are real and anxious seekers. And how are they seeking? I have been pained to see such persons, often intelligent persons, blindly groping about as for the profoundest secret. They have no distinct idea of what it is they want, what they are to obtain, what they are to do. All that they seem to know is, that it is something to be wrought in their souls, and something on which their salvation depends. They go about from one meeting to another, from one master in Israel, or from one Revival preacher, or from one experienced person to another, and say, "Tell us what this thing is, that is to be done in us; how did *you* feel when you were converted? How was it? *How* did the power of divine grace come upon you? What was the change in that very moment when you passed from death to life?" Well may the apostolic teaching speak to such, in this wise: "Say not who shall go up into heaven, that is to bring Christ down; or who shall go beyond the sea, to bring him near. For the word is nigh thee, in thy mouth and in thy heart, that thou shouldst do it." In your own heart, in the simplest convictions of right and wrong, are the teachings that you want. This, says the Apostle, "is the word of salvation which we preach; that if thou wilt believe in thy heart, and confess with thy tongue that Jesus is the Christ, thou shalt be saved." That is, if thou wilt have a loving faith in Jesus Christ as thy Guide, Example and Saviour, and carry that faith into open action, and endeavour to follow him, thou shalt be saved. In one word, if thou wilt be like Christ, if thou wilt imbibe his spirit and imitate his excellence, thou shalt be happy; thou shalt be blessed; blessed and happy forever. But the spirit, the loveliness of Christ, is no mystic secret. It is known and read of all men. It requires no mysterious initiation to instruct you in it. I do not object, of course, to seeking for light, or to seeking aid from men, from the wise and experienced; but I do object to your seeking from them any initial or mysterious knowledge of what religion is. Let you stand, alone, upon a desolate island, with the Gospel in your hands; and then and there, do thou read that sacred page, and pray over it, and strive patiently to bring your heart into accordance with it; to bring what is already in you, your love and trust, up to conformity with it; and you are in the way of salvation.

Oh! sad and lamentable perversion; that the greatest good in the universe, the very end of our being, the very point of all sublime human attainment, the very object for which rational and spiritual faculties were given us, should be a mystery; that the very light by which we must walk, must be utter darkness, and that all we can do is, to put out our hand and grope about in that darkness; that the very salvation, in which all the welfare of our souls is bound up, should be a dark enigma, and that all we can do is to hope that we shall some time or other know what it is. No, says the Apostle, "the world is nigh thee, in thy mouth and in thy heart that thou shouldst do it; *that* is the salvation which we preach."

XXIII.

ON THE IDENTITY OF RELIGION WITH GOODNESS, AND A GOOD LIFE.

IF A MAN SAY, I LOVE GOD, AND HATETH HIS BROTHER, HE IS A LIAR; FOR HE THAT LOVETH NOT HIS BROTHER WHOM HE HATH SEEN, HOW CAN HE LOVE GOD WHOM HE HATH NOT SEEN?—1 John iv. 20.

FROM these words I propose to take up again the subject of my last discourse. I have shown, that saving virtue, or whatever it be that is to save men, is commonly regarded, not as the increase or strengthening of any principle that is already in them, but as the implantation in them of a principle entirely new and before unknown. I have endeavoured to make this apparent, by a statement in several forms of the actual views that prevail of religion and of obtaining religion. I have shown, that with regard to religion or grace in the heart, the common feeling undoubtedly *is*, that it is a mystery, a thing which the people do not comprehend, and which they never expect to comprehend but by the experience of regeneration.

I may now observe, in addition, that all this clearly follows from the doctrine of total depravity. This doctrine asserts that in our natural humanity there is not one particle of true religion or of saving virtue. Of course, human nature knows nothing about it. The only way in which we can come at the knowledge of moral qualities, is by feeling them in ourselves. This is an unquestioned truth in philosophy.

If we have no feeling of rectitude or of religion, we can have no knowledge of it. It follows, therefore, from the doctrine of universal and total depravity, that to the mass of men, religion, as an inward principle, must be a mystery, an enigma, a thing altogether incomprehensible.

This position—held by many Christians, but rejected by not a few, and presenting, in my opinion, the most momentous point of controversy in the Christian world—I have proposed to discuss with a freedom and seriousness proportioned to its immense importance.

With this view, I proposed to consider its bearings on the estimate and treatment of religion, the culture of religion, and its essential vitality and power.

The first of these subjects I have already examined, and I now proceed to the second.

The next topic then, of which I was to speak, is religious culture, or what is commonly called growth in grace. I cannot dwell much upon this subject; but I must not pass it by entirely.

A mystery, a mystic secret in the heart, cannot be cultivated. A peculiar emotion, unlike all well-known and clearly defined emotions of goodness or veneration, cannot be cultivated. It may be revived from time to time; it may be kept alive in the heart by certain processes, and they are likely to be very mechanical processes; the heart, like an electric jar, may ever and anon be charged anew with the secret power;. but to such an idea of religion, *cultivation* is a word that does, in no sense, properly apply. To grow daily in kindness and gentleness, to be more and more true, honest, pure and conscientious, to cultivate a feeling of resignation to the Divine will and a sense of the Divine presence; all this is intelligible. But in proportion as the other idea of religion prevails, culture is out of the question. And on this principle, I am persuaded, you will find many to say, that the hour of their conversion, the hour when they received that secret and mysterious grace into their hearts, was the brightest hour of their religious experience. Look then at the religious progress of such an one. I do not say that all converts are such; but suppose any one to be possessed with this idea of religion as altogether an imparted grace; and how naturally will his chief effort be, to keep that grace alive within him! And where then is culture? And what will be his progress? Will he be found to have been growing more generous and gentle, more candid and modest, more disinterested and self-denying, more devoted to good works, and more filled with the good spirit of God? Will those who know him best, thus take knowledge of him that he has been with Jesus, and say of him, "he was very irascible and self-willed, twenty years ago, but now he is very gentle and patient; he was very selfish, but now he is very generous and self-forgetting; very close and penurious, but now he is very liberal and charitable; very restless and impatient, but now he is calm and seems to have a deep and immovable foundation of happiness and peace; very proud and self-sufficient, but now it seems as if God and Heaven were in all his thoughts, and were all his support and resource." I hope that this change of character does take place in some converts; I would that it did in many; but I must say, that in so far as a certain idea of conversion prevails, the idea of a new and mysterious grace infused into the soul, it is altogether unfavourable to such a progress.

And yet so far has this idea infected all the religion of our times, that Christianity seems nowhere to be that school of vigorous improvement which it was designed to be. Religion, if it is anything befitting our nature, is the very sphere of progress. All its means, ordinances and institutions have this in view, as their very end. But surely it is very obvious and very lamentable to observe, how much religious observance and effort there is, which goes entirely to waste, which does not advance the character at all. Think of our churches, our preaching, our Sabbaths; how little do they avail to make us better? How little do they seem to be thought of as seasons, means, schools of improvement! Must we not suspect that there is some error at the bottom of all this? And now suppose that men have got the notion that that something which is to prepare them for heaven, is something entirely different from charity, honesty, disinterestedness, truth, self-government, and the kindly love of one another; and would not this be the very notion to work that fatal mischief, the very notion to disarm conscience and rational conversion of all their power?

You will recollect that, some time since, a national ship belonging to the Imaum of Muscat, visited our shores. Its officers, who I believe were intelligent men, freely mingled with our citizens, and saw something of society among us. And what do you think was their testimony concerning us? On the point now before us, it was this: They said that there is no religion among us. And what now, you will ask, was their own idea of religion? I answer, it was analagous to the very idea which I am controverting in this discourse. Religion with them was not the general improvement of the character—nothing of the kind; but a certain strictness, a certain devoutness, a particular *way* of attending to religion. Wherever these persons were found, at whatever feast or entertainment provided for them, when the hour of prayer prescribed for Mussulmens arrived, they courteously desired leave to retire to some private apartment, to engage in the prescribed devotions. They found not these things among us, and they said, "there is no religion in America." But do you believe that these Arabian followers of the prophet, were better men than the Christian people upon whom they passed this judgment? No; you say, without denying their sincerity, that they had wrapped up all religion in certain peculiarities; and you deny, and very justly deny, that this view of religion is either just or useful. You say, on the contrary, that it is very dangerous; that it is unfriendly to the true improvement of character; that according to this way of thinking, a man may be a very good Mussulman and a very bad man. And this is precisely what I say of that idea of religion among ourselves which wraps it up in peculiarity; which finds its essence in certain beliefs, or in certain experiences, that are quite severed from general goodness and virtue. And I say, too, that according to this theory, a man may be a very good *Christian*, and yet a very bad man; may consider himself pious, when he is not even a humane man; not generous, nor just, nor candid, nor modest, nor forbearing, nor kind; in short, that he may be a man on whom falls that condemnation which the Apostle pronounces on him who says, "I love God, and hateth his brother."

But now it may be said, that the doctrine which I have delivered, is a very dangerous doctrine. "To tell a man," it may be said, "that there is some good in him on which he is to build; that religion consists essentially in the culture of what is already within him; that there are natural emotions of piety and goodness in him which he is to cultivate into a habit and a character; will not all this minister to self-complacency, sloth, negligence and procrastination? Will not the man say, well, I have some good in me, and I only need a little more, and I can attend to that, any time. I need not trouble myself; events perhaps will improve my character; and all will be well, without much effort or concern on my part. And especially, I need not go through this dreadful paroxysm of a conversion; I have nothing to do but to improve."

I might answer, that it is no new thing for a good and true doctrine to be abused. I do not know but it is abused by some among us. Indeed I fear that it is. Let me proceed at once, then, to guard against this abuse; and to show, as I have promised, that the doctrine which I advocate is one of essential vitality and power in religion.

Let us illustrate this by one or two comparisons. You wish to teach some man a science. Would you think it likely to awaken his zeal and earnestness, to begin by telling him, not only that he knows nothing about the science in question, but that he has no natural capacity for understanding it; that he has no elements in him of that knowledge in which you wish to instruct him; but that he must first have some special and supernatural initiation from heaven into that knowledge, and then he may advance; that till this is done, nothing is done, and that when this is done, all is done; all, that is to say, that is essential to his character as a man of science, all that is necessary to prepare him for a successful examination? Would it further your object to instruct him in this way? You wish to teach music to your pupil. You wish to arouse him to attend, and to labour for accomplishment. Would it be well, to tell him that he has no musical ear, and that he can do nothing till this is given him? You desire to train a youth to high physical accomplishment, to the exercises of the gymnasium or the riding school, to feats of strength or agility; a branch of education that deserves more attention than it is receiving among us. Would you avow to your pupil, that there is one preliminary step to be gained before you could proceed at all; that he had no muscles, no aptitude; and that, until these are given him, he can do nothing? Alas! when I look at the wonderful feats of some public performers, magicians as they are called, and as they seem to the people; and when I know that all this is the result of careful and patient training, I cannot help saying, would Christians exercise themselves in this way, to what might they not attain? "And these do it," says the Apostle, "for an earthly crown, but ye labour for a heavenly." Alas! I am compelled to say again: *every* school of learning, seems to be more successful than the Christian school! And why? let me ask. Have not all other schools their difficulties to surmount as well as the Christian? Why then is it that this is so lame and inefficient, but because there is some radical error at the very foundation? Let us see Christians labouring, ay, and denying themselves, as men of science and art and skill do, and should we not witness some new result?

So I contend they would labour, or at the least, would be far more likely to labour, if they were put in the right way and were impressed with the right convictions. What is the way? What are the convictions? What does our doctrine say to men? What does it say to them with regard to conversion, to progress, and to preparation for heaven?

With regard to conversion, it says, " you must *begin* the work of self culture; resolutely and decidedly you must enter upon the Christian path. If that era of solemn determination has never come to you, then it *must* come, or you are a lost man. With a feeling as solemn, as profound, as absorbing, as ever possessed the heart of any convert to mysterious grace, you must begin. *He* may think that the saving work is done upon him in an instant; *you* must not think so. That is all an error proceeding from a false interpretation of certain figurative language of Scripture; such as " new birth," " new creation"—figurative phrases which apply to the soul, only so far as the soul's nature will admit; and it does not admit of an instant's experience being the preparation for heaven. He who has received this instantaneous communication, may think that in that moment he has got a grace, a something—a something like a pass-word to heaven; but *you*, if you will have any reason in your religion, must not think so. If you think at all, you cannot think so. If you imagine, you may imagine what you will. And truly, it is no moderate stretch of imagination that is here supposed. For if an instant's experience is enough to prepare the soul for heaven, I must wonder why a life was given for it. No, in one moment we can only begin. But that beginning must nevertheless be made. What is never begun, is never done. On that great resolve, rests the burden of all human hope. On that great bond is set the seal of eternity. If we have never made that bond with our souls to be true and pure; if we have never taken up that resolve, I see not how we can be Christians. If all our impulses were good, we might yield ourselves up to them. If there were no temptations, we should need no purpose. If there were a tide in the ocean of life that set right towards the desired haven, we might cast ourselves upon it and let it bear us at its will. But what would you expect, if a ship were loosened from the wharf, and without any course set, or any purpose to make a voyage, it were to take such fate as the winds and waves might send it? You know what its fate would be; to founder amidst the seas or to be wrecked on the shore; it would reach no haven. And so upon the great deep of life, a moral voyage is to be made; amidst winds and waves of passion, and through clouds and storms of temptation and difficulty, the course must be held; and it will not be held, if it is not firmly set. Certainly, no man will make the voyage, unless he is determined to make it. How many launch forth upon the ocean of life without any such determination; and their ship is swayed this way and that way by unseen currents, and is carried far astray by smooth tides and softly breathing winds; but surely, unless a time comes, when the thoughtless mariner arouses himself, and directs his course and spreads his sails for the haven, he will never reach it!

I must lay this emphatic stress upon beginning; and I would that it might be a point of personal inquiry. I will use no intrusive liberty with your thoughts; but I would say, have you begun? Have you resolved? for there is nothing on earth so much requiring a resolve. Let not this matter then, be wrapped in mystery. In clear reality, let it stand before us; in close contact, let it come to us. There is something wrong, of which the soul is conscious. The resolve required is this; to do it no more. There is some secret indulgence, some bosom sin. The resolve is, to tear that sin from the bosom, though it be dear as a right hand or a right eye. Some duty, or course of duties, is neglected; the resolve is to set about it, this day, this hour. In short, the resolve is, a great, strong, substantial purpose to do right in all things; it is to set up the standard of duty as that beneath which we will walk all our life through; to give our hearts without any reserve to God, to truth and sanctity and goodness.

This is what our doctrine says in regard to conversion. And now what does it say, on the subject of progress? Does the message which it delivers, minister to sloth, negligence, or procrastination? What does it say? Your life's work is growth in goodness and piety. It is a daily work, or it is no work at all. Every day you must advance. Practical religion is self-culture. God has given you a natural piety, and a natural benevolence, as he has given you a natural reason. With one as with the other, your business is culture. The seed is in you, as the seed of the coming harvest is in the soil. Every thing depends on culture. Does it discourage the industry of the husbandman to tell him that the seed is provided, and planted in the earth; that there is a germ that will grow if he will take care of it? Nay, that is the very reason why he will work. Or does he refuse to work, because it is necessary that God's sun and air quicken the soil? And why any more that God's spirit must shine and breathe upon his soul?

In this rational and generous self-culture, is the secret of spiritual strength. There is nothing which most men so much feel as the want of vitality and earnestness in their religion. Their talk about it is dull and mournful; their prayers are cold and reluctant; their interest is languid, their Sabbaths and their religious meetings in conference-rooms and school-houses, are heavy and sluggish! And why is all this? It is, provided they are sincere, because their views of religion are irrational, mystical, essentially uninteresting; because the thing in question, is severed from the living fountains of all true emotion. Let me state it to you thus. You have a friend, a dear and lovely friend; and towards that being your affections are not dull and sluggish. But why is that friend dear and lovely? Because generous and noble-hearted, kind and gentle, full of disinterestedness and purity and truth? Then I tell you that your friendship is a part of religion. It is of the same nature as religion. It is no other than a portion of the beauty of the Divinity that is shed forth in the heart of your friend. Again, you have an enthusiasm for all that is morally sublime and beautiful. The patriot that dies for his country; the martyr that calmly goes to the stake, when one word, one little word uttered, will give him life and fortune, and splendour, and he will not speak that false word; the patient and heroic sufferer amidst pain and calamity; the great sufferer when he breathed the prayer, Father, forgive them; these, win admiration, draw tears from you perhaps, as you think of them. And again, I tell you that this is a part of religion. Once more, you have an *interest* in this matter. Surely you would be happy. Uneasiness, destitution, self-inflicted pain are hard to bear. But was ever a soul, full of the love of God, full of kindness and gentleness, full of serenity and trust; was ever such a soul essentially **unhappy**? How then can fainting and famishing creatures, gather in converse around this fountain of all healing and comfort, and not be thrilled with inexpressible emotion? Let me suggest one more thought. There is one great Being who is the first and chiefest object of religion—God! And God is every where. Can there be indifference where it is felt that God is? And he is every where. In the crowded meeting, in thy lonely and retired walk, in the ever lovely, holy and beautiful nature that is spread around you, in the silent and star-lit dome of heaven, **and** beneath your humble roof, in all that fills it with comfort and joy and hope, ay, or touches it with disciplinary sorrow, in all, God is: the nearest, the holiest; the greatest, the kindest of beings; and can indifference live in that sublime and blessed presence?

Now what is religion? It is not merely to feel all this, at certain times and seasons, but it is to make it the reigning habit of our minds. To feel it, is comparatively easy; to form it into the very structure of our souls, is quite another thing. I cannot very well understand how any man should want the feeling: but I can very well understand, how he should want the character. For this it is precisely, that is the greatest and rarest of all human attainments. This it is, to have Christ formed within us, the hope of glory. Jesus, the blessed Master, lived that perfect life. In him each good affection of the humanity, had its fullness, its permanence, its perfection. How reverend, how holy, how dear, how soul-entrancing, is that incarnate loveliness; God in him, God with us; the brightness of the Father's glory and the express image of his person! Oh! could we be like him! all our ungoverned agitations, all our vain longings, all our distracting passions, all our needless griefs and pains, would die away from us; and we should be freed from the heavy, heavy burden of our sins! I almost fear, my friends, so to express myself; lest it should be construed into the hackneyed and whining lamentation of the pulpit, and should win no respect, no sympathy with you. No, it is with a manly grief, with an indignant sorrow, and shame, that every one of us should lament, that he has not more unreservedly followed the great and glorious Master!

And let me add, that this is no visionary nor impracticable undertaking. It is what we all can do, with God's help, if we will. It is what is bound upon us, by the simplest perceptions of rectitude in our own souls, bound upon us by the very feelings of conscience and obligation which God has implanted within us.

Finally, it is what we must do, if we would attain to happiness here or hereafter. The hours are stealing on, when the veil of eternity shall part its awful folds, and the great and dread hereafter shall receive us. Solemn will be that hour! Lightly do we hear of its daily coming to one and another round us now; little do we think of what it was to them; but so will not be its coming—with lightness or with little thought—so will not be its coming to us. The gathering and swelling thoughts of that hour, no one can know but he who has felt it drawing nigh. Earth recedes; and earth's ambition, gain, pleasure, vanity, shrink to nothing; and one thought spreads all around and fills the expanding horizon of eternity—am I ready? Have I lived so, as to meet this hour? And believe me, in no court of human theology, must that question be answered. No imaginary robe of another's righteousness—I speak not now of God's mercy in Christ; that, we may be sure, will be all that mercy consistently can be; no mystic grace claiming superiority to all deeds of mercy and truth ; no narrow, technical hope of salvation garnered up in the heart, will avail us there; but the all-deciding question will be—what were we? and what have we done? What were we, in the whole breadth and length of all our good or all our bad affections? That awful question we must answer for ourselves. No one shall be there to answer for us. No answer shall be given in there, but that which comes from every day and hour of our lives. For there is not a day nor an hour of our lives, but it contributes to make us better or worse; it has borne the stamp of our culture or carelessness, of our fidelity or our neglect. And that stamp, which our life's experience sets upon our character, is—I speak not my own word, but God's word—that stamp is the very seal of retribution.

Does this seem, my friends, but a sad and stern conclusion of the matter; not encouraging to our hopes, nor accordant with the mercy of the Gospel? The Gospel? Is it a system of evasions and subterfuges and palliatives, to ease off the strict demand of holiness? No, let theology boast of such devices, and tell men that as they have sowed so shall they *not* reap; but believe me, the Gospel is the last thing to break the everlasting bond that connects happiness with goodness, with purity. And who would have it otherwise? Who *would* be happy, but on condition of being good, and in proportion as he is good? What true man asks, that over his corrupt and guilty heart, while such, may be poured a flood of perfect bliss? Our nature may be fallen and low; but that flood would sweep away the last vestige of all its honour and worth. God never created a thing so vile as that would be. No, it is a noble being that he has given us, though, alas! it be marred and degraded; and upon the eternal laws of that being, must we build up our welfare. It is a glorious privilege so to do; to do what the noble Apostle spoke of as his own law and hope, when he said,—and be assured, that must be our law and hope—" I have fought a good fight, I have finished my course, I have kept the faith; henceforth there is laid up for me a crown, which the Lord, the righteous Judge, will give me in that day; and not to me only, but to all who love his appearing."

XXIV.

SPIRITUAL INTERESTS, REAL AND SUPREME.

JESUS ANSWERED THEM AND SAID, VERILY, VERILY I SAY UNTO YOU, YE SEEK ME, NOT BECAUSE YE SAW THE MIRACLES, BUT BECAUSE YE DID EAT OF THE LOAVES AND WERE FILLED. LABOUR NOT FOR THE MEAT WHICH PERISHETH, BUT FOR THAT MEAT WHICH ENDURETH UNTO ETERNAL LIFE.—John vi. 26, 27.

The contrast here set forth, is between a worldly mind and a spiritual mind: and so very marked and striking is it, that the fact upon which it is based may seem to be altogether extraordinary, a solitary instance of Jewish stupidity, and not applicable to any other people, or any after times. Our Saviour avers that the multitude who followed him, on a certain occasion, did so, not because they saw those astonishing miracles, that gave witness to his spiritual mission; but simply, because they did eat of the loaves, and were filled. Yet, strange as it may seem, the same great moral error, I believe, still exists; the same preference of sensual to spiritual good, though the specific exemplification of the principle can no longer be exhibited among men. But let us attend to our Saviour's exhortation. "Labour not for the meat that perisheth, but for that meat which endureth unto eternal life." The word *labour*, refers to the business of life. It is as if our Saviour had said, work, toil, care, provide, for the soul. And it is in this sense of the word, as well as in the whole tenor of the passage, that I find the leading object of my present discourse: which is to show that spiritual interests, the interests of the mind and heart, the interests of reason and conscience, however neglected, however forgotten amidst the pursuit of sensual and worldly objects, are nevertheless real and supreme; that they are not visionary because spiritual; but that they are most substantial and weighty interests, and most truly deserving of that earnest attention, that laborious exertion, which is usually given to worldly interests.

So does not the world regard them, any more than did the Jews of old. It is written that the "children of this world are wiser in their generation"—i. e. after their manner wiser, "than the children of light." But the children of this world, not content with this concession, are apt to think that they are every way wiser. And the special ground of this assumption, though they may not be aware of it, is, I believe, the notion which they entertain that *they* are dealing with real and substantial interests. Religious men, they conceive, are occupied with matters which are vague and visionary, and which scarcely have any real existence. A great property is something fixed and tangible, sure and substantial. But a certain view of religion, a certain state of mind, is a thing of shadow, an abstraction vanishing into nothing. The worldly-wise man admits that it may be well enough for some people; at any rate, he will not quarrel with it; he does not think it worth his troubling himself about it; his aim, his plan, his course, is a different one, and—the implication is—a wiser one.

Yes, the very wisdom implied in religion is frequently accounted to be wisdom of but an humble order; the wisdom of dulness or of superstitious fancy or fear; or at most, a very scholastic, abstract, useless wisdom. And the very homage which is usually paid to religion, the hackneyed acknowledgment that it is very well, very proper, a very good thing; or the more solemn, if not more dull confession of "the great importance of religion;" and more especially the demure and mechanical manner in which these things are said, proclaim as plainly as any thing can, that it has not yet become a living interest in the hearts of men. It has never, in fact, taken its proper place among human concerns. I am afraid it must be said, that with most men, the epithet most naturally attaching itself to religion, to religious services, to prayers, to books of sermons, is the epithet, *dull*. And it is well known, as a fact, very illustrative of this state of mind, that for a long time, parents in this country were wont to single out and destine for the ministry of religion, the dullest of their sons.

I know of nothing more important, therefore, than to show that religion takes its place among objects that are of actual concern to men and to all men; that its interests are not only of the most momentous, but of the most practical character; that the wisdom that winneth souls, the religion that takes care for them, is the most useful, the most reasonable of all wisdom and discipline. It is of *the care of the soul*, then, that I would speak; of its wisdom, of its reasonableness, of its actual interest to the common sense and welfare of men.

The ministry of the Gospel is often denominated the care of souls; and I consider this language, rightly explained, as conveying a very comprehensive and interesting description of the office. It *is* the care of souls. This is its whole design, and ought to be its whole direction, impulse, strength, and consolation. And this, too, if it were justly felt, would impart an interest, an expansion, a steady energy, a constant growth, and a final and full enlargement to the mind of the Christian teacher, not surpassed, certainly, in any other profession or pursuit in life. Whether the sacred office has had this effect to as great an extent as other professions, is, to the Clergy at least, a very serious question. I am obliged to doubt whether it has. Certainly, to say that its spirit has been characterized by as much natural warmth and hearty earnestness as that of other pursuit; that its eloquence has been as free and powerful as that of the Senate and the Bar; that its literature has been as rich as that of poetry or even of fiction; this is more than I dare aver.

But not to dwell on this question; it is to my present purpose to observe that the very point, from which this want of a vivid perception of religious objects has arisen, is the very point from which help must come. Men have not perceived the interests of the mind and heart to be the realities that they are. Here is the evil; and here we must find the remedy. Let the moral states, experiences, feelings of the soul, become *but* as interesting as the issue of a lawsuit, the success of business, or the result of any worldly enterprize, and there would be no difficulty; there would be no complaint of dullness, either from our own bosoms or from the lips of others. Strip off from the inward soul those many folds and coverings—the forms and fashions of life, the robes of ambition, the silken garments of luxury, the fair array of competence and comfort, and the fair *semblances* of comfort and happiness—strip the mind naked and bare to the view; and unfold those workings within, where feelings and principles make men happy or miserable; and we should no more have such a thing as religious indifference in the world! Sin there might be, outbreaking passion, outrageous vice, but apathy there could not be. It would not require a sentiment of rectitude even; it would hardly need, that a man should have any religion at all, to feel an interest in things so vital to his welfare. Why do men care as they do for worldly things? Is it not because they expect happiness, or think to ward off misery with them? Only let them be convinced then, that happiness and misery depend much more upon the principles and affections of their own minds, and would they not transfer the greater portion of their interest, to those principles and affections? Would it not result from a kind of mental necessity, like that which obliges the artisan to look to the mainspring of his machinery? Add, then, to this distinct perception of the real sources of happiness, an ardent benevolence, an earnest desire for men's welfare; and from this union would spring that spiritual zeal, that ardour in the concerns of religion and benevolence, of which so much is said, so little is felt; and of which the deficiency is so much lamented. I am willing to make allowance for constitutional differences of temperament, and indeed for many difficulties; but still I maintain that there is enough in the power of religious truths and affections to overcome all obstacles. I do maintain, that if the objects of religion were perceived to be what they are, and were felt as they ought to be, and as every man is capable of feeling them, we should no more have such things among us, as dull sermons or dull books of piety, or dull conferences on religion, than dull conversations on the exchange or dull pleadings at the bar, or even than dull communications of slander by the fireside.

I have thus far been engaged with stating the obvious utility and certain efficacy of the right conviction on this subject. But I have done it as preliminary to a closer argument for the right conviction. Let **us,** then, enter more fully upon consideration of the great spiritual interest. Let us, my brethren, enter somewhat at large, into the consideration of religion as an interest; and of the place which it occupies among human interests. Among the cares of life, let us consider the care of the soul. For it is certain that the interior, the spiritual being, has as yet obtained no just recognition, in the maxims of this world.

The mind indeed, if we would but understand it, is the great central power, in the movements of this world's affairs. All the scenes of this life, from the busiest to the most quiet, from the gravest to the gayest, are the varied developments of that same mind. The world is spread out as a theatre for one great action, the action of a mind; and it is so to be regarded, whether as a sphere of trial or of suffering, of enjoyment or of discipline, of private interest or of public history. Life, with all its cares and pursuits, with all its aspects of the superficial, the frivolous and the gross, is but the experience of a mind. Life, I say—dull, plodding, weary life, as many call it, is, after all, a spiritual scene; and this is the description of it that is of the deepest import to us.

I know and repeat, that the appearances of things, to many at least, are widely different from this representation. I am not ignorant of the prevailing and wordly views of this subject. There are some, I know, who look upon this life as a scene not of spiritual interests, but of worldly pleasures. The gratifications of sense, the opportunities of indulgence, the array in which fashion clothes its votaries, the splendour of entertainments, the fascinations of amusement, absorb them; or absorb, at least, all the admiration they feel for the scene of this life. Upon others, again, I know that the cloud of affliction descends; and it seems to them to come down visibly. Evil and trouble are to them, mainly things of condition and circumstance. They are thinking chiefly of this thing as unfortunate, and of that, as sad; and they forget that intrinsic character of the mind which lends the darkest hue, and which might give an aspect of more than earthly brightness, to all their sufferings. And then again, to the eyes of others, toil presents itself; with rigid sinews and strong arm, indeed, but weary too—weary, worn down with fatigue, and perhaps disconsolate in spirit. And to its earthly-minded victims—for victims they are with that mind—it seems, I know, as if this world were made but to work in; and as if death, instead of being the grand entrance to immortality, were sufficiently commended to them, as a rest and a release. And last of all, gain, the master pursuit of all, since it ministers to all other pursuits, urges its objects upon our attention. There are those, I know, to whom this world—world of spiritual probation and immortal hope as it is,—is but one great market-place; a place for buying and selling and getting profit; a place in which to hoard treasures, to build houses, to enjoy competence, or to lavish wealth.

And these things, I know, are called interests. The matters of religion are instructions; ay, and excellent instructions; for men can garnish with epithets of eulogium, the objects on which they are to bestow nothing but praise. And such, alas! are, too often, the matters of religion; they are excellent instructions, glorious doctrines, solemn ordinances, important duties; but to the mass of mankind, they are not yet interests. That brief word, with no epithet, with no pomp of language about it, expresses more, far more, than most men ever really attribute to religion, and the concerns of the soul. Nay, and the interest that is felt in religion—I have spoken of dulness—but the *interest* that is felt in religion, is often of a very doubtful, superficial, unreal character. Discourses upon religion, excite a kind of interest, and sometimes it might seem, as if that interest were strong. And strong of its kind, it may be. But of what kind is it? How deep, how efficient is it? How many are there, that would forego the chance of a good mercantile speculation, for the moral effect of the most admirable sermon that ever was preached? Oh! no: then it is a different thing. Religion is a good thing by the by; it is a pleasant thing for entertainment; it is a glorious thing to muse and meditate upon; but bring it into competition or comparison with real interests, and then, to many, it at once becomes something subtile, spiritual, invisible, imperceptible: it weighs nothing, it counts nothing, it will sell for nothing, and in thousands of scenes, in thousands of dwellings in this world, it is held to be good for nothing! This statement, God knoweth, is made with no lightness of spirit, though it had almost carried me, from the vividness of the contrast which it presents, to lightness of speech. How sad and lamentable is it, that beings whose soul is their chief distinction, should imagine that the things which most concern them, are things of appearance! I said, the vividness of the contrast; yet in truth it has been but half exhibited. It seems like extravagance to say it, but I fear it is sober truth, that there are many whom the very belief, the acknowledged record of their immortality, has never interested half so deeply as the frailest leaf on which a bond or a note is written; many whom no words of the Gospel ever aroused and delighted, and kindled to such a glow of pleasure, as a card of compliment, or a sentence of human eulogium! Indeed, when we draw a line of division between the worldly and spiritual, between the beings of the world and the beings of the soul, between creatures of the outside and creatures of the intellect and of immortality, how few will really be found among the elect, the chosen and faithful! And how many who could scarcely suspect it, perhaps, would be found on the side of the world—would be found among those who in their pursuits and judgments, are more affected by appearances than by realities; who are more powerfully acted upon by outward possessions, than by inward qualities; who, even in their loftiest sentiments, their admiration of great and good men, have their enthusiasm full as much awakened by the estimation in which those men are held, as by their real merits.

And when we consider all this, when we look upon the strife of human passions too, the zeal, the eagerness, the rivalship, the noise and bustle, with which outward things are sought; the fear, the hope, the joy, the sorrow, the discontent, the pride of this world, all, to so great an extent fastening themselves upon what is visible and tangible; it is not strange that many should come almost insensibly to feel as if they dwelt in a world of appearances; and as if nothing were real and valuable but what is seen and temporal. It is not altogether strange, that the senses have spread a broad veil of delusion over the earth, and that the concerns of every man's mind and heart, have been covered up and kept out of sight, by a mass of forms and fashions, and of things called interests.

And yet, notwithstanding all these aspects of things, I maintain, and I will show, that the real and main interest which concerns every man lies in the state of his own mind; that habits are of far more consequence to him than possessions and treasures; that affections, simple and invisible things though they be, are worth more to him, than rich dwellings, and broad lands, and coveted honours. I maintain, that no man is so worldly, or covetous, or voluptuous—that no man is so busy, or ambitious, or frivolous, but this is true of him. Let him be religious or not religious; let him be the merest slave of circumstances, the merest creature of vanity and compliment that ever existed; and still it is true, and none the less true, that his welfare lies within. There are no scenes of engrossing business, tumultuous pleasure, hollow-hearted fashion, or utter folly, but the deepest principles of religion are concerned with them. Indeed, I look upon all these varied pursuits as the strugglings of the deeper mind, as the varied developments of the one great desire of happiness. And he who forgets that deeper mind, and sees nothing, and thinks of nothing, but the visible scene, I hold to be as unwise as the man, who, entering upon the charge of one of our manufactories, should gaze upon the noisy and bustling apparatus above, should occupy himself with its varied movements, its swift and bright machinery and its beautiful fabrics, and forget the mighty wheel, that moves all from beneath.

But let us pursue the argument. The *mind*, it will be recollected, is that which is happy or unhappy, not goods and fortunes; not even the senses; they are but the inlets of pleasure to the mind. But this, as it is a mere truism, though a decisive one in the case, is not the proposition which I am to maintain. Neither am I to argue on the other hand, that the mind is independent of circumstances; that its situation, in regard to wealth or poverty, distinction or neglect, society or solitude, is a thing of no consequence. As well say

SPIRITUAL INTERESTS, REAL AND SUPREME. 389

that its relation to health or sickness is a thing of no consequence. But this I say and maintain, that what every man has chiefly at stake, lies in the mind; that his excellence depends entirely upon that; that his happiness ordinarily depends more upon the mind itself, upon its own state and character, than upon any outward condition; that those evils, with which the human race is afflicted, are mainly evils of the mind; and that the care of the soul, which religion enjoins, is the grand and only remedy for human wants and woes.

The considerations which bear upon this estimate of the real and practical welfare of men, may be drawn from every sphere of human life and action; from every contemplation of mankind, whether in their condition, relations or attributes; from society, from God's providence, from human nature itself. Let us, then, in the first place consider *society*, in several respects: in a general view of the evils that disturb or afflict it; in its intercourse; in its domestic scenes; in its religious institutions; and in its secular business and worldly condition. These topics will occupy the time that remains for our present meditation.

It is the more desirable to give some latitude to this part of our illustration, because it is in social interests and competitions especially, that men are apt to be worldly; i. e., to be governed by considerations extrinsic and foreign to the soul. The social man, indeed, is often worldly, while the same man, in retirement, is after his manner devout.

What then are the evils in society at large? I answer, they are, mainly, evils of the mind. Let us descend to particulars. Some, for instance, are depressed and irritated by neglect; and others are elated and injured by flattery. These are large classes of society around us; and the first, I think, by far the largest class. Both are unfortunate; both are wrong, probably; and not only so, but society is wrong for treating them in these ways; and the wrong, the evil in every instance, lies in the mind. Some again want excitement, want an object; and duty and religion would fill their hearts with constant peace, and with a plenitude of happy thoughts. Others want restraint, want the power to deny themselves, and want to know that such self-denial is blessed; and true piety would teach them this lofty knowledge; true piety would gently and strongly control all their passions. In short, ennui and excess, intemperance, slander, variance, rivalship, pride, and envy,—these are the miseries of society, and they are all miseries that exist in the mind. Where would our account end, if we were to enumerate all the things that awaken our fears, in the progress and movements of the social world around us? Good men differ, and reject each other's light and countenance; and bad men, alas! agree but too well; wise men dispute, and fools laugh; the selfish grasp; the ambitious strive; the sensual indulge themselves; and it seems, at times, as if the world were going surely, if not swiftly, to destruction! And why? Only, and always, and every where, because the mind is not right. Put holy truth in every false heart, instil a sacred piety into every worldly mind, and a blessed virtue into every fountain of corrupt desires; and the anxieties of philanthropy might be hushed; and the tears of benevolent prayer and faith might be dried up: and patriotism and piety might gaze upon the scene and the prospect with unmingled joy. Surely, then, the great interests of society are emphatically the interests of religion and virtue.

Gather any circle of society to its evening assembly. And what is the evil there? He must think but little, who imagines there is none. I confess that there are few scenes that more strongly dispose me to reflection, than this. I see great and signal advantages, fair and fascinating opportunities for happiness. The ordinary, or rather the ordinarily recognised evils of life, have no place in the throng of social entertainment. They are abroad indeed, in many a hovel and hospital, and by many a wayside; but from those brilliant and gay apartments they are, for the time, excluded. The gathering is, of youth and lightness of heart and prosperous fortune. The manly brow flushed with the beauty of its early day, the fair form of outward loveliness, the refined understanding, the accomplished manner, the glad parent's heart, and confiding filial love, and music and feasting, are there; and yet beneath many a soft raiment and many a silken fold, I know that hearts are beating, which are full of disquietude and pain. The selfishness of parental anxiety, the desire of admiration, the pride of success, the mortification of failure, the vanity that is flattered, the ill-concealed jealousy, the miserable affectation, the distrustful embarrassment,—that comprehensive difficulty which proceeds to some extent indeed from the fault of the individual, but much more from the general fault of society,—these are the evils from which the gayest circles of the social world need to be reformed; and these too, are evils in the mind. They are evils which nothing but religion and virtue can ever correct. The remedy must be applied where the disease is, and that is to the soul.

But now follow society to its homes. There is, indeed, and eminently, the scene of our happiness or of our misery. And it is too plain to be insisted on, that domestic happiness depends ordinarily and chiefly upon domestic honour and fidelity; upon disinterestedness, generosity, kindness, forbearance; and the vices opposite to these, are the evils that embitter the peace and joy of domestic life. Men in general are sufficiently sensible to this part of their welfare. Thousands all around us, are labouring by day and meditating by night, upon the means of building up in comfort and honour, the families, with whose fortunes and fate their own is identified. Here, then, if any where—here in these homes of our affection, are interests. And surely, I speak not to discourage a generous self-devotion to them, or a reasonable care of their worldly condition. But I say, that this *condition* is not the main thing, though it is commonly made so. I say that there is something of more consequence to the happiness of a family, than the apartments it occupies, or the furniture that adorns them; something of dearer and more vital concernment, than costly equipage or vast estates or coveted honours. I say, that if its members have any thing within them, that is worthy to be called a mind, their main interests are their thoughts and their virtues. Vague and shadowy things they may appear to some; but let a man be ever so worldly, and this is true; and it is a truth which he cannot help: and all the struggle of family ambition, and all the pride of its vaunted consequence and cherished luxury, will only the more demonstrate it to be true.

Choose, then, what scene of social life you will; and it can be shown beyond all reasonable doubt, that the main concern, the great interest there, is the state of the mind.

What is it that makes dull and weary services at church; if, alas! we must admit that they sometimes are so. A living piety in the congregation, a fervent love of God, and truth, and goodness, would communicate life, I had almost said, to the dullest service that ever passed in the house of God: and, if destitute of that piety, the preaching of an angel would awaken in us only a temporary enthusiasm. A right and holy feeling would make the house of God, the place for devout meditation, a place more profoundly, more keenly interesting, than the thronged mart, or the canvassing hall, or the tribunal that is to pass judgment on a portion of our property. Do you say that the preacher is sometimes dull, and that is all the difficulty? No, it is not all the difficulty; for the dullest haranguer that ever addressed an infuriated mob, when speaking their sentiments, is received with shouts of applause. Suppose that a company were assembled to consider and discuss some grand method to be proposed, for acquiring fortunes for themselves—some South-Sea scheme, or project for acquiring the mines of Potosi; and suppose that some one should rise to speak to that company, who could not speak eloquently, nor in an interesting manner: grant all that; but suppose this dull speaker could say something, could state some fact or consideration, to help on the great inquiry. Would the company say that they could not listen to him? Would the people say that they would not come to hear him again? No, the speaker might be as awkward and prosaic as he pleased; he might be some humble observer, some young engineer; but he would have attentive and crowded auditories. A feeling in the hearers would supply all other deficiencies.

Shall this be so in worldly affairs, and shall there be nothing like it in religious affairs? Grant that the speaker on religion is not the most interesting; grant that he is dull; grant that his emotions are constitutionally less earnest than yours are; yet I say, what business have you to come to church to be passive in the service, to be acted on, and not yourselves to act? And yet more, what warrant have you, to let your affections to your God depend on the infirmity of any mortal being? Is that awful presence that filleth the sanctuary, though no cloud of incense be there; is the vital and never-dying interest which you have in your own mind; is the wide scene of living mercies that surrounds you, and which you have come to meditate upon; is it all indifferent to you, because one poor, erring mortal is cold and dead to it? I do not ask you to say that he is not dull, if he is dull; I do not ask you to say that *he* is interesting; but I ask you to be interested in spite of him. His very dulness, if he is dull, ought to move you. If you cannot weep with him, you ought to weep for him.

Besides, the weakest or the dullest man tells you truths of transcendent glory and power. He tells you that "God is love;" and how might that truth, though he uttered not another word, or none but dull words; how might that truth spread itself out into the most glorious and blessed contemplations! Indeed, the simple truths are, after all, the great truths. Neither are they always best understood. The very readiness of assent is sometimes an obstacle to the fulness of the impression. Very simple matters, I am aware, are those to which I am venturing to call your attention, in this hour of our solemnities; and yet do I believe, that if they were clearly perceived and felt among men at large, they would begin, from this moment, the regeneration of the world!

But pass now from the silent and holy sanctuary, to the bustling scene of this world's business and pursuit. "Here," the worldly man will say, "we have reality.

Here, indeed, are interests. Here is something worth being concerned about." And yet even here do the interests of religion and virtue pursue him, and press themselves upon his attention.

Look, for instance, at the condition of life, the possession or the want, of those blessings for which business is prosecuted. What is it that distresses the poor man, and makes poverty in the ordinary condition of it, the burden that it is? It is not, in this country,— it is not usually, hunger, nor cold, nor nakedness. It is some artificial want, created by the wrong state of society. It is something nearer yet to us, and yet more unnecessary. It is mortification, discontent, peevish complaining, or envy of a better condition; and all these are evils of the mind. Again, what is it that troubles the rich man, or the man who is successfully striving to be rich? It is not poverty, certainly, nor is it exactly possession. It is occasional disappointment, it is continual anxiety, it is the extravagant desire of property, or worse than all, the vicious abuse of it; and all these too are evils of the mind.

But let our worldly man, who will see nothing but the outside of things, who will value nothing but possessions, take another view of his interest. What is it that cheats, circumvents, overreaches him? It is dishonesty. What disturbs, vexes, angers him? It is some wrong from another, or something wrong in himself. What steals his purse, or robs his person? It is not some unfortunate mischance that has come across his path. It is a being in whom nothing worse resides, than fraud and violence. What robs him of that, which is dearer than property, his fair name among his fellows? It is the poisonous breath of foul and accursed slander. And what is it, in fine, that threatens the security, order, peace and well-being of society at large; that threatens, if unrestrained, to deprive our estates, our comforts, our domestic enjoyments, our personal respectability and our whole social condition, of more than half their value? It is the spirit of injustice and wild misrule in the human breast; it is political intrigue, or popular violence; it is the progress of corruption, intemperance, lasciviousness, the progress of vice and sin, in all their forms. I know that these are very simple truths; but if they are very simple and very certain, how is it that men are so worldly? Put obligation out of the question; how is it that they are not more sagacious and wary with regard to their interests? How is it that the means of religion and virtue are so indifferent to many, in comparison with the means of acquiring property or office? How is it that many unite and contribute so coldly and reluctantly for the support of government, learning, and Christian institutions, who so eagerly combine for the prosecution of moneyed speculations, and of party and worldly enterprises? How *is* it, I repeat? Men desire happiness; and a very clear argument may be set forth to show them where their happiness lies. And yet here is presented to you the broad fact—and with this fact I will close the present meditation; that while men's welfare depends mainly on their own minds, they are actually and almost universally seeking it in things without them; that among the objects of actual desire and pursuit, affections and virtues, in the world's esteem, bear no comparison with possessions and honours; nay, that men are every where and every day, sacrificing, ay, sacrificing affections and virtues, sacrificing the dearest treasures of the soul, for what they call goods, and pleasures, and distinctions.

Lightning Source UK Ltd.
Milton Keynes UK
UKHW022026071218
333658UK00010B/826/P